Strangers at the Gates
Movements and States in Contentious Politics

This book contains the products of work carried out over four decades of research in Italy, France, and the United States, and in the intellectual territory between social movements, comparative politics, and historical sociology. Using a variety of methods ranging from statistical analysis to historical case studies to linguistic analysis, the book centers on historical catalogs of protest events and cycles of collective action. Sidney Tarrow places social movements in the broader arena of contentious politics, in relation to states, political parties, and other actors. From peasants and Communists in 1960s' Italy, to movements and politics in contemporary Western polities, to the global justice movement in the new century, the book argues that contentious actors are neither outside of nor completely within politics, but rather that they occupy the uncertain territory between total opposition and integration into the polity.

Sidney Tarrow (PhD, University of California, Berkeley, 1965) is Maxwell M. Upson Professor Emeritus of Government at Cornell University. His recent books are *Power in Movement* (Cambridge, revised and updated edition 2011); *Contentious Politics* (with the late Charles Tilly 2006), *The New Transnational Activism* (Cambridge 2005); *Transnational Protest and Global Activism* (coedited with Donatella della Porta 2004); *Dynamics of Contention* (Cambridge, with Doug McAdam and Charles Tilly 2001); and *Contentious Europeans* (with Doug Imig 2001). He is currently researching the relations among war, rights, and contention.

For Jonathan, Owen, Gabriel, and Jamie

Strangers at the Gates

Movements and States in Contentious Politics

SIDNEY TARROW
Cornell University

CAMBRIDGE
UNIVERSITY PRESS

CAMBRIDGE UNIVERSITY PRESS
Cambridge, New York, Melbourne, Madrid, Cape Town,
Singapore, São Paulo, Delhi, Mexico City

Cambridge University Press
32 Avenue of the Americas, New York, NY 10013–2473, USA

www.cambridge.org
Information on this title: www.cambridge.org/9781107402010

First published 2012

Printed in the United States of America

A catalog record for this publication is available from the British Library.

Library of Congress Cataloging in Publication data
Tarrow, Sidney G.
   Strangers at the gates : movements and states in contentious politics /
Sidney Tarrow.
      p.   cm.
Includes bibliographical references and index.
ISBN 978-1-107-00938-7 (hardback) – ISBN 978-1-107-40201-0 (paperback)
   1. Social movements – History.   2. Social action – History.
   3. Collective behavior – History.   4. Social change – History.
   5. Political sociology.   I. Title.
HM881.T374   2012
303.48'409182109045–dc23   2011034034

ISBN 978-1-107-00938-7 Hardback
ISBN 978-1-107-40201-0 Paperback

Contents

Tables and Figures

Tables

Figures

Preface and Acknowledgments

This book assembles and reflects on work I carried out over four decades in Italy, France, and the United States, and in the territory between social movements, comparative politics, and historical sociology. Because of its heterodox pedigree, I do not expect all of my readers to be equally engaged by everything in the book. Time has also not been on my side. Consider: while Chapter 2 draws on work I did in Italy when Communism was still a living force there, the final chapter was written when that country was being fleeced by a vain huckster with an implanted hairline and a taste for young women. Readers will have to search deep and hard to find continuity in these essays.

Moreover, the book gives short shrift to general intellectual developments in the social sciences as the work collected here was done – such changes as the impact of rational-choice theory and constructivism, historical institutionalism, and path dependency. Had I stopped to place it in these broader developments, the book would have been twice as long and more ponderous. But it was deeply influenced by events in the periods in which it was done. The Berkeley Free Speech movement that raged outside my window at the University of California in Berkeley influenced Chapter 2; the Civil Rights Movement affected my thinking about American contentious politics in Chapter 3; state breakdown, insurgency, and terrorism in the post–Cold War world led me to return to the French Revolution in Chapter 4; the 1968 movements triggered my analysis of policy impacts in Chapter 9; the current era of globalization affected how I studied the transnational movements examined in Chapters 11 and 12; and the explosive events in the Middle East in 2011 shaped the reflections in the coda. The book also reflects changes in how contentious politics and social movements have been studied since the 1960s, when there was a paradigmatic shift from a tradition that assessed the influence of structural cleavages on social movements to new and more "political" paradigms.

Yet the reader searching for continuity will find it in the relationships the book records among social movements, political parties, and political institutions. That triangular relationship affects how activists think and act, so it should also shape how analysts examine their trajectories. If they are to prosper, activists balance trying to bring about change with operating in what Gramsci called the "trenches and fortifications" of existing society. The history books are full of tales of those that do not make this adjustment, but those who survive succeed in negotiating the tensions at the gates of the polity. This book explores various facets of the basic ambiguity of being outside of institutional politics but working within the polity.

No scholar who studies contentious politics for more than four decades walks alone. Although I cannot mention all my fellow travelers, a few colleagues and collaborators cannot go unrecognized. As the late David Apter was introducing me to the challenges of comparative analysis, his friend Joseph LaPalombara was exposing me to the intricacies of Italian politics. These two teachers, future colleagues and friends, were the dual guideposts for a sometimes disoriented traveler as he labored on his first book, *Peasant Communism in Southern Italy*.

A colleague – like me, of a certain age – once remarked that it is somehow embarrassing for mature academics to continue to pride themselves through the number of books and articles they publish; better, he argued, to think in terms of the quality of the young people they have worked with. I fully agree: the privilege of collaborating with young scholars of the quality of Bill Ascher, Jeff Ayres, Donatella della Porta, Antonina Gentile, Jennifer Hadden, Doug Imig, Ariel Levite, David S. Meyer, Tsveta Petrova, Sarah Soule, Sonia Stefanizzi, Alan Stern, and Mary Frase Williams was a high point of my career. All have gone on to bigger things.

If this book has anything to contribute to the study of France it is due to the guidance of the late Annick Percheron, and to Guy Michelat and René Mouriaux, all of CEVIPOF (The Center for the Study of French Political Life), which served for years as a magnet for students of France. In Italy, the late Alberto Spreafico and Aris Accornero helped me keep my feet in the churning currents of Italian politics. In Berkeley, Jack Schaar introduced me to a richer brew of American politics than the thin gruel I had encountered in the *American Political Science Review*. In New Haven, Robert Dahl and Fred Greenstein showed me that American politics has a great deal to teach a comparativist, while at Cornell my colleagues in comparative politics reminded me that Western Europe is not the only place in which contentious politics flourishes. As I dipped into the murky waters of transnational politics, my friends Peter Katzenstein, Bob Keohane, and Kathryn Sikkink were patient guides.

My not-so-silent partners in exploring the byways of political contention were and remain Doug McAdam and the late Charles Tilly. When I would reach a particularly dicey patch in preparing this book, I often felt Chuck looking over my shoulder from beyond the grave; and when Doug read what I had produced, I treasured his typically gentle but pointed comments. As I reached into the uncertain territory of transnational politics, a frequent companion was Donatella della Porta, who transmuted from student to junior colleague to senior scholar as I watched in awe.

Too many people read and commented on individual chapters in this book for me to recognize them all. Eitan Alimi, Lew Bateman, Breno Bringel, Valerie Bunce, della Porta, Lars-Erik Cederman, Hadden, Steve Hellman, Jeff Isaac, Ira Katznelson, Mark Lichbach, McAdam, David Meyer, and Martin Shefter were the kind of nonfinicky critics an author treasures. Ryan Morfopoulos prepared the bibliography with unflagging attention to detail.

Susan Tarrow never failed to believe that work that sometimes seemed too all-over-the-place might some day come together. She read every word in the manuscript of this book – often more than once – and responded to my errors with patience and understanding. Only she can know how much she means to me.

Ithaca, New York
June 2011

Introduction

"Strangers at the gates"? Why not "strangers *outside* the gates"? Or "strangers *assaulting* the gates"? This book investigates the role of movement activists and activist organizations in the vaguely delimited borderland between contentious and routine politics. It takes up the insight of the great British historian, E.P. Thompson, that grain protesters in eighteenth-century England were engaged in what he called "collective bargaining by riot" (Thompson 1971). It expands on the path-breaking work of Charles Tilly (1978, 1984, 1986, 1995, 2006) linking the study of states with that of contentious politics. And it traces my own contributions from the largely structuralist perspective I took earlier to a more interactive and process-based approach I adopted in recent years.

I will argue in this book that although the internal lives of social movements are important in themselves, activists choose their repertoires and frame their appeals in the light of their relations to a broader map of both contentious and routine politics. As a result, they not only demand change but also accommodate inherited understandings and ways of doing things. They are "strangers at the gates" operating on the boundaries of constituted politics, culture, and institutions. I will argue, finally, that changes in regimes result from these intersections among contentious actors, members of the polity, and political regimes.

When I look back at the work assembled in this book I can see how this interactive perspective developed over the course of my research. When I began to study what I came to call "contentious politics," young scholars like myself were more taken with structural accounts than with models of the political process. Those who came from a Marxist background struggled to see in the contradictions of capitalism the sources of the behavior they were observing; but that was hard to do in the conditions of the 1960s, when the western working class appeared to be integrated within those structures. In reaction, those who came from non-Marxist backgrounds searched for substitutes for the working class in the students, the new middle class, and groups that were dislocated by the changes in advanced capitalism (Offe 1985; Touraine 1971). This was interesting in itself, because mainstream work on what was then called "collective action" was influenced by implicitly conservative functionalist and pluralist views. My generation rebelled against both these views and embraced the participatory and reformist messages of the movements of the 1960s.

But as these movements faded and many of their veterans entered institutional politics, disillusionment grew. By the 1980s, many had moved on from studying movements to examining the machinery of power and the incentives of power holders. The 1990s produced yet another disillusionment among scholars who thought they had seen in the collapse of Communism the End of History and now saw neoliberalism, xenophobia, and inequality in its place. When September 11, 2001 ushered in the new century with blood, challengers to the polity were exiled to the status of "The Other" and students of contention were sidelined to the study of "outsiders." Only the revival of contention on the once-unpromising terrain of the Middle East as the second decade of the century began brought a hopeful renaissance of work on contention, not unlike what we (now older) scholars experienced in the 1960s.

The fifty-odd years of research on social movements between these two cycles of contention were ripe with theoretical and empirical contributions. In the wake of the 1960s, scholarship on social movements expanded to new and promising strands of theory and research. First, there was a "cultural turn" that placed more emphasis on the phenomenology of contention – its framing, its identities, its emotions – than on its ultimate sources in social structure. Second, a "world systems" perspective tried to retain the broad historical sweep of Marxism without its teleological mission. Third, an organizational approach retained the structuralist cast of older theories while shifting attention to movements' internal lives. All three strands of research opened scholarship to new ways of studying contention.

But there were problems: the cultural turn tended to reduce the clash of movements and their opponents to contests about discourse; world systems theory was too occupied with "Big Structural Changes" to pay much attention to interactions on the ground; and a focus on the internal structure of movement organizations gave less attention to movements' interactions with other actors and institutions in the polity.

At the same time, a heterodox group of scholars in both Europe and the United States began to focus on movements' relationship to their political systems. They developed an approach – loosely known today as the "political process model" – that explored movements' relationships with political parties, interest groups, opponents, and institutions. Scholars working in this tradition tried to build a synthetic model: they embraced the culturalists' emphasis on framing; the actors in their analyses were movement organizations; and their attention centered on the political process and on the opportunities and constraints it offered challengers.

This book grew out of that orientation, which will be outlined in more detail in Chapter 1. Its driving theme is that movement activists balance trying to bring about change – sometimes revolutionary change – with operating in what Gramsci called the "trenches and fortifications" of existing society. How they negotiate that tension, and the results of the solutions they fashion for public policy, political culture, and regime change, are the questions I hope the book will address. If it has an underlying claim it is that challengers are neither as independent of the polity as they like to portray themselves, nor as ensnared in institutional politics as many later become. They are "strangers at the gates" who operate on the boundaries of the polity, in an uneasy position that explains much of the ambiguities and contradictions in their strategies, composition, and dynamics. They are part of a broader system of conflict and cooperation I call "contentious politics."

By this term McAdam and Tilly and I did not mean to cover all of politics but more than "social movements": the broader term refers to interactions in which actors make claims bearing on someone else's interests, leading to coordinated efforts on behalf of shared programs in which governments are involved as targets, initiators of claims, or third parties (McAdam et al. 2001). Within this arena, movements intersect with each other and with institutional actors in a dynamic process of move, countermove, adjustment, and negotiation. That process includes claim making, responses to the actions of elites – repressive, facilitative, or both – and the intervention of third parties, who often take advantage of the opportunities created by these conflicts to advance their own claims. The outcomes of these intersections, in turn, are how a polity evolves.

This move to envelop the study of social movements within a broader field of contentious politics has been part of a broader shift in comparative politics and international relations toward the systematic study of processes and mechanisms in the last decade (George and Bennett 2005). As a result, the study of contentious politics has become one of the most exiting arenas for interdisciplinary work in the social sciences:

- Instead of focusing on single social movement actors, scholars have increasingly focused on the spaces in which actions of actors at the gates of the polity and of actors within the polity interact;
- Instead of focusing on particular events, scholars are turning to longer and more complicated episodes and trajectories of collective action, reaction, and regime change;
- Instead of focusing only on western contention, the field has expanded to the study of postsocialist and third world countries;
- Rather than center only on social movements, the field has expanded to include nationalism, civil wars, guerilla insurgencies, and religious, ethnic and nationalist conflicts;[1]
- And although much of the work generated by the new paradigm has focused on *political* contention, there has been an expansion of the study of

---

[1] Despite path-breaking work by students like Lars-Erik Cederman and Luc Giradin (2007), Stathis Kalyvas (2006), and James Fearon and David Laitin (2003), students of civil wars still seem to be talking a different language than students of social movements, even when their concepts run along parallel lines; for a review that calls attention to this disjunction, see my "Inside Insurgencies" (2007).

contention to a host of other institutional realms, from firms, schools and school systems to the military, churches, and economic structures (Binder 2002; Katzenstein 1998, Rojas 2007, Soule 2009).

This Book

This book will employ an interactive, dynamic approach to explore where social movements fit in a series of episodes of contention, past and present. Episodes of contention are broader – and last longer – than social movement campaigns. Think of the American civil rights movement, usually identified with the movements of "the sixties." Many of the key events in that episode began much earlier, for example, with Roosevelt's opening of federal employment to African Americans (Kryder 2000) and Truman's Cold War–born civil rights policies (McAdam, Tarrow, and Tilly 1999 [1982]). Moreover, many of the outcomes of that movement went well beyond the goals of its movement organizations – for example, in life-course changes that could be seen only decades later (McAdam 1998). By focusing excessively on "hot" periods of movement collective action, scholars have underspecified both the mechanisms that lead to these periods of conflict and their long-term outcomes.

This led me to see the need to embed the study of social movements in history.[2] Chapter 1 reflects on the influence of five major theorists who have used the historical approach to study contentious politics: Marx, Lenin, Gramsci, Tocqueville, and Tilly. It then turns to contemporary theories of social movements. It concludes with a sketch of my own approach, which will be illustrated in the rest of the book. The next three chapters can be read as one-sided conversations with Gramsci, Tocqueville, and Tilly. Chapter 2 returns to the southern Italian peasant movement that I studied in the 1960s – showing how it intersected with the Communist Party and the Italian state in the light of Gramsci's theory. Chapter 3 turns to the United States in the early nineteenth century, arguing – *pace* Tocqueville – that between the Revolution and the Civil War, movements and political parties were in constant interaction. Chapter 4 turns to the French Revolution, showing, in the light of Tilly's work, how state-building impacted on the character of contention and on the future of democracy in that country.

Parts II and III explore the linkages among movements, parties, and institutions, arguing that we can only understand social movements when we place them in a broader framework of contentious politics and look at them over extended periods of time. Think of elections: political scientists who study them rarely take note of social movements, while movement scholars are almost as indifferent to studies of elections (McAdam and Tarrow 2012). Chapter 5

---

[2] I recall a colleague who was working on social networks in the Netherlands. When I observed that Dutch networks were historically structured along confessional lines, he proudly pronounced: "I am only interested in the structure of networks; the rest is mere history!" This book is marinated in "mere history."

examines the relations among parties and social movements in general, while Chapter 6 illustrates the complexities of these relations in Italy in the 1960s and 1970s. Part III focuses on the dynamics of contention, in which challengers and polity members are mutually engaged in cycles of collective action. In Chapter 7 I examine three major ways in which contentious events have been studied by major exponents of the study of contentious politics. It closes with the implications of these approaches for the study of cycles of contention. The internal dynamics of cycles and their relationship to the repertoire of contention are the subject of Chapter 8, developed in studying the Italian cycle of the 1960s and 1970s.

Part IV turns to the ambivalent relations between contention and movement outcomes. Chapter 9 analyzes the reforms that resulted from the Events of May 1968 in France. It traces the decline of mobilization and its effects on reformism in the educational sphere – a failure that still haunts the French educational system today. Chapter 10, "What's in a Word," examines the linkages between contentious episodes and changes in language. It takes the "cultural turn" in social movement studies one more turn: linking changes in language to the political changes produced by new forms of contention.

Part V turns to contention beyond the gates of the nation-state. Ever since the birth of the social movement, movements have been associated with state development. How do internationalization and globalization challenge this duality? Chapter 11, "Rooted Cosmopolitans and Transnational Activists," asks whether a new stratum of activists is developing outside the nation-state in response to these processes, or if we should continue to look within the gates of national politics for the sources of "global" social movements. Chapter 12 asks whether distinct transnational opportunity structures have been developing in the complex processes of internationalization that have developed since the end of World War II or whether transnational contention takes place through relational processes between the domestic and international spheres. It ends with a coda reflecting on the striking similarities in revolutionary trajectories between a previous revolutionary cycle – 1848 – and the one that spread across the Middle East as this book was completed.

This book by no means attempts to cover all aspects of contentious politics. For example, only in Part V will I return to the classical theme of the relations between structural change in the global economy and contentious politics. The turn to the political process has been a productive one for the study of social movements; if nothing else, it helped to escape the iron grip of Marxist determinism. But it may also have distracted scholars' attention – including this one – from the deeper mechanisms and processes that drive people to mobilize on behalf of causes greater than themselves: processes like the historical expropriation of peasants from their land, the deskilling of workers whose only property is their skill, and broader processes like globalization and democratization.

These are the kinds of issues that animated our theoretical predecessors – Marx and Engels, Lenin, Gramsci, Tocqueville, and Tilly. It is to these theorists that I will first turn in Chapter 1.

Theories of Contentious Politics

Networks Never Lie. – or, at least, by telling us who people hang around with, they offer hints about where they stand. That seems to have been the case for those who studied contentious politics in recent decades.

In 1993 and 1994, two new networks of social movement scholars were established by the International Sociological Association (ISA):

- The Research Committee on Social Classes and Social Movements (RC47), created with largely French-Canadian, Brazilian, German, and English board members in 1993;[1] and
- The Research Committee on Social Movements, Collective Action, and Social Change (RC48), formed by Dutch, Polish, American, and Italian board members in 1994.[2]

Over the nearly two decades of its history, RC47 showed a remarkable degree of continuity, judging by both country representation and individual members on its board, with Brazilian scholars in the lead with nine "presences," Canadian ones with eight, the United States with seven, and Germany, Italy, and the United Kingdom with five, over its eighteen-year history. But even these figures underestimate the degree of continuity: from its founding, RC47 had a clear imprint of former students of French sociologist Alain Touraine, who moved from a structuralist to a poststructuralist position during his long and distinguished career. Although there were only three French representatives on its board over the years, from its beginnings, RC47, like its founder Louis Maheu,[3] had a clear Tourainian stamp.

---

[1] Go to www.isa-sociology.org/rc47.htm, visited on April 25, 2011.
[2] Go to www.isa-sociology.org/rc48.htm, visited on April 25, 2011.
[3] Maheu is best known by anglophone audiences for his edited book, *Social Movements and Social Classes: The Future of Collective Action*. Sage Publications, 1995.

Some of the material in this chapter is drawn from the third edition of my *Power in Movement* (2011a).

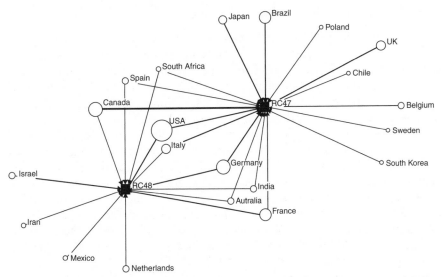

FIGURE 1.1. Board Members and Countries of Origin of ISA Sections RC47 and RC48. *Source:* Author's calculations.

There was greater circulation of elites in RC48, with nine American presences, five from Israel, four each from India, Germany, and the Netherlands, and the rest of the board members scattered among eight other countries. And although there have been structuralists and poststructuralists on the boards of RC48 – most notably, the late Alberto Melucci – its members figured more centrally in the "social movement canon" in American and European social movement research. Figure 1.1 symbolically suggests the cleavage in the "social movement community" over the past two decades by showing which countries are represented in the two networks and how many times representatives of each country appeared and where.

Why should we care about the bipolar committee structure of an international professional association that meets once every four years, has no power to define research paradigms, and may not even appear on the curriculum vitae of its members? Figure 1.1 shows three things: first, that, however imperfect, there are transnational links among students of social movements, and this has produced a lot more comparative and collaborative work than was the case a few decades ago (van Skelenburg et al. 2012); second, it shows that the cleavages that have marked the study of contentious politics in individual countries for decades are also present at the international level; and, third, it shows that this cleavage is broadly organized along a single main axis: between macrostructural approaches that focus on the exogenous causes of social movements (RC47) and process-based approaches that focus on the endogenous social movement sector (RC48. The (partial) shift from the first to the second – from structure to action, to put it crudely – is the theme of this chapter and the underlying trend of the work collected in this book.

From Contentious Politics to Social Movements

Over the past few decades, students of contentious politics have made great strides in examining both historical and contemporary social movements – especially the civil rights, feminist, peace, environmental, and radical rightwing movements in the West. But they have left to specialists the rich evidence of labor movements, revolutionary movements, nationalist, ethnic, and religious movements coming from other sectors of research and from other parts of the world – notably, from the global South, from which a growing strand of theorizing has come. This tendency to closure is unfortunate because it elides rich sources of data on contentious politics and makes it more difficult to understand the long-term relationship between changes in social structure and their effects on different forms of contention. For example, did the social movement form emerge from capitalism, the formation of modern states, or some other structural development? These "structural" questions have tended to be elided as scholars – including this one – focused more and more precisely on the endogenous lives of social movements.

An older tradition of theory – beginning with Marx on the left and Tocqueville on the liberal right – focused on a broader range of movements and placed them in the historical context of the rise of capitalism and state building. It is from within this broad tradition that I take my theoretical bearings in this chapter. But the chapter will also survey more recent approaches that center on the contemporary phenomenology of social movements. This is the tradition that has come to be called the "political process" approach, even if it deals with much more than politics. This newer tradition has helped us understand such processes as mobilization and demobilization, the framing of contentious political action, and how social movements mobilize resources on behalf of their claims.[4] But in its focus on the internal lives and proximate environments of social movements, it has left in the background the connections between long-term social change and contentious politics. The problem we face today is how to connect the long-term rhythms of social change from the classical tradition to the shorter-term dynamics of contentious politics.

Many sociologists trace the lineage of social movement theory to the negative reactions that followed the French Revolution and to the outrages of "the crowd" that the revolution brought onto the historical scene. While such authors as Tarde (1989) and Le Bon (1977) make a convenient starting point, their work was in fact less about organized social movements than about crowd psychology. Emile Durkheim (1964) gave this tradition a scientific imprimatur, arguing that collective action arises from alienation and anomie. But he had nothing specifically to say about social movements. In contrast, this book sees conflicts between challengers and authorities as a normal part of society. This is why I will begin with theorists who saw conflict inscribed in the very structure

---

[4] For literature reviews that survey these developments in more detail, see McAdam et al. 2009. For a more sustained presentation of this tradition, see della Porta and Diani 1999.

of society – Karl Marx, Vladimir Lenin, and Antonio Gramsci on the left and Alexis de Tocqueville and those who followed him on the liberal right. The chapter then turns to more recent theorists who have taught us a great deal about the micropolitics of contention but less about how it relates to long-term social change.

Marx and Engels, Lenin, and Gramsci

Marx and Engels, Lenin, and Gramsci, were all macrostructuralists, regarding structural changes in society as the primary causes of social conflict and the contentious politics that followed from them. To Marx's original focus on macrostructural change, Lenin added attention to movement organization, arguing for a revolutionary vanguard strategy to institute revolutionary change. Gramsci embraced Leninism, but added to it a sensitivity to culture, and argued for the insertion of the revolutionary party in the "trenches and fortifications" of capitalist politics. But this was the closest these Marxist theorists came to specifying the properties of politics that revolutionary movements would need to engage with. None of them examined how structure could be turned into action.

Marx, Engels, and Class Conflict

The earliest theorists of social movements, Marx and Engels, conceived of revolution as a macrohistorical episode related more to a society's structural development than to questions of individual volition or collective choice. And while they saw collective action rooted in social structure, they left little room for the political mechanisms that induce individuals to mobilize and interact with opponents and institutions. People will engage in collective action, they thought, when their social class comes into fully developed contradiction with its antagonists. In the case of the proletariat, this meant when capitalism forced workers into large-scale factories, where they lost the ownership of their tools but developed the organizational resources to act collectively. Chief among these resources were class consciousness and the trade unions. It was the rhythm of socialized production in the factory that would pound the proletariat into a class "for itself" and give rise to the unions that would shape its future.

Although there are many more elegant (and more obscure) formulations of this thesis, Marx and Engels put it most succinctly in *The Communist Manifesto*:

> The advance of industry, whose involuntary promoter is the bourgeoisie, replaces the isolation of the labourers, due to competition, by their revolutionary combination, due to association.... The real fruit of their battle lies, not in the immediate result, but in the ever-expanding union of the workers. (Tucker, ed. 1978: 481 and 483)

Marx dealt summarily with a problem that has worried activists and theorists ever since: why members of a group who "should" revolt when history provides the "objective conditions" for revolt often fail to do so. Concerned with the problem that the workers' movement could not succeed unless a significant proportion of its members cooperated, he developed a number of explanations for why this kind of class mobilization was so difficult to accomplish, focusing on the role of intermediate classes and political groupings, the role of ideologues in weakening the socialist dispositions of workers, and the effectiveness of political ideologies and forms of collective mystification. For our purposes the most important thing to note is that Marx thought the problem would resolve itself when capitalism's contradictions ripened and the solidarity that came from years of toiling side by side with others like themselves opened the workers' eyes to their real interests.

We now know that as capitalism developed, it produced divisions among the workers and mechanisms that integrated them into capitalist democracy. We also know that through nationalism and protectionism, workers often allied with capitalists, suggesting that an independent analysis of the political process was needed to understand when they would engage in class-based contention. A form of consciousness also had to be created that would transform economic interests into revolutionary collective action.

But how would such consciousness emerge, and more importantly, *who* who would initiate its emergence? Because Marx had never seen a modern political party or union, he lacked a developed understanding of both these requisites of political leadership. And because he worked far from the complexities of working-class culture, he underspecified the political conditions that would be needed to provide opportunities for workers' revolutionary mobilization (1963: 175). Only in some of his political writings, like *The Eighteenth Brumaire of Louis Bonaparte* (1978) do we find hints of how Marx thought structural conflicts would translate into processes of contention in moments of rupture.

Lenin and the Vanguard Party

The first of these problems – that of leadership – was the major preoccupation of Lenin, who, as founder of the Bolshevik Party and principal leader of the Russian Revolution of November 1917, established himself as Marx's most politically effective follower. Drawing not only from the failure of the Western European proletariat to transcend corporate or "trade union consciousness," but also on the less-developed situation of Russia, Lenin refused to wait for objective conditions to ripen but proposed instead creating an elite of professional revolutionaries (1929: 52ff.). Substituting itself for Marx's proletariat, this "vanguard" would act as the self-appointed guardian of the workers' real interests. When that vanguard, in the form of the Russian Bolshevik Party, succeeded in gaining power, it transposed the equation, substituting party interest for that of the working class (and ultimately, in its Stalinist involution, substituting the will of the leader for that of the party). But in 1902 – when Lenin's pamphlet "What Is To Be Done" was published – this was too far in the future to see. To Lenin, it seemed that organization was the solution to the workers' collective action problem.

With the virtues of hindsight, we can see that Lenin's organizational amendments to Marx's theory were a particular response to the historical conditions of Tsarist Russia. In superimposing an intellectual vanguard on the young and unsophisticated Russian working class, he was adapting Marx's theory to the context of a repressive state and to the backward society it ruled – both of which retarded the development of class consciousness and inhibited mass collective action. Lenin's vanguard theory – put forward as a universal recipe for revolution – was actually an adaptation to the repressive and backward conditions of Imperial Russia, with all the deformations that that adaptation entailed.

Nobody knows what a "mature" working class in a liberal political system would have done had it come to power independently: for once Leninism took hold in Russia, the working class movement in Europe split and was partially destroyed and the entire international system was transformed. The theory of the vanguard was an organizational response to a historical situation in which the working class was unable to produce a revolution on its own. Applied indiscriminately to the world Communist movement, with little regard to social and political opportunities and constraints, it led to the failure of the proletarian revolution and, indirectly, to fascism.

Gramsci and Cultural Hegemony

A better understanding of these problems became the principal concern of a range of thinkers – Rosa Luxemburg, Gyorgy Lukacs, Karl Korsch, and Antonio Gramsci – who together developed what the historian Perry Anderson has called "Western Marxism" (Anderson 1976). Dispirited by the failure of the Russian Revolution of 1917 to spread to the West, these thinkers, who had embraced Leninism in the excitement created by that revolution, came to realize that under Western conditions, vanguard forms of organization would not be sufficient to raise a revolution.

In terms of his impact on the subsequent development of social and political theory, the most important of these figures was Gramsci, who began his career as an orthodox Leninist who thought that the conditions of rural Italy were like those that had thrown Russia into revolution. After being clapped into prison by Benito Mussolini, he began to understand that what had worked for Lenin in Russia turned into a catastrophe for Western Communists. Although more backward than its neighbors, Italy nevertheless approximated the conditions of a modern civil society, and the vanguard party that Gramsci joined ended up as a sect of isolated militants – *pochi ma buoni* (few but good ones).

Gramsci's mature writings centered on the fact that the development of revolutionary working class consciousness had to be a collective *project*, rather than a preordained outcome. This takes him closer to a political process approach than his predecessors. For him, it would be necessary to develop the workers' consciousness, and he therefore conceived of the worker's movement as a collective intellectual, one of whose prime tasks was to create a new political culture. This idea is central to Gramsci's work on Machiavilli, on whom he drew in his prison writings on *Notes on Machiavelli*. In that essay, Gramsci saw the modern party as a modern version of *The Prince*. This idea was Leninist in inspiration, if not in tone. He saw in *The Prince* "a creation of concrete imagination which could work upon a dispersed and disintegrated society to stimulate and organize its general will" (1955: 3). "The modem Prince," he wrote, "the myth-prince, cannot be a real person, a concrete individual; it can only be an organism ... the political party, which, time and again ... knows how to form a new type of state" (Ibid.: 5).

This was a subtle but an important change. It led Gramsci to add to Lenin's organizational solution two key theorems: first, that a fundamental task of the party was to create a historic bloc of forces around the working class (1971: 168); and, second, that this could only occur if a cadre of "organic intellectuals" was developed from within the working class to complement the "traditional" intellectuals in the party (6–23). Both innovations turned out to hinge on a strong belief in the power of culture. In 1924, he wrote:

> The error of the party has been to have accorded priority in an abstract fashion
> to the problem of organization, which in practice has simply meant creating
> an apparatus of functionaries who could be depended on for their orthodoxy
> towards the official view. (1971: lxii)

Gramsci's solution to the cultural hegemony of the bourgeoisie was to recognize the need to produce a counter-cultural consensus among the workers, give them a capacity for autonomous initiatives, and build coalitions between them and other social formations. The process would be a long and a slow one, requiring the party to operate within the "trenches and fortifications" of bourgeois society, proselytize among nonproletarian groups, and learn how to deal with cultural institutions like the church.

But Gramsci's solution posed a new dilemma, for he provided no guide to how the battle within the gates of bourgeois society would be fought (1971: 229–239). Nor did he differentiate between countries according to whether the opportunities for revolution would be strong or weak. Moreover, if the party as collective intellectual engaged in a long-term dialogue between the working class and bourgeois society, what would prevent the cultural power of the latter – what Gramsci called "the common sense of capitalist society" – from transforming the party, rather than vice versa? Lacking a theory of political mobilization and paying insufficient attention to the state, Gramsci's solution to the collective action problem – like Marx and Lenin's – substituted a kind of political faith for detailed political analysis.

Dependencia and World Systems Theory

The macrostructuralist persuasion did not die with Gramsci. Responding to the social and political changes of the postwar years of economic revival, two groups of scholars with an internationalist orientation began to specify the old Marxist approach into a historical and comparative political economy approach. The first group, most common in Latin America and the United

States, came to be called the "dependency theorists."[5] Focusing on the terms of trade between northern capitalist countries and the dependent peripheral trading partners, these writers argued that peripheral countries needed to take protectionist measures to counterbalance the control exercised by core countries over the prices of their (mainly primary) exports. This eventually broadened into a structural theory of "development and underdevelopment" (Furtado 1964), which went so far as to argue that a condition of the development of the core capitalist countries of the North was the underdevelopment of the third-world periphery.

Dependency theorists were largely concerned with the conditions of late capitalist development in the periphery, but a second school, "world systems theory," was deliberately more global and historical. The founder of this school, Immanuel Wallerstein, went back to the first wave of globalized capitalism in the sixteenth century and posited that the class structure that Marx had seen in largely European terms was also global (1974). Capitalism spread across the world, he argued, not only because capitalists found new markets and needed new consumers in the global "periphery," but because they in some sense "used up" the sources of cheap labor in their own domestic economies.

This idea of capitalism expanding to find new sources of cheap labor was the guiding insight of Wallerstein's collaborator and chief interpreter, Giovanni Arrighi, who added to Wallerstein's twofold distinction of core and periphery the concept of the "semiperiphery," an intermediate zone that served, in some ways, as mediator between the capitalist core and its noncapitalist periphery. Each zone of the world, in Arrighi's view, passed through stages of development and crisis, each expansion recruiting new sources of labor until the entire planet was conquered for the capitalist enterprise (Arrighi ed. 1985; Arrighi 1990 and 1994). What Arrighi, and his collaborator, Beverly Silver (2003), crucially added to Wallerstein's theory was that labor in these countries did not remain indefinitely inert, but as it organized and mobilized, wages rose to a level at which capitalists moved on to newer and more peripheral locales, where the process of exploitation and mobilization would begin all over again. This in turn produced moving waves of "anti-system movements" (Arrighi et al. 1989).

This notion of mobile capital triggering the formation of labor movements and capital's response to capital's mobility excited a generation of students disappointed with classical Marxism but unwilling to embrace mainstream sociology. But neither the *dependencia* theorists nor the world systems school went much further than this in specifying the institutional and political variations that conditioned the formation of such movements; their inherent structuralism, wedded to their globalist convictions, left the organization, the ideology,

---

[5] Of the many writers on dependency theory, the most notable are: its founder, economist Raúl Prebisch (1950), its major American proponent, Paul Baran (1957) and two major Latin American proponents, Celso Furtado (1964) and sociologist and later President of Brazil, Fernando Henrique Cardoso (1979).

and political opportunities and constraints of "antisystemic movements" in the shadows. The current age of globalization provided scholars associated with the world systems' perspective with a new wave of movements that could be connected to capital's internationalization (Evans 2005; McMichael 2005). But because their theory allowed little space for noneconomic factors, neither school spent much energy specifying which movements were "antisystemic" and which were products of distinct political contexts in different parts of the world.

Weber, Tocqueville, and Their Modern Followers

The classical non-Marxist theorists – Tocqueville and Weber – were more attuned to the intricacies of the political process than the Marxists, yet they too began from structural properties of modern societies.[6] For Max Weber and his student, Robert Michels, the fundamental structural development of modernity was the rise of legal-rational bureaucracy, which affected both modern states and political parties and movements (Weber 1991; Michels 1962). States, Weber argued, evolve from traditional forms of authority to charismatic leadership to legal rationalism, most concretely reflected in the development of bureaucratic administration. Political parties and movements, Michels added, are diverted from their revolutionary messages as bureaucratic managers replace militants and displace their goals in favor of preserving the organization.

The trouble was that while Weber understood the power of the modern state far better than his Marxist opponents, he had little conception of the give-and-take of politics that put the state in motion in relation to society. Even Michels, who identified with the Left until later in his life, had only a one-sided view of the relationship between contentious actors and the state. He argued for a unilinear development of bureaucracy within political parties and movements that ignored their interaction with the political process (Zald and Ash 1966).

If we are looking for a classical theorist who did focus on political contention, we cannot do better than to turn to Alexis de Tocqueville. In both his *Recollections of the 1848 Revolution* (1992) and in his *Old Regime and the French Revolution* (1955), Tocqueville made clear his commitment to liberalism, his fear of strong states, and his distrust for democracy. What he tells us about contentious politics is more ambiguous because he drew his conclusions from the far-from-universal lessons of the French Revolution, which he abhorred.

Tocqueville saw that revolution as the result of both broad structural determinants and of distinctively French cultural developments. He began with a structural question: "Why did the revolution break out in France?" and answered: because the Old Regime's centralization denuded the aristocracy and other corporate groups of their positive functions, reducing them to

---

[6] This section draws on a recent article, "Red of Tooth and Claw: The French Revolution and the Political Process – Then and Now" published in *French Politics and Society* (Tarrow 2011b).

parasitic burdens on society and leaving France bereft of its "natural" sources of civic initiative and balance (1955: x). Stripped of intermediate bodies, lacking a buffer between state and society, Frenchmen became "self-seekers practicing a narrow individualism and caring nothing for the public good." The result was jealous egalitarianism, sporadic and uncontrolled mobilization, and, ultimately, the revolution: "a grim, terrific force of nature, a new fangled monster, red of tooth and claw" (1955: xiii).

Although best remembered for this structural theory of the revolution's origins, Tocqueville also had a cultural view of its causes. In explaining why the revolution spiraled from the relatively liberal phase of 1789 to the dogmatism and violence of the Terror, he placed primary responsibility on the intellectuals who were the Old Regime's shining lights. These *lumières*, he proposed, had laid the philosophical groundwork for the abstract notions of popular sovereignty that would characterize French revolutionary thought and drive the republic to the Terror. While the centralization of the Old Regime was the ultimate cause of state breakdown, the writings of its philosophical opponents were the efficient cause of its radicalization.

The cultural and structural facets of Tocqueville's thought came together in a kind of hydraulic model: because the centralization of the Old Regime had throttled France's "free institutions" – its municipal councils, its provincial assemblies, and the Estates General – it left a vacuum that was filled by men of letters. "The politicization of literature," writes Roger Chartier, "was thus at the same time a 'literarization' of politics transformed into an expectation of rupture and a dream of an 'ideal world'" (Chartier 1991: 12). This dual movement reduced the "complex of traditional customs" that Tocqueville treasured to a few "simple, elementary rules deriving from the exercise of the human reason and natural law" (Ibid.).

What is most interesting about Tocqueville for our purposes is that his views were so deeply influenced by French history that he missed most of the contention that was brewing in America as he wrote *Democracy in America*: the enormous amount of religious enthusiasm in the 1830s; the conflicts on the frontier that had led to the Whiskey Rebellion; and the implications of the federal system that he so admired for the coming Civil War. If he marveled that the "excess of democracy" he found in America did not lead to the collapse of democracy (1960), it was just such an excess, in his view, that led to the destruction of French liberties. Because his image of contention came from the French revolution – "red of tooth and claw" – Tocqueville missed the proximity of social movements to ordinary politics in the United States.

What did a conservative liberal like Tocqueville have in common with his Marxist enemies? Very little, ideologically speaking, but both Marx and Tocqueville were structuralists – the former in classist, and the latter in statist terms. And both Tocqueville and Gramsci had strong affinities to culturalism, the former in the influence of intellectuals on politics and the latter in the concept of the party as collective intellectual. As for Lenin, his unspoken adaptation of the Bolsheviks to the conditions of the Tsarist autocracy was a striking parallel to Tocqueville's insistence on the heritage of the Old Regime in France. These modern culturalist and structuralist tropes would reappear in the 1960s and 1970s in the neo-Tocquevillian culturalist, François Furet, and the neo-Tocquevillian structuralist, Theda Skocpol.

Furet and Skocpol

Until the recent revival of Tocqueville studies in the 1980s, the French thinker was largely remembered as a student of institutions – the institutions of the Old Regime in France and the decentralized institutions of American democracy across the Atlantic. But his theory of the nefarious influence of the French Revolution was revived in the historical work of French historian François Furet while his structural approach was revived in the work of American Theda Skocpol.

Following Tocqueville, Furet drew a causal link from the abstract thought of the Enlightenment intellectuals to the excesses of the Terror (1981; 1992). Fittingly, he used the bicentennial of the revolution in 1989 to attack the Jacobins and their contemporary successors (Kaplan 1993; Tarrow 2011a). This move was historiographic but it was also political. By the 1980s, Furet was deeply implicated in the politics of the Fifth Republic. Looking backward, he linked the Terror to the abstractions and simplifications of Enlightenment theory; but looking to the present, he saw it as the source of the Leninist deviations of the French Left. If this sounds like Tocqueville it was no accident: Furet was an avid admirer of his nineteenth-century predecessor. Of course, Tocqueville could not have imagined the horrors of the Gulag, and Furet had the advantage of seeing first-hand how Marxist theory had twisted the mentality of his former Communist comrades. Yet the two had this in common: neither was very interested in the political processes within the revolution that produced the first experiment with a revolutionary state (Furet 1992: 312).

A less politically inflected inheritance of Tocqueville's teaching came from the American historical sociologist, Theda Skocpol (1979; 1994). Skocpol placed the French Revolution in a comparative framework with the Russian and Chinese Revolutions, seeing all three as the joint result of international pressures, agrarian conflicts, and statist factors. The enduring popularity of her work is due to the fact that it combined sociological and statist structuralism. In explaining the origins of three great social revolutions she combined an emphasis on agrarian class relations with an acute attention to state fiscal crises, in interaction with international vulnerability. When she turned to revolutionary *outcomes*, state structure loomed even larger in Skocpol's vision, while international factors receded into the background. As for the revolutionary political process – the dynamic of political culture, coalition building and leadership – Skocpol's statism left little space for the political process, a lacuna that her critics were quick to observe.[7]

---

[7] The corpus of criticism of Skocpol's book would fill a review article on its own. For her encyclopedic, and sometimes acerbic, reply to some of her critics, see the conclusion to her *Social*

Contemporary Theorists

While there were major differences between the Marxists and Tocquevillians in how they saw contentious politics, these differences pale in comparison with the newer traditions of research on social movements in Western Europe and the United States. While some Western European theorists, like Alain Touraine and Claus Offe, attempted to update Marxian structuralism by finding substitutes for the working class, American theorists focused increasingly on the phenomenology of social movements: how individuals are mobilized into movements; their organizations and resources; how they frame collective action; and how they interact with the political system. There remained a structuralist component in both sets of theories, but in the Tourainian version it devolved into a search for "real" movements at "higher" levels of history, while in the second, structure came to be specified as the proximate "political opportunity structure" and no longer as the broad structural changes examined by the theorists surveyed earlier in this chapter.

Both sets of theorists came only after the interwar period and World War II left an imprint in the form of theories of collective behavior.

Collective Behavior Theories

Fascism and its wartime atrocities produced a largely negative image of social movements. A first generation of theory was a response to the dislocations and destruction of the interwar and World War II periods. Influenced by the horrors of Stalinism and Nazism, many scholars saw social movements driven by alienation and social disorganization (Hoffer 1951; Kornhauser 1959). If that generation was influenced by any theorist, it was Emile Durkheim, who had little to say about social movements but who famously coined the term "anomie" to describe the psychological state of people unhinged from traditional social moorings (Durkheim 1964). Freud and his followers added a psychological dimension to the theory, especially in the hands of Erich Fromm, whose work united his psychological training with his experience of fascism (1969).

In academia, this perspective was adopted by collective behavior theorists like Neil Smelser, Ralph Turner, and Lewis Killian. These scholars lacked the fear of Hoffer and Kornhauser that movements would lead to totalitarianism, but they retained the core idea that contention resulted from dysfunctions in the working of society (Smelser 1962; Turner and Killian 1987; see

Revolutions in the Modern World, 1994. In her later work, Skocpol softened her elemental statism, added the relevance of urban classes and interclass coalitions to the overworked peasantry, and admitted that professional revolutionaries and ideologies help to make revolutions (1994). But her work remained largely free of cross-fertilization with the softer political structuralism that was developing in the social movement field; with the microhistorical emphasis on agency that was advancing the culturalist study of revolutions (Selbin 1993); with the deeper cultural approaches pioneered by Lynn Hunt (1984); the rational choice approaches of Popkin (1977) and Taylor (1988); or with the ambitious syncretism of Goldstone (1991), Wickham-Crowley (1992), and Goodwin (1994; 2001). These intersections would be far more advanced in contemporary theories of social movements.

the review in McAdam 1999 [1982]). The postwar period produced a largely negative image of social movements. All this was to change in the 1960s and 1970s.

The "New" Social Movement School

When, in the late 1960s, the institutionalized politics of the postwar decades were challenged by worker, student, and generalized discontent, just as the ruthless nature of state socialism was being exposed by the Soviet invasion of Czechoslovakia, scholarly certitudes were shattered as well. In Western Europe the most obvious casualty was the notion that the working class was a radical social movement's necessary class basis. In Germany, Claus Offe (1985), in Italy Alberto Melucci (1985, 1989), and in France the school founded by Alain Touraine distanced themselves deliberately from Marxism, yet continued to link movements to class structure and to place movements in a historical progression of types of society. Because it was Touraine whose work had the widest international influence, this section gives more attention to his work than to that of Offe or Melucci.

Growing out of a background in industrial sociology, Touraine formulated what he called an "actionist sociology," which actually reproduced many of the concepts of Marxist structural historicism. He began by rejecting the Marxist idea of the inevitable radicalization of the industrial class struggle, arguing that the "institutionalization of the labor conflicts which transform the worker's movement into a truly political force has made it lose its role as a central social movement" (Touraine 1981: 12). Following the 1968 student revolts, Touraine took up a political position closer to the new intellectual left than to the classical Marxist left-wing parties. Following the events of May 1968, for example, he put forward the idea that the revolt, despite its obvious limits, heralded a new era in history, a thesis which he worked out in more detail in his subsequent collection of essays entitled *La société postindustrielle*" (Touraine 1965; quoted in Rucht 1991: 358–359).

But although distancing himself from Marxism and founding what he called "actionist" sociology (1965), Touraine continued to think in structural-historicist terms. Society is divided into three systems. The highest system, he declared, is based on two fundamental components: historicity – "its capacity to produce the models by which it functions"; and class relations – "though which these orientations become social practices." Social movements emerge at this level where "Touraine situates the category of 'dominance' and the realm of class conflict, and thus of social movement activities" (Rucht: 363). Politics and political struggles are found only at a second level, what he called the "institutional system," where political struggles and political movements occur. But these struggles and movements are inferior to real social movements, a term that Touraine reserved for conflicts at the level of "historicity." At a third level is what Touraine calls "the organizational system," to which he gives little attention, because his main interest is with the highest level at which social movements emerge.

But movements do not emerge at all times and for all purposes. In order to be counted as "true" movements, Touraine required them to have three aspects: *identity*, which refers to the conscious self-definition of a social actor; *opposition*, through a conflict that constitutes and organizes the actor; and *totality*, which refers to the realm in which actors "strive for domination." The social movement, Touraine writes, is "a collective behavior which is not directed towards the values of a social organization or towards participation in decision-making systems, but towards the stake of class conflicts" (Touraine 1973: 365). Other social formations are mere political movements or "deficient forms" which "may well be the heralds of a coming social movement" (Rucht 1991: 365).

Note that, although declaring himself not a Marxist, Touraine nevertheless insisted that every society has a main class relation that organizes antagonistic pairs of movements. "Social movement and class struggle are synonymous expressions," he wrote in 1981; "there exist no class relations separable from class action, from its cultural orientations and from the social conflict in which the movement occurs" (1981: 84). This idea Touraine maintained over much of his career, even while arguing that particular social actors and the axis around which they oppose one another shift over the different stages of social development, from agrarian, merchant, industrial, to postindustrial societies (Rucht: 366–367).[8]

Not all post-1968 social movement scholars were smitten with Tourainian abstractions. A group of mainly younger scholars were moving away from the class-based macrosociology that had guided earlier European scholarship but toward a focus on movements' interactions with the polity. Instead of the working class, they focused on the new middle-class sectors; instead of the labor movement, they turned to movements in favor of peace, the environment, and feminism. A landmark was the comparative analysis of environmental groups in Europe and America by Dieter Rucht (1990). A second was the comparative work on terrorism in Germany and Italy by Donatella della Porta (1995). A third, which partially hearkened back to the structuralism of the Marxist tradition in its emphasis on social cleavages, was the work of Hanspeter Kriesi and his collaborators on the politics of new social movements in four European countries (Kriesi et al. 1995). But it was in the United States that class-based structuralism had little purchase

---

[8] Oddly, in this final phase of Touraine's career the struggle is no longer over the means of production but over the access and distribution of knowledge. "As a consequence of this potential for total self-production, conflicts no longer focus on a specific societal subsystem but may emerge everywhere, including in institutions such as schools, universities, hospitals, or homes for elderly people" (Rucht: 367). Touraine's reluctance to let go of the idea that class is the basis of social movements did not prevent him from investigating movements whose class basis would be hard for most observers to discern (See Touraine et al. 1978; Touraine et al. 1980; and Touraine et al. 1981). Only toward the end of his career did he return to the working class movement but the logic of his writing remained in the structural-historicist mode in which politics appears as a secondary subsystem to history and class.

and that scholars increasingly turned to the endogenous world of social movements.

Resource Mobilization

Inspired by the same new wave of contention that led Touraine to search for a substitute for the working class, a group of younger American scholars saw activism in the light of the organizational level that Touraine ignored. Peopled by fresh young faces often active in civil rights and the antiwar movement, animated by the desire to see wrongs righted and democracy advanced, these movements showed scholars the capacities, the wholesome democratic instincts, and the social ties that bound their activists to each other – the very opposite of what that earlier scholars, influenced by the interwar and wartime periods, had uncovered (Keniston 1968). And rather than "anomie" producing collective action, these scholars found vital emotional energies and cognitive liberation in the new generation of activists (Piven and Cloward 1972; 1979; McAdam 1999 [1982]).

This new work had a second feature as well – greater concreteness and specificity. Disheartened by the loose and inclusive way in which the term "movement" had been employed by their predecessors, the new generation zeroed in on movement *organizations,* drawing on the vigorous strain of organization theory that had developed in American sociology and observing the tremendous organizational growth in America and Western Europe in the postwar years (McCarthy and Zald 1973; 1977). This "resource mobilization" tradition gave American social movement research a concrete object of study and led practitioners to focus on the birth, death, and transformation of movement organizations, using the empirical tools of organizational analysis (Minkoff 1995) and survey research (Klandermans 1984).

But in their desire to inter the older "collective behavior" approach, many of this new generation of scholars – especially in the United States – elevated movement *organizations* to the center of attention. That translated into a healthy attention to the structural, organizational, and behavioral facets of movements, but it gave less attention to what movements actually *do.* Do they protest? Do they socialize their militants and members? Does social movement action extend to lobbying, a form of action that is more typically seen as part of the interest group universe (Zald 2000)? Or do movement organizations negotiate the space between contention and convention, using more contentious or more routine actions according to the opportunities and threats of the moment and the issues at stake?

One line of work that grew out of this focus on movement organization was based on the new statistical approaches coming out of population ecology. Rather than focus on individual movement organizations, population ecologists like Debra Minkoff (1995) and Susan Olzak (1992) studied the birth, death, and temporal clustering of organizations. A second line of work, referred to obliquely in the introduction to this chapter, was the study of social networks: scholars like Mario Diani (1995), Roger Gould (1995), and Maryjane Osa

(2003) traced the linkages among movement organizations. But although these scholars were all concerned with organizational changes over time, their models were essentially static. Not so the work of Charles Tilly, who focused his work on longer-term contentious episodes.

Tilly and the Political Process Approach

In friendly contrast to this "resource mobilization" approach, which focused on movement organizations, Charles Tilly and his students broadened their interest to what Tilly called "contentious events" (Tilly 1995), and what others, who followed his lead, called "protest events" (Jenkins 1985; McAdam 1999 [1982]; Tarrow 1989) or "conflict events (Olzak 1992). Tilly's work was deeply attuned to history (1986); to the interaction between contention and changes in political regimes; and to the broad canvas of political conflict and regime change (1995). Scholars influenced by him, like Ronald Aminzade (1983), Michael Hanagan (1980), Craig Jenkins (1985) Ted Margardant (1979), Doug McAdam (1999 [1982]), Susan Olzak (1992), Michael Schwartz (1976), Mark Steinberg (1999), this author (1989), and Wayne te Brake (1998), also strove to place episodes of contention in their historical and geographic contexts.

By focusing centrally on what happens in episodes of political contention, Tilly and his students developed a new method for studying collective action – the systematic cataloguing and analysis of contentious events. Variants of this approach, surveyed in Chapter 7, were: the "event history" method, which borrowed methodological tools from organizational sociology to systematically track sequences of events like ethnic conflict (Olzak 1992), the environmental movement (Vasi 2009), and the shantytown protests that marked the antiapartheid movement in the United States (Soule 1997, 1999); the systematic study of great events, which, in the hands of historical sociologists like William Sewell, helped to show how events like the taking of the Bastille were historical hinges in bringing about structural change (Sewell 1996); and the textual reading of chains of events that marked Tilly's final contribution to the field (2008a). The systematic analysis of contentious events is perhaps the most unique contribution of scholars of contentious politics to the social sciences (Klandermans and Staggenborg eds. 2002).

In summary, whether American or European, working historically or on recent periods of contention, contemporary scholars made great strides in understanding the endogenous processes – recruitment, mobilization, political structuring – that lead people to engage in contentious collective action. They specified the nature of the organizations engaged in contentious politics. However – the present author included – they did not work nearly as hard to analyze the broader structural realations among movements, parties, and states. In order to do so, the "movement" in social movements would need to be put in motion through the deliberate study of how contention occurs, who engages in it, and the events that mark its beginnings, its development, and its demobilization.

Interactive Contention

That social movements should be seen in a dynamic framework is not a
new idea. But the problem with both the resource mobilization and political process approaches as they developed in the United States is that they
were so movement-centered that it was difficult to track how movements
interact over time with other elements of the polity. In the classical political
process model, movement organizations, political opportunities, the framing
of contention, and the forms of collective action were loosely connected in
predicting mobilization, but the causal links among these factors were seldom well specified or integrated with routine politics (McAdam et al. 2001:
17, 43–44).

   Think of the relations between social movements and the courts. We know
well that movements often use legal strategies, as the civil rights movement did
in the United States even before the 1950s; and we know that legal frameworks
affect movement strategies and outcomes – for example, the "permitting" that
regulates marches in Washington, DC (McCarthy, Schweingruber, and McPhail
1999). But these are empirical observations: we have no general theory that
accounts for the relations between social movements, the courts, and legal systems, although work on "legal mobilization" has provided a start in this direction (Sarat and Scheingold eds. 2006). So far, we have not devised a means
for systematically bringing the elements in contentious politics together and
putting them into motion. Scholars could only begin to answer these questions
if they took apart episodes of contention into their component mechanisms
and processes. Or so I have argued, among others who think that a focus
on social mechanisms may provide an answer (Hedström and Swedberg eds.
1998; Mahoney et al. 2009; McAdam et al. 2001; Tilly 2000).

Mechanisms and Processes

In the classical political process approach, actors respond to opportunities
and threats; they frame their movements around cognitive liberation or, more
broadly, collective action frames; and they create movement organizations or
activate old ones. There is nothing wrong here, as far as it goes. But the action
in this model was lodged in the boxes of a static paradigm, rather than in the
mechanisms and processes that connect the elements in the paradigm to each
other and to other actors.

   In the last decade, a mechanism-and-process approach to social action has
gained ground, both in the social sciences in general and in the study of contentious politics in particular. A first move in this direction was made in the 1980s
in the path breaking work of David Snow and his collaborators, who specified different forms of social movement framing (Snow et al. 1986). Scholars
like Sarah Soule were also studying mechanisms – particularly the complex of
mechanisms that constitute diffusion (Soule 1997, 1999, 2004). Doug McAdam
made a similar move in his work on the strategic interaction between the civil
rights movement and authorities (1983). More recently, Ann Mische specified

a variety of relational mechanisms in her study of networks of Brazilian youth movements (Mische 2008).

What are mechanisms? Definitions abound but something like a consensual view is that mechanisms are a delimited class of changes that alter relations among specific sets of elements in identical or closely similar ways over a variety of situations (McAdam et al. 2001, *Mobilization* 2010). Mechanisms compound into processes, regular combinations and sequences of mechanisms that produce similar transformations of those elements. Some mechanisms and processes – such as the attribution of opportunity or threat, the adoption of new performances, and the construction of new identities – are familiar from the classical social movement paradigm; but others – like identity shift and actor constitution – draw deliberately on the new culturalist approaches to social movements. The systematic study of the mechanisms of contention are one way – certainly not the only one – to break the traditional cleavage between structure and action.

This takes me to the "Dynamics" project that shaped the contributions later in this book. In the early 2000s, in *Dynamics of Contention,* my collaborators, Doug McAdam and Charles Tilly, and I tried to build a comparative and historical exploration of the mechanisms and processes of contention (2001). Though it built on the classical political process approach, we wanted to design a relational approach to contentious politics by specifying the mechanisms and processes that appear not just in social movements, but in all forms of contentious politics. The book focused to some extent on the factors contributing to the emergence of contentious action and to some extent on its outcomes, but most of its message centered on the relational processes of contention between inputs and outcomes.

Three main types of mechanisms were identified and explored in that book:

- *Dispositional mechanisms,* such as the perception and attribution of opportunity or threat;
- *Environmental mechanisms,* such as population growth or resource depletion;
- And *relational mechanisms,* such as the brokerage of a coalition among actors with no previous contact by a third actor who has contact with both.

A historical example from that book is how a set of environmental, cognitive, and relational mechanisms combined to trigger the American Civil War. Older scholars had seen slavery as the fundamental cause of the war between the states, an explanation that was modified as it became clear that the North's original war aims did not include ending bondage. Then the economic splits between an expanding North and a static South came into play as scholars saw an expanding industrial northern economy coming into conflict with a static and agrarian South. More recently, new institutionalists have pointed to congressional decision making as a primary cause (Weingast 1998).

But seeking to identify a final cause for a major historical episode of contention is both fruitless and deceptive: in the onset of the Civil War, a combination of environmental, cognitive, and relational mechanisms were at play;

- *Environmental mechanisms:* the population of the North and West were expanding rapidly, leading to a wave of restless western farmers who feared that if slavery were allowed to penetrate their region their farms would become uncompetitive;
- *Dispositional mechanisms:* there was a growing cognitive shift between North and South as northerners saw southerners as lazy parasites living off the labor of their slaves and southerners saw northerners as money-grubbing capitalists;
- *Relational mechanisms:* finally, the mechanism of brokerage came into play as the new Republican party brought together Northern abolitionists with Western free-soil farmers and part of the old Whig party (McAdam et al. 2001: 163–171).

This account oversimplifies a complex and contradictory historical episode. Historians would cringe at the idea that three kinds of mechanisms explained the outbreak of the most searing conflict in American history. But note that if it rested wholly on the action of a "social movement" – the abolitionists – it would be grossly inadequate. Equally inadequate was the revisionist view that structural changes somehow explained the breakdown of the antebellum political consensus. Focusing on mechanisms places movements in dynamic interaction with a host of other forces – institutional and noninstitutional, structural and political – to provide a more rounded account of the coming of the American Civil War.

Dynamics claimed that the same strategy could help to explain other major episodes of contention by disaggregating historical narratives into their constituent mechanisms and processes. We compared democratization in Switzerland and Mexico; revolution and failed revolution in Nicaragua and China; and nationalism in the construction of unified Italy and in the destruction of the Soviet Union, among other cases. That book was imperfect, but it illustrated how a relatively small number of mechanisms and processes drive a wide variety of contentious episodes, sometimes producing revolutionary change and sometimes the reconstitution of existing power relations.

Dynamics was not an isolated effort. In the last decade, the mechanism-and-process approach to contentious politics has made progress, especially among younger scholars. For example, in a 2011 issue of *Mobilization,* a number of mostly younger scholars came together to explore and extend the mechanism-and-process approach. Mark Beissinger applied a mechanistic approach to the "color revolutions" in the former Soviet bloc; Roger Karapin surveyed a number of mechanisms in the American women's movement of the late nineteenth century to trace spirals of opportunity and threat; Daniel Sherman examined the mechanisms that were triggered in local opposition to the storing of low-level radioactive waste in the United States; Michael Heaney and Fabio Rojas demonstrated how coalition formation and narrowing affected the American peace movement between the beginning of the Iraq War and the election of Barack Obama; and Bogdan Vasi showed how opposition to the U.S. Patriot Act diffused during the same period (all in *Mobilization* 2011).

The mechanism-and-process approach is not without its problems, as critics were quick to point out (see the criticisms in *Mobilization* 2003, and the self-criticisms in *Mobilization* 2011). There have been a number of criticisms: of the term's conceptual vagueness, proliferation of mechanisms adduced, and lack of methodological rigor in the production of mechanism-based analyses. There has also been criticism of "mechanism talk," that is, resort to mechanisms whenever there is the need to explain unexplained variance. What *Dynamics* and cognate work over the last decade *did not do* was to bridge the gaps between structural and process-based approaches.

In the first part of this chapter, I surveyed the contributions of several of the great structural theorists of contentious politics: Marx, Lenin, and Gramsci on the left; Weber, Michels, Tocqueville on the center-right, and their successors, *dependencia* and world systems theorists in the "capitalist" tradition and Furet and Skocpol in the "statist" one. Though giving some attention to the cultural constitution of contention, all these theorists were fundamentally structuralist: they derived the incentives for collective action from either social structure or state structure. But none of them specified theoretically how the structural variables they featured translate into the processes of contentious politics: how challengers organize themselves; seize and create opportunities; and frame contention so as to attract supporters and engage in dialogue with opponents and the state. Gramsci came closest to a political process approach to contention, but as we will see in the next chapter, his idea of inserting the communist movement into the "trenches and fortifications" of civil society lacked specificity and opened the door to contradictions.

As we saw in the second part of the chapter, these lacunae in the structuralist approach were attacked by theorists who paid greater attention to the political process. In the United States, McAdam and Tilly, and in Europe, della Porta, Rucht, and Kriesi and their collaborators were exemplars of this shift from structure to process. Both McAdam and Kriesi acknowledged social change and social cleavages at the ultimate sources of contention but only Tilly gave as much attention to capitalism and state building as he did to the political process. By focusing on political opportunities, resource mobilization, movement framing, and the forms of contention that challengers use, scholars – including this one – simply assumed that broad social change is somehow responsible for starting a process of mobilization that results in the formation of social movements and, more generally, in contentious politics.

How can we bridge the chasm between structural and process approaches without falling into the "old structuralism" that Tilly criticized (2008b)? Tilly left us before he could complete his project of constructing a unified analytical framework to study contentious politics. But in his analysis of state building and capitalism, he moved toward a closer linkage between structural processes like capitalism and state building and "local" mechanisms and processes than anyone working in the field of contentious politics. For example, Tilly argued that war – the most extreme form of contention – was at the origin of the state-building projects of early modern Europe (Tilly 1990). State building in turn produced the need for rulers to extract resources; to standardize their populations; educate elites to staff the army and the state; produce the resources the state needed; distribute goods and services; and reconcile and pacify the interests of different population groups affected by the state-building project. From a sequence that began with war making and state building, he argued, modern states both created contention and fashioned instruments to deal with it (see Chapter 3).

These are not the mechanisms and processes that are usually seen as internal to social movements, mechanisms like recruitment, mobilization, and framing. But this is exactly the point: If we want to connect the structural preconditions of contention we saw in part one to the internal processes we saw in part two, we will have to find ways to linking structure and process in a dynamic framework. To accomplish this linkage, much work remains to be done. Some of that work will be attempted in the chapters that follow.

I

MOVEMENTS IN HISTORY, HISTORIES OF MOVEMENTS

2

Peasants and Communists in Southern Italy

When, as a green American graduate student, I arrived in southern Italy in the fall of 1963 to study the Communist Party and the peasant movement, it was with a conviction common to my generation that social movements were "good," states were "bad," and political parties were more-or-less useless in producing social change. Note that this was orthogonal to the reigning orthodoxy in the study of collective behavior, which saw contention as the result of "dysfunctions." But it resonated with Anthony Downs' recent claim that most parties gravitate toward the political center (1957) and with Giovanni Sartori's argument that Italy suffered from "polarized pluralism," a system in which extremist parties were blocked from legitimate participation (1966). Between Downs and Sartori, what was left for parties as agents of change?

In the Italy of the 1960s I found grist for both Sartori's and Downs' theories in the Italian Communist Party (PCI). In the late 1940s, that party had intervened in the relations between the land-hungry peasants and the Italian state, but it seemed only to have succeeded in restraining their energies. The party wanted to gain power, but in an Italy still occupied by the American army, contention on the toe of the peninsula would have upset its plans to pacify the country. The immediate result, as this chapter will show, was to call rhetorically for "the land for those who work it!" but also to moderate the violent energies of the peasants. The long-term result was to denude the party of the passion and commitment that had brought the peasantry to its door in the first place.

In the early 1960s, a new left around the journal *Quaderni Rossi* began to aim its intellectual darts at this ambivalent position of the PCI and by the late 1960s, student and worker movements seemed to be outflanking the party on the left. Young progressive scholars like myself were quick to associate with this movement. Inspired by Gramsci (see Chapter 1), I cheered the peasantry that had fought for ownership of the land in the years following World War I (Gramsci 1963); and through lenses shaped by Weber and Michels I criticized the PCI as a bureaucratic brake on the peasants' energies.

This view was heavily shaped by the structuralist ontology common to my generation: the Communists, I argued, were shackled by the structures in which they found themselves: first, by the "backward" conditions of the South: then by the region's fragmented agrarian structure and fractured civil society – which Gramsci had characterized as a "great social disaggregation" – and, finally, by its leaders' petit bourgeois origins (Tarrow 1967a). If the peasants who had rebelled against the power of the *latifundia* received only slivers of land at the hands of a conservative Christian Democratic-led government, this was the result of their demobilization at the hands of the PCI (Tarrow 1967a: ch. 12). Or so I argued.

But something was missing from this account. After all, it was a Communist minister of agriculture who had passed the first land reform act in 1946. Moreover, the PCI had intervened actively in the relations between the peasants and the state to organize the struggle for the land. Finally, the party that I saw shaped by the "backwardness" of the South was hardly southern: born in the North, it was the product of an industrial/commercial culture and a working class with a solid sense of discipline. Seeing it as the product of the "backward" political culture of the South gave the party little agency. Or so I later decided as a "recovering structuralist" (Tarrow 2005). This chapter reproduces the original structuralist account of that episode; the conclusion will return to this episode with a reinterpretation of the findings that draws on the perspective I developed toward contentious politics in the intervening decades.

Marxism and the Peasantry

Each of the Marxist theorists examined in Chapter 1 of this book had a position on the role of the peasantry. In *The Eighteenth Brumaire of Louis Bonaparte*, Marx had famously dismissed the peasants as no more than "potatoes in a sack of potatoes" (1963: 123–124). Dreaming of the collapse of capitalism in the long term, he failed to see that revolutions are made in the much shorter term and might depend on the disposition – radical or reactionary – of the rural masses. The Social Democrats who inherited Marx's mantle were even more short-sighted about the peasantry, attempting to appeal to them for votes while cavalierly informing them that they would eventually disappear into the proletariat (Mitrany 1961: ch. 3).

Non-Western Marxists like Mao tse-Tung, who was chastened by the massacre of the Shanghai proletariat in 1925, turned to the peasants as the core of the revolution (Schram 1967). Although the peasants were the motor force in defeating the Japanese occupiers and then the Chinese Nationalists (Selden 1971), that revolution was also heavily infused with nationalism (Johnson 1962). At the same time, Indonesian Communists (PKI) were relapsing into a kind of "folk communism" (Benda 1966; McVey 1970). Lacking an organizational weapon, this left the party prey to destruction in the army coup of 1965. In India, in contrast, where Communist parties had to deal with caste and religious differences as well as class and agrarian cleavages, there were both revisionist and sectarian distortions (Overstreet and Windmuller 1959; Zagoria 1971). Once Marxist leaders compromised Marx's single-minded focus on the proletariat, they were prone to lose their way.

Lenin was more politically astute. Writing of a society – Tsarist Russia – in which the peasantry was overwhelmingly the largest class, he hoped to divide the poor peasants from more substantial *kulaks* and attract them to communism with the hope that they would gain ownership of the land (1972). When the revolution did break out, and peasants and peasant/soldiers played a major role in it, Lenin's vision appeared to be validated. But we know what eventually happened: encouraged to become small landholders under the "New Economic Policy," the *kulaks* were eventually herded into collective farms and decimated by Stalin when they resisted (Mitrany 1961: ch. 7).

Gramsci, the Peasants, and the Southern Question

Gramsci's views were more complicated and deeper "inside the gates" of Italian society.[1] At first he adopted the view that when the Italian revolution broke out, the peasants – especially in Southern Italy – would serve as a diversionary force to divide the repressive efforts of the state between North and South. But as he reflected on Italian conditions from his prison cell in the 1930s, Gramsci's view of the peasantry took a major turn. He came to believe that the peasant masses could be brought to play a major role in constructing working class hegemony.

Gramsci remained every inch a Leninist, as his attraction to Machiavelli shows (1955). In his thought, the party would be a "collective intellectual" that would meld the anarchic energies of the southern peasantry with the more disciplined militancy of the northern workers. But this posed another problem: if the party, as Gramsci proposed, was to excavate for itself a position in the "trenches and fortifications" of Italian society, that society was *two* societies – an industrial, highly organized North and an agrarian disorganized South – what Gramsci called "a great social disaggregation" (1963: vol. II: 68). He was confident that the party could manage these differences; but there was a tension between his theory of the party and his model of its adaptation to its various societal and cultural settings.

We can portray these tensions graphically with a simple structural typology. Parties of the left could be mass parties – like the Italian Socialists that Gramsci had abandoned when he became a Communist – or they could be parties of cadres like the one that Lenin had constructed in Russia. Orthagonally, the societies they were attempting to conquer could be peasant societies – as Russia was in 1917 – or advanced capitalist states with strong civil societies like the societies of Western Europe. The two sets of structural variations potentially produce four types of party, as Figure 2.1 suggests:

---

[1] Although he was the son of a petit-bourgeois public servant, Gramsci's background in Sardinia gave him a better sense of what life was like in a poor rural region than either Marx or Lenin had. For a short biography that stresses these origins, see Fiori 1971.

Type of Party

	Mass party	Party of cadres
Agrarian Society	Mass	
	Movement	Vanguard

Type of

Society

	Advanced	Class-	
	capitalist	mass	Sect
	Society		

FIGURE 2.1 A Typology of Marxist Parties and Societies.

* *Vanguard parties:* Leninist parties in agrarian societies
* *Social-Democratic parties:* class-mass parties in interwar Europe
* *Sects:* Leninist parties trying to penetrate advanced societies
* *Mass movements:* class-mass parties in agrarian societies

From his prison cell, Gramsci recognized that the attempt to create a vanguard party in an advanced society failed miserably after World War I and produced only a narrow sect of isolated militants – *pochi ma buoni* (few but good ones). This was an experience he did not want the party to repeat after fascism's end. Yet he did not want the party to emerge from the war as a facsimile of the social democratic parties that Michels criticized either. His solution was to try to produce "a party of a new type," which would combine the two types noted previously: a combination of a vanguard party prepared to attack the summit of the Italian state and a class-mass base embedded in the "trenches and fortifications" of society.

Gramsci contributed two important ideas to his party's future ideology: the first was the idea of the party as the modern Prince. This idea was Leninist in inspiration, if not in tone. He saw in *The Prince* "a creation of concrete imagination which could work upon a dispersed and disintegrated society to stimulate and organize its general will" (1955: 3). The modern equivalent of Machiavelli's Prince is the political party and its sublime mission is to organize a new collectivity.

> The modern Prince, the myth-prince, cannot be a real person, a concrete individual; it can only be an organism ... the political party, which, time and again ... knows how to form a new type of state. (Ibid.: 5)

A second aspect of Gramsci's thought concerned the backward and "disaggregated" nature of southern Italian society and its role in the future revolution. Presaging the dependency theory of the 1960s, North and South were not united nationally, but colonially; "The bourgeoisie of the North," he wrote, "has subjected the South of Italy and the Islands to the status of colonies for exploitation" (1963: vol. 2: 50). The South was ruled by an agrarian bloc of landed proprietors and intellectuals who were paid off by their northern bosses through parliamentary deals. The peasant was helplessly tied to the agrarian bloc through clientele relations with the landholders. Semifeudal contractual relations dominated economic life, preventing the peasantry's emergence as a modern social force. Left to themselves, the peasants of the South would dissolve into a "disorganized mass, a chaotic disorder of exasperated passions." Organized by the proletariat of the North, they could be an engine of the revolution. "The proletariat," Gramsci wrote, "will destroy the southern agrarian bloc in the degree that it succeeds, through its party, in organizing ever larger masses of poor peasants in autonomous and independent organizations (Ibid.)

Several points are significant about Gramsci's formulation. First, it separated North and South theoretically and admitted that special efforts were needed to organize the southern peasants. Second, the relationship was bilateral. "The workers of the factory and the poor peasants," he writes, "are the *two energies* of the proletarian revolution" (Ibid: 79; emphasis added). Third, the alliance was to be revolutionary and socialist, rather than tactical and democratic, and there was no doubt about proletarian hegemony. Instead of what he called the "magic formula" of the division of the *latifundia,* Gramsci proposed a "political alliance between workers of the North and peasants of the South to overthrow the bourgeoisie from the power of the state" (Ibid).

The "organizational weapon" that emerged from these two central ideas – the party as the modern Prince and the alliance of northern workers and southern peasants – would have a strong potential for revolution in an underdeveloped area like the South. With allowance made for his sensitivity to Italian conditions, this was close to Lenin's model for a revolutionary party in a backward society. "Spontaneity" was rampant in the "disaggregated" southern peasantry, while the party as modern Prince was the embodiment of "consciousness." The parallel to Lenin's model, we may assume, was not lost on Gramsci, even as he reflected on the failure of the revolution in the West after World War I.

But these ideas ran at cross-purposes to a second idea: the embedding of the party in the "trenches and fortifications" of Italian society. Where those "trenches and fortifications" were part of a backward agrarian society, like Russia's, they offered little purchase for the party, which had succeeded in 1917 only by attacking the summit of the state. In an advanced capitalist society with a large and disciplined working class like Northern Italy's, Gramsci reasoned, those trenches and fortifications were strong, and a party that wanted to gain power there would need to root itself within them. But in the disorganized agrarian South, where such a proletarian cadre was not available, a party that sought a position in "the trenches and fortifications of civil society" was more likely to reflect that weakness, and produce an unstructured rural mass movement. That is exactly what happened in Southern Italy in the years following World War II as the party applied its strategy from the North to the stark regional differences between the two regions, as I will show below. In the next section I will turn to these "two societies" to demonstrate the great variations in "trenches and fortifications" that the Communist Party had to deal with in Italy after World War II.

Two Italies

"Italy," Joseph LaPalombara wrote in 1964, "represents two distinct cultures, the relatively dynamic and industrial North and the relatively stagnant South" (1964: 37). The disparity between the regions was not merely one of degree: it was a structural cleavage, observed by generations of statesmen and intellectuals, extending into the economic, social, and political systems and presenting concrete obstacles to political integration.[2] While exhaustive analysis of Italian dualism is impossible in this context, several basic indicators suggest the breadth of the gaps between North and South (SVIMEZ 1961).

Economically, Italy has long been a "dual economy," with a dual labor market and a dual structure of industry (Lutz 1962: ch. 5). The North was industrial, the South agricultural: out of fifty-eight northern provinces, thirty-five had more than half of the working population in nonagricultural activities in the 1960s, while in the South only four provinces out of thirty-two had more than 50 percent of the active population outside agriculture. In the industrial sector, most southern workers were found in the small-scale traditional sector, while only 200,000 were employed in the large-scale modern sector. In agriculture, the stable and productive commercial and family farms of the North contrasted sharply with the unstable tenancies and *latifundia* of the South.

Historically, we can trace the emergence of modern social organization in the North to the typical western processes of commercialization and industrialization: commercialization set up a marketing and credit network while industrialization reshaped social stratification through the discipline of the factory process (Apter 1965: 68). The South, in contrast, remained a fragmented developing society because commercialization, caused by the influx of northern goods after national unification in 1861, was not accompanied by industrialization; social roles were undermined by commercialization, but in the absence of industrialization, they remained transitional and disorganized.[3]

---

[2] The classical sources on the cultural cleavage between North and South are found in Gaetano Salvemini, *Scritti sulla questione meridionale* (Turin: Einaudi, 1955); Francesco Saverio Nitti, *Scritti sulla questione meridionale* (Bari: Laterza, 1958); Giuseppe Fortunato, *Il Mezzogiorno e lo stato italiano* (Bari: Laterza, 1911). The most important works on the historical development of the South are collected in Bruno Caizzi (ed.), *Antologia delta questione meridionale* (Milano: Comunitá, 1955); and Rosario Villari (ed.), *Il Sud nella storia d'Italia* (Bari: Laterza, 1961).

[3] We find indicators of the South as a fragmented developing society in the atomization of business enterprise and in the network of unstable and transitional roles in agriculture. The average industrial firm in the South employed 2.4 workers in the 1960s, as opposed to 7.5 workers in the North; only 13 percent of southern firms had joint-stock ownership, as compared to 46 percent in the North; and twice as many southerners (27.3 percent) working in industry were owners

Without a strong industrial sector, the attention of all major social groups focused on the land, with results that soon became pathological (Hobsbawm 1959). The middle class, urban, aggressive, and entrepreneurial in the North, was unproductive, provincial, and land-oriented in the South (Salvemini 1955). The family retained an importance in socialization and economic allocation in the South that was far greater than its equivalent in the North. In a society in which modern forms of social organization failed to crystallize, the family was a solidarity unit of almost pathological consistency.[4] In agriculture, the situation was still more fragmented. Until the agrarian reform of 1951, much of the land was operated by small renters, share tenants and day laborers on plots with no farmhouse or equipment. These marginal operating units were not "farms" in any significant sense of the word, nor were they commercial operations. Many peasants shifted from one occupational role to another, while others (*figure miste*) held several occupational roles at once. The fragmentation of contractual ties between owners and peasants prevented the formation of horizontal secondary organizations, inhibiting both economic development and political aggregation.

The fragmented nature of southern Italian society had critical effects on southern politics. Politics in the North had long been organized according to typical western patterns, with groups and parties growing out of the broad functional and class groupings of an industrial society. In the South, in contrast, a formal representative system disguised what amounted to a massive system of clienteles. *Clientelismo* grew out of the narrow vertical ties of a fragmented agricultural system. Organized by the liberal middle class of the provinces, which held a strategic role in landholding, it used the fulcrum of local government for patronage, and sent local notables to parliament to make up shifting majorities for national politicians (transformismo). Structurally, the clientele pattern meant that broad functional interests were not readily represented in politics, where personal favors and patronage were dominant.

The distortions of the system were patent; one reached the apex of authority not by merging one's demands in a horizontal membership group, but by linking up to a hierarchical chain of personal acquaintance that might begin in the network of neighborly relations and reach up to the state bureaucracy with little adjustment in structure. The clientele chain soon grew too long for effective political allocation. It was this, and not a conspiracy by the industrialists of the North, that made the South ineffective in the national political arena; faced by the well-organized interest groups of Milan, Turin, and Genoa, southern clienteles were unable to bargain effectively because they could trade only in personal favors. Even a "monolithic" party like the PCI was profoundly affected by the dualism of the political system.

and directors than in the North (12.8 percent), suggesting the dominance of the family enterprise over modern forms of business (SVIMEZ 1961: 336–38).

4 This was clearly not the view of Edward Banfield (1958), who saw the South's familism as "amoral."

Italian Communists in Italian Society

Under the postwar leadership of Palmiro Togliatti, Gramsci's successors strove to create "a party of a new type" – one which would be both a vanguard and a mass party. Returning from Moscow in 1944, Togliatti said "We are the party of the working class; but the working class has never been foreign to the nation," thereby launching what came to be called the *Via Italiana al Socialismo*.[5] This was more than just a new version of the popular front strategies of the interwar period. Its major characteristics were: (1) participation in parliament and in elections and local government; (2) a strategy of alliances that at the same time emphasized the party's proximity to the Socialists, "sincere democrats" and the progressive wing of the Christian Democratic Party; (3) an ideology of "reform of structure" as the preferred means of constructing socialism in Italy; and (4) activity in local government, cooperative associations and stores, which both developed an efficient class of PCI administrators and tied the economic interests of large numbers of people to the party.

The party's strategy had an impact on its membership, its organization, behavior, and internal unity. First, the typical party member was no longer a dedicated militant whose entire life was devoted to party work. Interviews and questionnaires carried out with PCI federal secretaries in the 1960s showed that only 10 to 15 percent were full-time activists (Tempi Moderni 1960: 50). Moreover, the number of party members decreased rapidly after 1956 and the ratio of members to voters changed from one member for every three voters in 1956 to one member for every 4.8 voters in 1963. Finally, the ideological preparedness of even the most militant party cadres was weak. In 1962, a party report concluded that "the problem of launching an elementary activity of ideological education in the party on a wide scale remains an urgent one."[6]

Second, the classical unit of disciplined party activity – the cell – was progressively weakened, while the larger and more heterogeneous party section became more prominent. The shift was not coincidental; the *Via Italiana* was geared more closely to the loose, horizontally linked party sections than to the narrow, vertically linked cells. Between 1950 and 1963, the number of PCI cells decreased from 54,000 to 33,000 while the number of sections increased from 10,200 in 1951 to 11,000 in 1961. Factory cells also became less important in contrast to the more heterogeneous neighborhood cells and sections.

Third, the PCI paid primary attention to parliamentary and electoral activity and was not observed to dedicate itself to conspiratorial activities. The

---

[5] Togliatti's speeches and writings are collected in three volumes: *Il Partito; La Via italiana al socialismo;* and *Sul Movimento operaio internazionale,* all published by Editori Riuniti of Rome in 1964. See in particular his "Promemoria sulle questioni del movimento operario internazionale e della sua unità," published posthumously in 1964 in *Sul Movimento operaio internazionale,* pp. 361–376.

[6] These data are drawn from the official statistics published by the party in the 1960s, in particular from *Forza e attività del partito,* 1954, *L'organizzazione del PCI,* 1961, *L'organizzazione del partito,*1962, and *Dati sull'organizzazione del PCI,* 1964.

increased importance of the party section was related to this emphasis, for the traditional cell structure was useless in winning elections, while the section functioned as a typical party club. In the trade-union field, after 1948 the party-dominated Confederazione Generale Italiana del Lavoro (CGIL) shunned the political strike weapon and concentrated upon bread-and-butter union issues. In summary, although it was sometimes classified as an "anti-system party" (Sartori 1966: 147), the PCI operated well within the gates of Italian politics.

It was possible to interpret this strategy in purely tactical terms in 1944 when Togliatti returned from Moscow and the presence of Allied troops made revolution impossible. But after a brief return to orthodoxy in the late 1940s, the party's revisionism, if anything, increased (Togliatti 1964: 361–376). It would prove impossible to talk reformism for twenty years and then carry off a revolution. This would be made brutally manifest when a wave of "extraparliamentary" movements arose in the 1970s and the party – seeing its chance to gain a share of power evaporating – cooperated with its conservative opponents in squelching these movements, which one critic called the party's "unwanted children" (della Porta and Tarrow 1986). It was in the South that the ambiguities in the party's basic model were most glaringly present. On the one hand, a strategy designed for the North was applied mechanically to a region with a completely different social structure. And on the other, its leaders' desire to integrate the party into the "trenches and fortifications" of Italian society led to its infiltration by many of the most problematic characteristics of the society of the Mezzogiorno.

Dual Polity and Dual Party

Four dimensions are particularly interesting in comparing the PCI in northern and southern Italy: the composition of the membership; the party organization; the leadership; and its ideology.

Party Membership

The membership of the PCI in northern Italy was concentrated in the medium and large-sized cities, while party membership in the South was dispersed in the countryside. Membership in the North was stable as well as concentrated: new members in that region composed less than 6 percent of the total in the early 1960s while, in the South, the party suffered from rapid turnover, with new members amounting to 13.9 percent, during these years, while it was losing an average of 45,000 members a year (PCI 1962: 21).

The sharpest difference in the membership of the PCI in the North and South stems directly from the different social composition of the two regions: a working class cadre was at the center of the party in the North and was much less present in the South, while the peasantry was the bulwark of the party in the South (with 42 percent of the members) and less present in the North (30 percent). A historical factor colors the composition of the PCI membership

in the South: the absence of a significant labor movement to provide the experience and the cadres for political activity (PCI 1964).

Secondly, the Communist Party in southern Italy differed from the northern
wing of the party in the relative importance of intellectuals and students in its
membership. While 25.8 percent of the PCI's members lived in the South, 40
percent of the intellectuals registered in the party and 60 percent of its student
members were southerners (Ibid.: 22–27). The importance of intellectuals in
the South increased moving up the hierarchy from ordinary members to active
cadres. Figures released in 1954 indicated that over 30 percent of the members
of the party's provincial federal committees in the South were students, techni-
cians, intellectuals, or other professionals, as compared to less than 18 percent
in the North, where the workers were dominant. Reflecting the more conservative, Catholic society of the South, women members were also concentrated in
the North. Eighteen percent of the party's female members lived in the South
as opposed to 82 percent who lived in the North (Ibid.).

The paradox of the *Via Italiana* in southern Italy was that the PCI had as
its largest membership bloc a group with the poorest organizational potential. Rather than a popular mass party based on the organized support of the
urban proletariat, the PCI had the membership outline of a poor peasant's
party in a fragmented developing society, with an intellectual leadership group
and a scattering of worker and middle class groups. Not only was its major
membership group dispersed and poorly organized; unlike the urban and rural
proletariat of the North, it was a group whose social aspirations belonged to a
rearguard and not a vanguard.

Party Structures

In its network of party sections, cells, and factory cells, the differences within
the PCI between North and South were linked to the socio-political structure
of each region. Seventy percent of the party's sections, 68 percent of its cells,
and 92 percent of its factory cells were found in the North in the mid-1960s
(Ibid.: 29–63). In the large-scale industries of the major cities and the commer-
cialized agriculture of the central provinces, these units operated with relative
regularity and precision. Moreover, a panoply of secondary units – recreational
groups, adult classes, and economic organizations – were articulated around
the nucleus of the party cell and section.

In the South, party organizations were less numerous and less articulated
than in the North, and the differentiation of program between party and mass
organization was far less clear. While 30 percent of the party sections were in
the South, only 11.4 percent of its cells, and less than 8 percent of its factory
cells were found there. The decrease in articulation from level to level meant
that the PCI organizational pyramid was virtually inverted with respect to that
of the North. In many places, there were more sections than cells, and the cells
were reported to be far too large to permit their political use (Ibid.). Secondly,
the number of secondary and mass organizations surrounding the party cells
and sections was far smaller than in the North. In the absence of these groups,

the section was often the single manifestation of the party in the southern village. The party member went there to meet his friends and gossip, to play cards and watch television. Surprisingly, 42 percent of the PCI sections in this impoverished region had television sets in the 1960s, as opposed to only 16 percent in the North (Ibid.: 45).[7]

A third organizational characteristic of the PCI in Southern Italy was the lack of a strategic differentiation between the programs of the party and the policies of the mass organizations. Launched in the region in an organizational vacuum, the party was compelled to recruit many members spontaneously and to fulfill many of the functions, which normally fall to labor and other mass secondary groups. A number of party front groups were formed, but these inevitably drew upon the same cadres. As one party intellectual wrote, "very often the Communist Party, the Socialist Party, the Chambers of Labor and the Cooperatives were nothing but different faces of a single popular movement" (de Pasquale 1956: 543). In some provinces, the membership of the party exceeded that of the unions – an inversion of the classical Communist organizational weapon. The division seemed to depend upon which group had arrived first after Fascism. In interviews, party leaders complained that local cadres often found it difficult to distinguish between the tasks of the party and the tasks of the mass organizations.

Organizational difficulties are encountered by all militant political parties in their early phases, but the PCI in Southern Italy appeared to have been permanently affected by these problems. Why this should be so relates to the socio-political milieu of Southern Italy. To quote a party document: "Experience has shown the great difficulty in organizing the masses of the southern peasants and, above all, of grouping them in organizations by category, because of their indeterminate social character" (Comitato centrale 1951a: 197). This was particularly true in the more backward areas of the region. In interviews, party leaders complained that it was often difficult to find more than a handful of peasants who belonged to a clear occupational category.

The Communist Party in Southern Italy developed with a style of organization that was distinctly different from its style in Northern Italy. A resolution of the Central Committee defined the problem this way: "A multiplicity of popular assemblies, of committees for the land and other democratic organizations of an elementary type are necessary to give a primary and simple form of organization to masses of the people who are not socially concentrated and homogeneous" (Comitato centrale 1951b: 230). This pattern of organization

[7] The only PCI units in which the southern portion of the party carried its organizational weight were the *circoli* of the Communist Youth Federation: 22.1 percent of the national total were found in the region. Women's cells, on the other hand, were extremely underrepresented in the South, with 7.1 percent of the national total. To one party leader, this resulted not only from the modesty of women in the region, but from resistance from PCI leaders. He writes, "Conceptions which assign to women a subaltern and a marginal role in society are not yet overcome by the PCI" (Valenza 1960: 7).

reached its apogee in the PCI-led movement for the occupation of the *latifundia* in 1950 (Tarrow 1967a: ch. 11). Yet twenty years after the party began its activity in the South, its organizations still had an amorphous and fluctuating character (Ibid.: ch. 8).

Leaders and Leadership Roles

As might be expected when dealing with political leadership in dualistic political settings, the backgrounds and career patterns of Communist leaders in Northern and Southern Italy differed sharply. Southern Italian Communist leaders were mainly middle- or upper-middle-class individuals with urban backgrounds. Forty-eight percent of the party's national level leadership from the North were of lower- or lower-middle-class origin, while only 34 percent of the southern leaders came from these groups. Eighteen percent of the northern leaders were middle class, compared to 28 percent in the South; and 19 percent of the northern leaders were of upper-middle or upper-class origin, compared to 32 percent in the South.[8]

From data collected by the author on PCI provincial leaders, marked contrasts in educational levels also emerged between the two leadership groups: while provincial secretaries in the North were evenly divided between those who had had elementary or medium level education and and those with secondary or college backgrounds, almost two-thirds of the southern leaders had graduated from high school or college and little more than a third ended their education in elementary or high school. Indeed, there was a chronic overabundance of intellectuals in the PCI in this backward region.[9] Some of these were transplants from the North but most were home-grown teachers, lawyers, and other professionals, descendents of the petit bourgeois intellectual class that Salvemini and Gramsci wrote about.

The southerners were more likely to be newcomers to politics while the northerners were more experienced. Turning again to the national leadership, 58 percent from the South were full-time professional politicians, as opposed to 67 percent from the North. Half as many southerners were the sons of Communist Party members, and very few had siblings, wives and children who were or had been members of the party. On the provincial level, 53 percent of the northern leaders had entered the party from the Resistance movement, compared to only 24 percent in the South, reflecting the largely northern location of the Resistance against fascism. The largest group of southern provincial leaders were recruited into politics while in college or during professional careers (28 percent), or from the peasant or labor movements (36 percent). In the North, in contrast, 11 percent came from intellectual pursuits and 19 percent joined the party from the labor movement.

---

[8] These data were graciously provided me by Professor Gianfranco Poggi, then of the University of Edinburgh, from a study of the Carlo Cattaneo Institute. They were eventually published in Giorgio Galli and Alfonso Prandi, *La partecipazione politica in Italia* (1970).

[9] These and the following data are reported in detail in Tarrow 1967a: ch. 9.

The roles assumed by the leadership differed between North and South too. Since fewer paid officials were available to the party in the South, the provincial leaders in that region functioned more as generalists than in the highly articulated federations of the North. Interview and questionnaire responses indicated that 45 percent of the southern federations were staffed by one to five persons, 40 percent had six to ten persons and only 15 percent were staffed by more than ten. In the North, in contrast, only 13 percent of the federations had less than five full-time officials, 45 percent employed six to ten, and 42 percent were staffed by over ten functionaries.

The disjunction between city and countryside and between middle-class intellectual leaders and peasant members in the party in the South was attitudinal as well as organizational. Southern leaders tended to view the peasants paternalistically. The failure of a substantial peasant cadre to develop in the party may have been linked to such attitudes. As one leader complained, "The formation of a new type of cadre of popular extraction is bound to meet or even instigate a certain resistance and danger of distortion from the residues of clientelism in the bosom of the popular movement" (Valenza 1958: 865).

Not all of the differences in the two leadership cadres left the South at a disadvantage: southern provincial leaders were far more "political" – understanding "political" as oriented to public activities – and less "organizational" than their northern colleagues. Southern leaders, one informant suggested, "have more political sensitivity than leaders in the North" (Interview, Naples, April 1964). Another informant, a member of the party's national secretariat said,

> The cadres in the South are more politically sensitive, more flexible, more sensitive to the political nature of their problems. In the South, traditionally, everything is decided politically, for in a disorganized society, it is the relations between individuals, which solve problems. In the North, in contrast, we deal more with concrete classes and opposing groups, and less with contacts on a personal level. In the leaders of the South, therefore, political sensitivity and ideological subtleties are more important. (Interview, Rome, May 1964)

Yet the greater political capacity of the southern leaders was damaged by their organizational weakness. As another informant in the national party organization said,

> The differences between northern and southern leaders are the differences in the characteristics of the regions. The northerner is more of a formalist; the southerner is more versatile but he is less organizationally oriented. (Ibid.)

The characteristic described as "political sensitivity" by many party informants shaded into personalism in relationships with followers and the opposition. In interviews, provincial leaders in the South stressed such qualities as "prestige," "honesty," and "seriousness" as the factors which recommend them to the admiration of their fellow citizens. In the North, party leaders were more concerned with presenting a united face to the opposition. Southern leaders were far more conscious of the need to establish a network of ties with local elites than northerners, who interpret the Leninist policy of alliances as the affair of the national party organization, pointing to relations with the Vatican rather than to interaction with village priests. In their relations with the rank and file, the southern leaders reported spending much of their time helping job seekers, writing letters of recommendation for students, and trying to resolve the legal disputes of the peasants. Two-thirds of the northern provincial leaders perceived their roles predominantly in organizational terms, while almost two-thirds of the southerners included mainly political factors in their role perceptions (Tarrow 1967a: ch. 9).

Ideology

The essence of PCI ideology after 1945 was the uneasy cross-fertilization of Gramsci's ideas with Togliatti's *Via Italiana al Socialismo*. Under Togliatti, Gramsci's idea of the party as the modern Prince lost its Leninist components and was interpreted almost entirely in terms of Togliatti's emphasis upon national solidarity. In the North the party operated with an increasingly reformist political ideology, and with positive results. For the *Via Italiana* was a strategy designed for an industrialized society with a strong and disciplined working class. Emphasis was placed upon trade union action and structural reform within the capitalist system. Party theoreticians adopted revised views on the evolution of capitalism, and party leaders talked of "insertion" in the processes of neocapitalism to influence its direction. As a leading labor intellectual wrote, "The CGIL does not try to prevent the modernization of Italian capitalism. Instead of opposing neocapitalist solutions *a priori*, we each time oppose more advanced and equally realistic and concrete solutions" (Anderson 1962: 153).

But in the South, the synthesis of the *Via Italiana* with Gramsci's formulations was less happy. The party ignored his concept of a creative working class impelling a peasant motor force to revolutionary action in a bilateral relationship directed by the party. Instead, it called for a pluralistic system of alliances between many social groups, which suppressed the insurrectionary force of the peasants. A bilateral revolutionary partnership was expanded into "a system with the working class at its head ... and an alliance with the southern peasants, first, with the petit bourgeoisie, the intellectuals and the progressive medium bourgeoisie, isolating the conservative and the large bourgeoisie" (Scoccimaro 1945: 138). Retrospectively, party leaders claimed that "Gramsci reaffirmed the real unity between workers and peasants in the common battle for the *structural renewal* of the Italian state" (Ferri 1952: 10). The alliance had lost its revolutionary character.

With neither a Leninist party's organizational weapon nor its revolutionary goals, the PCI in the South fell prey to the "objective conditions" of its political setting in a backward and fragmented society. The whole concept of the party changed from the creative catalytic agent envisaged by Gramsci into an amorphous mass movement that cast its net through diverse social strata, seeking issues that could build an interclass coalition. As Togliatti wrote in a key theoretical article, "Because of the social disorganization of the South, we need an organization of a conspicuously broad, popular nature, *more than is necessary in the large industrial centres* [emphasis added]" (Togliatti 1954: 412).

Conclusions

What can this story about the failed strategy of the Communist Party in Southern Italy in the decades after World War II tell us tell us about the dilemmas of "strangers at the gates" in contentious politics?[10] The answer I offered as a young scholar was broadly structural (Tarrow 1967a): based on the very different structural conditions of North and South Italy, I argued, the backwardness, the social disorganization, and the land hunger of the South had negative impacts on the membership, organization, leadership, and ideology of a Marxist Party that was not native to the region.

This was not a bad explanation but with the distance of time, it now seems heavily overdetermined by social structure. After all, in a much more backward rural society like China's, Mao had developed a very different – and ultimately successful – *revolutionary* strategy. In an equally different one – Indonesia – a species of "folk communism" developed that was easily liquidated by the military coup in 1966. And in Kerala, India, a successful Communist experiment was developed (Nossiter 1982) and the Communists did very well electorally where dense land tenure patterns resembled those in Southern Italy (Zagoria 1971). Clearly, the strategy of the PCI in a peasant society like the *Mezzogiorno* could not have been as structurally determined as I thought.

Were the failures of Communism in Southern Italy due to what Marxists used to call "subjective conditions" – errors in appreciation and analysis of the party itself? Born in the factories and the resistance movement of the North, party leaders tried to restrain the peasants' robust energies and insert their struggle into the reformist *Via Italiana al Socialismo* that had been designed for an advanced western country. This, I argued, left the field open to the governing Christian Democrats to pass a tepid agrarian reform and co-opt the peasantry into a traditional system of clientelism and patronage. But this answer too was insufficient because it separated agency from structure. It was the combination of the party's strategy and the unpromising conditions of Southern Italy that produced the weaknesses in the party's membership, organization, leadership, and ideology documented previously and summarized in Figure 2.1.

As a still photograph of the PCI's dilemma in southern Italy in the 1950s and 1960s the typology in Figure 2.1 was not a bad portrayal. Under the party's leadership, the peasant movement took the form of a shapeless mass movement with neither the vanguard character of a Leninist Party nor the high level of organization of a social democratic one. But the logic of this analysis was

---

[10] These conclusions draw on reflections published four decades after the research reported in this chapter was carried out, in "Confessions of a Recovering Structuralist," published in *European Political Science* in 2006.

entirely static: all the action in the story was compressed into the boxes of Figure 2.1 and said nothing about the mechanisms that produced the party's dilemma in the South.

The PCI eventually transformed from a Marxist-Leninist Party to a "Party of Democracy and Socialism," then to "Democracy and Socialism" *tout court,* and finally to the mild-mannered "Democratic Party" of today. Those changes are generally accounted to the collapse of state socialism in the Soviet Union and its satellites between 1989 and 1992. But as we have seen here, the slope from revolutionary party to party of structural reform to reformist party was already present in the South long before the collapse of the Soviet bloc. In other words, it can be traced to the history of how the Italian Communists managed their ambivalent position at the gates of the Italian polity.

3

State Building and Contention in America

The previous chapter took its starting point from Gramsci's theory of the party. This one begins from Tocqueville's theory of American society. But because Tocqueville's views of contention were shaped by his experience of French revolution he found it hard to understand it in a country – the United States – in which it was wedded to routine politics. Three decades before the outbreak of the Civil War, he failed to see how quickly polity members in American politics can turn into "strangers at the gates" – and vice versa. He also saw religion – at times a ferocious source of contention in America – in largely institutional terms. And he failed to see how the institutional pluralism he so admired in America could produce the most savage episode of contention in American history – the Civil War.

The "Very Excess of Democracy"

It was during his and Gustave de Beaumont's swing to the South that Tocqueville met a Mr. Finley, a candidate in the congressional elections of 1830. The travelers had missed the raucous election that Finley, the scion of an old Maryland landed family, had contested in Baltimore. He told them of how the boos of the opposing party at a public assembly had continually drowned out his and his opponent's voices; and how there were several broken limbs. "But do you see nothing to fear in such disorderly and tumultuous assemblies," Tocqueville asked? "For my part," Finley answered, "I think the hustings system detestable. But it does not present the dangers you imagine. Our people is accustomed to that type of election. They know just how far they can go, and how much time they can devote to this sort of ancient saturnalia ... *the very excess of democracy partly saves us from the dangers of democracy* [emphasis added] (Tocqueville 1960: 83).

This chapter is a much revised version of my contribution to Anne Costain and Andrew McFarland, eds., *Social Movements and American Political Institutions* (1998). Ira Katznelson, Doug McAdam, and Martin Shefter offered thoughtful comments on a draft of the chapter.

How different from Tocqueville's experience of contentious politics in France, where an "excess of democracy" had led to the death of the France's first republican experiment and to the Terror! And how reassuring to him that electoral participation –however rude and plebian – saved America from the dangers of democracy. Distressed by the bloodletting, the collapse of legitimacy, and the excesses of democracy in his own country, the French traveler confided to the American candidate that such an electoral scene as he had described would be impossible in France: "You argue as a man who has never seen a people stirred by real and profound political passions. Everything with you up to now has been on the surface," he said to Finley. There have been no large substantial interests at hazard" (Ibid.).

America not "stirred by real and profound political passions"? Everything "on the surface"? No large substantial interests at hazard"? What of the American Revolution? The revival movements of the Second Great Awakening? The frontier populism of the age of Jackson? And the conflict over slavery that was gathering force even as he wrote? Tocqueville was one of the world's first and greatest comparativists. What was he thinking of?

One problem was that Tocqueville had never witnessed a national election himself in his travels in America (Altschuler and Blumin 2000:16).[1] Another was that the early 1830s was a period of relative social peace. But there was a deeper problem: Tocqueville failed to recognize how contentious America was because when he thought of contentious politics he thought of revolutionary France. A return to his view of France will not only show us where he went wrong, but will help to introduce the character of contentious politics in America and its relation to the state that Americans were building.

The French Connection

Tocqueville was the first theorist to write about the implications of the modern state for collective action. In his *The Old Regime and the French Revolution* (1955: pt. 2), he argued that it was state centralization that had produced the catastrophic patterns of contention in the French Revolution. His reasoning was complex: the centralized Old Regime had aggrandized itself by destroying intermediate bodies and reducing local autonomy. This process strangled civic participation and meant that when confrontation did break out – as it did in 1789 and again in 1830 and 1848 – it rapidly rose to the summit of the state, was extremely violent, and led to reaction. In contrast, in decentralized and weak states like the United States that Tocqueville and Beaumont traveled through in 1831, local self-government filled the gap left by a void in central authority; local autonomy stimulated self-help and association; political participation was robust; and contention was rooted in personal interest, avoiding "real and profound political passions" and diffusing conflict into a thousand

---

[1] It is interesting that Beaumont, who saw the same America as Tocqueville, was more struck by the indifference of Americans to politics than with their activism. See Altschuler and Blumin 2000: 16, for this observation.

rivulets, rather than centralizing and radicalizing it, as in France. This allowed democracy to flourish without the dangers it had brought to Tocqueville's own country (1960: 55).

Most American scholars who followed in Tocqueville's footsteps emphasized the American side of these perceptions and ignored the starting point of his calm view of American contention: the Terror – born of the dangerous democracy that destroyed the French monarchy and decimated his family (Schama 1989: ch.19). It was only in contrast to the French revolutionary experience that American contention could seem so peaceful. What Tocqueville saw in America was private association and robust local participation; the decentralized and private interest-laden character of politics made contention seem less of a danger than in France. Tocqueville's horror at the monarchical destruction of intermediary bodies in France led him to posit that a state without a centralized bureaucracy would produce an orderly associational politics without the dangers of democracy he had witnessed in France (1992: 61–68). Decentralization would produce something else as well: a flowering of routine political participation at the local level. "The cares of political life," Tocqueville wrote, "engross a most prominent place in the occupation of a citizen in the United States; and almost the only pleasure of which an American has any idea, is to take part in the Government, and to discuss the part he had taken" (1954: vol. II: 138).

With respect to the old French regime, we now know that Tocqeuville exaggerated both its degree of centralization and how thoroughly it had eviscerated society's intermediate bodies. In most of the country, the court had ruled only indirectly. Provincial *parlements* resisted the expansion of the tax system to pay for France's wars and were largely responsible for dragging down the monarchy in the 1780s. And the corporate spirit – if not the actual structure – of the prerevolutionary guilds and other intermediate bodies was alive among French craftsmen and workers long after the revolution ended (Sewell 1980; 1986).

In both state and society, Tocqueville saw in Jacksonian America a mirror image of the strong state and weak civil society that dismayed him in his native land. A July 4th celebration in Albany during his and Beaumont's journey to the West encapsulates his enthusiasm for the rich fabric of civic participation: "Perfect order that prevails. Silence. No police. Authority nowhere. Festival of the people. Marshall of the day without restrictive power. And obeyed. free classification of industries, public prayer, presence of the flag and of old soldiers. Emotion real" (1960: 128).

To be sure, America lacked the traditional corporate bodies whose passage Tocqueville so regretted in France. But it had a functional equivalent in the churches, interest groups, and town meetings that provided Americans with a buffer against state expansion and with a repertoire of instruments for self-help and political participation (1954: vol. I, pt. 2: ch. 4). With its flourishing associations and its vigorous civic and political life, America, he thought, would avoid the extremes of social egalitarianism and statist despotism that

France suffered from 1789 onward. But thirty years later, America erupted into the most savage war in its history. Why was Tocqueville so mistaken?

Politics and Movements in Antebellum America

If Tocqueville's image of a France bereft of intermediate bodies exaggerated both its societal atomization and the strength of its state, his obsession with the French experience made him insensitive to the tremendous amount of social activism that was gathering force in this country even as he wrote. For one thing, he misunderstood the contingent nature of the weakness of the antebellum national state; for a second, he left the relationship between association and contention in the shadows; most important, he misunderstood the reciprocal relations between contentious and conventional politics.

A State That Was Not So Weak

To begin with the first point, like many of his twentieth-century successors, Tocqueville thought the American state was weak. "In letters home, he wrote that 'in spite of anxiously searching for the government, one can find it nowhere.' There was no army, no taxation, no central government: 'The executive power is nothing'" (Kramnick 2007: xiii). But the Federalists had constructed a state that – although it looked nothing like European states – was effective for their purposes. It was marked by fiscal consolidation, debt reduction, diplomatic maneuver, and westward expansion (Bright 1984: 121–122). Their successors built roads, bridges, and the canals that carried Tocqueville and Beaumont on their voyage westward, and a national bank to provide cheap credit to the West.

If the state that Tocqueville found America in the 1830s looked weak, that was largely the outcome of political struggle. As Bright observes; "the periods of greatest paralysis in federal policy corresponded with the periods when party mobilization was the fullest and the margins of electoral victory the slimmest" (136). The American state had been weakened by a political stalemate between two expanding, sectionally based socio-economic systems (Ibid.: 121, 134), but it could expand in response to changes in the political and military environment. As Ira Katznelson writes:

> Both the American military and the state within which it was embedded have been underestimated badly, widely portrayed as weak, amateur, decentralized, negligible.... A fresh look at early American statebuilding through the prism of military spending, deployment and activity, especially in the period after the country's sovereignty and independence ... calls into question the conceptual apparatus and familiar empirical claims made about antebellum state formation." (2002: 87)

In the 1830s this was not yet apparent but by the end of the civil war, the American state had expanded into a "democratic leviathan," one that had begun to lay the foundations for the peculiarly American version of the welfare state (Bensel 1990; Skocpol 1992).

A Contentious Society

Nor was contention as absent from the shaping of the early American state as it seemed to Tocqueville. The example of Shay's Rebellion was before the founders to warn them that "organized opposition to seated authority quickly degenerated into lawless insurrection." This was one of the motives for calling the convention that produced the federal Constitution (Moore 1994: 80). Under the new government, Hamilton's fiscal reforms threatened western farmers, who "defied a federal tax on whiskey, terrorized the excise officers, robbed the mail, and closed the federal courts," fomenting the "Whiskey Rebellion (Wood 2009: 134).

Pennsylvania's western farmers presaged the mix of contained and transgressive contention that would become familiar in later decades. As Gordon Wood writes:

> While some western Pennsylvanians prevented enforcement of the tax by tarring and feathering and terrorizing excise collectors, others channeled their anger into extralegal meetings of protest. They sent petitions to Congress, organized assemblies and committees of correspondence, condemned the excise tax for being as unjust and oppressive as the Stamp Act of 1765, and ostracized everyone who favored or obeyed the excise law. (Ibid.)

The whisky rebels organized a social movement with both modern and traditional forms (Gould 1998; Tilly 1995). These Pennsylvania farmers were not alone. Since the Stamp Act agitation of the 1760s, and especially after the Revolution, Americans had grown accustomed to raucous and, at times, violent public manifestations. Orchestrated processions, mass religious revivals, the erecting of liberty trees and their destruction: these had become standard performances in public life (Altschuler and Blumin 2000: 22–23; Ryan 1989; Smithey and Young 2010).

Contention and Convention

Tocqueville's greatest error was in failing to see the reciprocal relationship between contentious and conventional politics. Like many of his successors, he saw social movements as part of the anarchic world of "collective action" outside the gates of politics. But movements, parties, and interest groups actually gravitate in an uneasy amalgam at the gates of the polity, intersecting around elections, legislatures, and the judiciary. This was already true of antebellum America, as Tocqueville's friend Finley well understood. "Americans of the nineteenth century," write Altschuler and Blumin, "ventured out for a variety of public events, of which political rallies were but one type" (65).

Take the most institutionalized form of public performance – the parade. "Parades typically celebrate the status quo," write Lee Smithey and Michael Young, "but with careful symbolic manipulation they may also level a challenge" (2010: 393). Parades in early America were civil celebrations organized to celebrate an important event, like the completion of the Erie Canal or Washington's birthday. At the same time, an elite temperance movement had developed under the leadership of Congregational or Episcopalian ministers, who frowned on these disruptive and well-lubricated processions (Ibid.: 400–401). But in the 1840s a new, more popular form of teetotalling developed in the form of the Washingtonian Temperance Society. The Washingtonians, according to Smithey and Young, "wrested the temperance cause from the wealthy and the religious" and adapted the form of the parade from its boozy antecedents "as a weapon in their movement against a hard-drinking culture." "In these instances, they conclude, "the gathered were also parading political contention" (401–402).

The habit of participating in public events spread from politics to commerce, entertainment and religious revivals. From the newspaper records they studied in Kingston, New York, for example, Altschuler and Blumin found

> a courthouse crowd of more than five hundred, with hundreds more turned away, who paid to hear *The Oratorio of Esther* in early 1859. Religious revivals and camp meetings could attract many hundreds of people every day for several weeks.... During the New York gubernatorial election of 1858, for example, a torchlight parade was held in Kingston, not to promote one or another candidate, but to celebrate the completion of the Atlantic telegraph. (Ibid.)

Under the umbrella of well-understood public performances, social movements moved easily into politics. Consider how quickly the anti-Masons turned themselves from an evangelical reform movement into a political party, holding America's first presidential nominating convention in 1831 (Moore 1994: 78). Or how effortlessly America's nineteenth-century immigrants were absorbed into the routines of American electoral democracy (Shefter 1986; Katznelson 1981). Or how inexorably the less radical abolitionists of the 1830s and 1840s were fed into the party system, joining breakaway Whigs and Free Soilers in the new Republican Party. Between the outdoor politics of social movements and the indoor politics of the party system there is surely a line to be drawn; but in the permeable American state, that line was fuzzy and was easily crossed – as it is today.

State Building and Contentious Politics

If one looked for the "dangers of democracy" that culminated in the French Terror, it would be hard to find them in ante bellum America. But the United States in the late eighteenth and early nineteenth centuries was literally bursting with collective action: the sabotaging of British rule and the raising of a popular army in the 1770s; the Shay's and Whiskey rebellions that followed the revolution and required troops for their suppression; the frontier mobilization that produced Jackson's presidency; the religious fervor of the Second Great Awakening that was "burning over" wide swaths of newly settled territory in New York and Ohio even as Tocqueville and Beaumont travelled through the region (Cross 1950): these episodes escaped the neat institutional pluralism that Tocqueville saw in his image of America.

The center of gravity of American social movements was still local in 1832 and this fit the Tocquevillian paradigm very well. But even before industrialization, in the cities of the Atlantic coast there was a lively workers' movement empowered with a strong dose of Painite republicanism (Wilentz 1984; Bridges 1986). Already, interchurch coalitions in places like Rochester were forming to oppose drink and Sunday work (Johnson 1978). And already, religious movements were laying the groundwork for abolitionism and feminism, and, indirectly, for the sectional conflict that culminated in the Civil War (Walters 1976: ch. 3).

America was not as exceptional as Tocqueville thought. He found in the United States what he thought France had lost – a flourishing associational life that he mistook for the equivalent of a lost corporate order. He found widespread elections that he mistook as a sign of universal citizen involvement in politics. But because he understood contention in the violent forms it had taken in France, he missed the intimate connections among contentious and routine politics in America. Three characteristics in particular would mark America's brand of contentious politics: the importance of religious movements, the multilevel nature of activism, and the intersections among social movements, association, and routine politics.

Religion and Contention in America

In his travels through America, Tocqueville came to the conclusion that religion is a political institution "which powerfully contributes to the maintenance of the democratic republic among the Americans" (*Democracy in America,* Kramnick edition, 2007: 244):

> It may be asserted that in the United States no religious doctrine displays the slightest hostility to democratic and republican institutions. The clergy of all the different sects hold the same language; their opinions are consonant to the laws, and the human intellect flows onward in one sole current. (Ibid.: 246)

Tocqueville was convinced that members of the clergy did not support any particular political persuasion and that they kept aloof from politics and public affairs. Religion, he was convinced, kept Americans "free from all trammels." Even revolutionaries were "obliged to profess an ostensible respect for Christian morality and equity, which does not easily permit them to violate the laws that oppose their designs" (249).

These ideas on the calming and apolitical nature of religiosity were fortified by Tocqueville's travels among the great and good in antebellum America. For example, in a long conversation with Joel Roberts Poinsett during his swing through the South, Tocqueville asked the former diplomat:

> Q: What do you think of the influence of religion on politics?
>
> A: I think that the state of religion in America is one of the things that most powerfully helps us to maintain our republican institutions. The religious spirit

exercises a direct power over political passions, and also an indirect power by sustaining morals. (1960:114)

Poinsett was not the first man to think so: in his Farewell Address, George Washington had seen religion as an indispensable support for political prosperity (Moore 1994: 71). But both seem to have regarded religion mainly as a form of social control and a source of moderation of the passions. Neither emphasized the noninstitutional side of religion or the ease, in America, with which religion could animate social movements and slide into political activism.

Like most upper-class gentlemen of his time, Tocqueville was more than ready to accept Poinsett's dictum (1954: vol. I: 310–326). He did notice the Temperance Societies that were already developing in reaction to a whiskey-sodden frontier society (1960: 212). But it was *institutional* religion that Tocqueville focused on as he travelled across central New York and not the buzzing, blooming and enthusiastic religious revival that was "burning over" central New York State in the 1830s (Cross: 1950). He missed the sabbatarian movement that was bringing together members of different denominations in interchurch coalitions to stamp out both Sunday work and drink (Johnson 1978: ch. 6), the antimasonic movement that grew out of these efforts (Ibid.: ch. 3), and the often-violent anti-Catholic Protestant crusade that was the dark side of American "republican" religion (Billington 1938).

Why did so sensitive an observer fail to detect the importance of religious movements in America? One reason is that much of Tocqueville's information about religion in America came from the upper-class gentlemen and established clerics he interviewed in his travels. Another is that his image of social movements was colored by his memory of the anticlericalism in the early phases of the French Revolution. Tocqueville did not recognize religious social movements when they took the form of temperance societies, revival meetings, bible and tract societies and travelling evangelists. In addition, while Tocqueville well understood the importance of private interest in driving American politics, he missed it completely in the world of religion.

Competing for Religious Consumers

Most observers of the role of religion in American politics focused heavily on the "Establishment Clause" of the First Amendment and Tocqueville's clerical interlocutors insisted over and over on the importance of the separation of church and state (1960: 82). But they frequently failed to see the equally important effects of the other half of the amendment, the one that permitted the free coinage of religious denominations. In the context of an anarchic, expanding, and soon continent-wide capitalist country, the First Amendment helped to produce a process of religious commodification (Moore 1994).

Even before the passage of the federal Constitution, American clerics had understood that they would have to "make religion *popular*, able to compete in a morally neutral and voluntaristic marketplace environment alongside all the goods and services of this world." Already, they were "caught up in a 'consumer revolution' stimulated by vast increases in manufacturing, capital, and leisure time" (Stout 1991: xvii). The trend was common to England and American colonies, but in America a written constitution gave denominational proliferation a juridical stamp of approval. As Lawrence Moore writes, "The environment of competition among denominations created by the First Amendment's ban on religious establishment simply accelerated the market rationale" (1994: 7).

In a laissez-faire market economy, where established religion was banned and free creation of new religious organizations was encouraged, it was but a short step to marketlike competition for supporters between religious entrepreneurs. Religious congregations competed for clients through print, revival meetings, the media, in workplaces, and in leisure activities. As Moore writes:

> Without an established church, they [religious leaders] could not depend upon the high social status that had formerly belonged to many of them as quasi-public officials. Churches and clerics held their own in American life, however much their relative authority in public life declined, but they had to drum up business both among wealthy and influential lay people and among the general population. (Ibid.: 69)

Religion competed with politics for Americans' attention (Altschuler and Blumin 2000: 7). But many evangelicals soon found that they could not pursue religious campaigns without entering the toils of organized politics (Carwadine 1993: ch. 7). It may be no accident that the great age of religious revivalism – the 1830s and 1840s – was also the period in which the modern American party system was born. It is also striking that the techniques of the revival meeting were strikingly similar to those of the mass movement – "large-scale efforts to try to control behavior by inventing new forms of publicity to stir people" (Moore 1994: 72). "In religious protest," writes Moore, Americans "flexed their muscles, cast off habits of deference, and felt the thrill of empowerment" (73). It was not long until religious leaders began to insist on the moral duty of Christians to lobby politicians and demand legislative changes on behalf of moral issues (75). The most portentous of these would be the religious cause of antislavery (Altschuler and Blumin 2000: 155).

Commodification led to competition. Moore analyzes in great depth how religious leaders competed for souls and eventually for profits (ch. 2). If the Jim and Tammy Bakkers of the twentieth century took the profit motive to new heights, they were working within a well-worn repertoire of religious entrepreneurship. But competition for parishioners can also lead to competition of another sort: to competitive outbidding for support which, in its more extreme forms, leads to radicalization. Much of the dynamic of early American religious movements arose out of the competition for souls. Just as cycles of protest are driven by the efforts of competing movement organizations to find new supporters and hold the loyalty of old ones, Protestant preachers outdid one another – and tried to outbid other forms of activity, like the theater – in adopting forms of proselytizing that would win them a larger share of the religious market (Moore 1994: ch. 2; Stout 1991: ch. 6).

The First Amendment saved Americans from a state-imposed official religion, but it also gave religious reformers the incentive to organize their parishioners much as social movement entrepreneurs organize activists. Consider the temperance movement. Like many social movements, temperance described a cyclical trajectory of activism and quietism, responding to favorable opportunities with greater activism and to the pressure of broader issues by lying low (Szymanski 2003). The separation of church and state and the free coinage of religious denominations in the presence of an expanding capitalist society not only produced the commodification of religion but created a quasi-permanent religious sector in a shifting relationship with the dynamic of political struggle.

Movements and American Institutions

One reason movements could survive periods of disillusionment and revive when the opportunity arose was because they learned to use the institutions of the political system in a differentiated manner. First, the federal Constitution gave them the opportunity to shift to different levels of the American federal system as realignments occurred, new parties took power at different levels of the system, and failure at one level led them to shift their activities to another level. And second, their tactics frequently blended the extrainstitutional contention of classical social movements with the institutional tactics of private associations – just as social movements do today.

Multilevel Movements

Tocqueville made much of the localism of American politics and certainly, the incremental expansion of the country westward and the traditions of local home rule created incentives for Americans to organize locally. But localism was less an institutional imperative than a political strategy, one that depended on political circumstances and could give way – as it did in the temperance and antislavery movements – to cross-local movement organization.

The federal system had been designed to govern territorial expansion, manage diversity, and split up potentially corrosive adversaries – and for seventy years it more or less achieved its aim. But as the events leading up to the Civil War showed, it could also provide strong points for territorial contention that could not be compromised through the give-and-take of institutional politics, at least in the forms that dominated the federal system before 1861. On the other hand, federalism also provided social movements with a variety of levels in which to operate.

The history of temperance shows how this mobility could operate. The radical wing of the movement favored a strategy of seeking constitutional prohibition of liquor, because it created "an established standard of right principles exerting its instructive influence upon public sentiment" (Szymanski 2003: 2). Agitation at the local level was at first frowned upon, "for it was wrong for the state to surrender its sovereignty, evade its duty and divest itself of responsibility on a matter vitally affecting the welfare of the state by shifting the decision to localities" (Ibid.). "By swamping the state legislatures with petitions, and by carefully navigating the quagmires of the amendment process and the party system," the drys managed to force prohibition referenda onto the ballot in eighteen states on whether to include prohibition in their constitutions (Ibid.).

Unfortunately for the movement, its higher-level referendum strategy failed in most states and at the federal level as well.[2] Reacting to this failure, and facilitated by local home rule, the Massachusetts Law and Order League and the more durable Anti-Saloon League turned to the local level. Localism allowed them, in the short run, to nibble at the small-scale illegalities and improprieties of local saloons and, in the long run, to build consensus around the broader goals of the movement through local prohibition efforts. As Szymanski observes:

> Instead of expecting its recruits to possess the "correct" beliefs about prohibition before participating in the movement, the Anti-Saloon League first sought to engage Americans in local prohibition skirmishes which barely dented the profits of the liquor industry, but which socialized them into the militancy of the broader movement. (Szymanski 2003: 4)

Localism, far from burying the movement in the meandering rivulets of private interest and local association, exposed nascent "dries" to the obstinacy of the liquor industry, and "unleashed the democratic potential of the decentralized American state" (Ibid.: 4). It provided the movement with a network of supportive associations, allowing them to gain tactical advantage where they were strong, engage members in confidence-building activities where they were weak, and allowed them to wait out the doldrums of unpromising political periods for new political alignments and opportunities (Rupp and Taylor 1987). Localism also allowed movements to build a basis of consensus around sympathetic candidates who exchanged their support for a movement's programs in the legislature for electoral support. Not only that: as regional and national networks of communication developed, the strategy of localism gave way to *trans*-local movements like the Anti-Saloon League, the Grange, and the Populists.

A contemporary example of multilevel politics can be seen in the shift of the Christian Coalition's activities from national agitation to state-level, intraparty organizing in the 1980s and 1990s (Moen 1996: 461–463; Usher 2000). In the 1980s, the coalition directed its support at voters through a barrage of media propaganda, and at the highest levels of the state through its support for Pat Robertson's candidacy for the Republican nomination to the presidency. But although increasing proportions of the electorate declared themselves sympathetic to the coalition's programs, little was gained from the Reagan or Bush administrations but pious platitudes and an antiabortion plank in the Republican platform.

---

[2] Szymanski notes that the voters of twelve states rejected it outright; in four others prohibition won fleeting victories; and as of 1900, only Kansas, Maine, North Dakota, New Hampshire, and Vermont had either constitutional or statutory prohibition. See Szymanski 2003: 2, for details.

By the early 1990s, under the skilled leadership of Ralph Reed, the coalition shifted its attention to the local and state levels of the party, using its internal machinery to gain seats at state nominating conventions and win congressional nominations for candidates sympathetic to its goals. By one informed estimate, by 1994, the coalition had taken control of the nominating process in seventeen state organizations of the Republican Party (Persinos 1994; Usher 2000). The American state provides many alternative access points for movements that are unable to achieve their goals at their chosen level of the political system.

But some issues, like slavery, could not be confined to the local level. "While temperance remained a state and local issue ... slavery could not be kept out of national politics" (Altschuler and Blumin 2000: 154). The federal government delivered mail, including the abolitionist tracts that southern states were increasingly inclined to ban; it governed the District of Columbia; and "most of all it conquered, purchased, and otherwise claimed vast amounts of land to the west of existing states, and supervised the process by which American citizens who moved on to this land formed themselves into new states" (Ibid.: 154–155). When a coalition of western farmers, eastern abolitionists and disenchanted Whigs elected Abraham Lincoln president and South Carolina seceded from the Union, the sectional standoff over slavery "could only be resolved through national political action" (Ibid.).

According to an old tradition in American sociology, social movements are part of a distinct universe called "collective behavior" which differs from "institutional behavior" in being outside the gates of routine politics (see Chapter 1). In this tradition, a clear distinction was made between uncontrolled, spontaneous, and emergent forms of collective action and those forms that are routine, operate within political institutions, and have clearly defined goals. In the former category we find social movements; in the latter are interest groups and parties. Movements in this tradition were defined in terms of tactics that were somehow "outside" of institutions, and their relationship to institutional politics remained elusive (McAdam, Tarrow, and Tilly 2001).

Recent trends call for greater efforts to relate movements to institutional politics. For example, since the 1960s it has been apparent to many observers that the repertoire of forms of collective action has expanded and that contentious action has become common among broad sectors of the population (Dalton 2006; Meyer and Tarrow eds. 1998). How does this affect the once-sharp analytical distinction between social movements and institutional politics? If the forms of collective action associated with social movements are also used by interest groups, civic associations, and, on occasion, by elected politicians, what remains distinctive about movements? Moreover, many social movements in western democracies *combine* institutional forms of activity – like legal maneuvering, educational activities, and lobbying – with more confrontational forms like demonstrations, sit-ins, and strikes. How can we differentiate social movements from interest groups when both are using the tools of computerized mailings, lobbying, and legal action as well as occasional confrontations with powerholders?

We can see these convergences between contention and convention in the post-1968 world of social movements, in the relations between elections and movements. Few political scientists who study elections take note of the role of social movements, while movement scholars are almost as indifferent to studies of elections (McAdam and Tarrow 2012). Yet movements and elections intersect in at least five ways: first, historically, many social movements developed under the umbrella of election campaigns, which legitimated – or at least permitted – their use of collective public actions (Tilly 1995); second, at times, movements transform themselves into parties, as did an important part of the "green" movement in Western Europe after the 1970s; third, movements often engage in electoral politics proactively because they see them as opportunities to advance their agendas, as the recent "tea party" movement did when it entered the Republican Party in 2010 (Tarrow 2011a: ch. 5); fourth, movements often react to elections by mobilizing against their outcomes – as in the so-called "color revolutions" in the Balkans and in the Caucasus after the turn of the century (Bunce and Wolchik 2011); and fifth, elections are frequently connected to the long-term fate of movement families.

What is surprising about the blending of electoral and movement politics is how "old" it is (Calhoun 1995; D'Anieri, Ernst, and Kier 1990). Consider the repertoire of contention used at one time or another by the temperance movement: from its origins in the 1830s to the passage of the Eighteenth Amendment, temperance utilized a broad repertoire of social movement organizing techniques and pressure tactics, ranging from education and proselytizing efforts in the schools and churches, to invoking legal restraints on the sale of liquor, to supporting candidates and lobbying, to mounting public demonstrations, to confrontational tactics, like invading taverns and staging public breaking of whiskey bottles (Blocker 1989).

The same was true of the Civil Rights Movement. From the legal strategy of the early 1950s, to the church-based mobilizations and sit-ins of the late 1950s, to the mass demonstrations and marches of the early 1960s, to the occasional recourse to violence in the late 1960s, the Civil Rights Movement ran the gamut of institutional and noninstitutional forms of contention. Part of its success was its ability to react strategically to elite responses (McAdam 1983; another part was the ability to move from unpromising locales to other cities, where television cameras might show the ruthlessness of local elites and induce the federal government to intervene on behalf of the movement; and part of it was the ability to trigger the intervention of federal forces in the local politics that was wedded to segregation (Vallely 2004).

The same can be said for the Women's Movement, which some scholars have sometimes interpreted as either "new" – and therefore radical – or "old" – and supposedly more moderate. A more historicized account shows that, at various times and in various circumstances, both the old and the new wings of the movement employed both institutional and noninstitutional tactics; the movement organizations that we see testifying before congressional committees today may be the same ones whose militants marched, demonstrated, sat-in, and raise consciousness among their constituencies yesterday. This is even a movement that excels at what Mary Katzenstein has called "unobtrusive mobilization" within such hierarchical institutions as the armed forces and the Catholic church (1990; 1998). What democratic theorist John Dryzek calls a "dualistic" strategy (1996: 485) has been part of the American social movement scene since the founding of the American state. Movements have sometimes been outside the gates of the American polity but those that endured maintained a shifting and delicate relationship to conventional politics.

Conclusions

Is there a special quality of American social movements that allows them to shift their activities between different levels and arenas of politics and to traverse the frontiers between conventional and confrontational collective action? Or is it simply that – as the world's longest-running electoral democracy – the American system showed the rest of the world earlier how contentious and conventional politics can intersect? We have seen how federalism both fostered hardened territorial movements like pro- and antislavery and provided movements like temperance with the institutional flexibility to operate at different layers of the polity. We have also seen how the First Amendment, together with a rampant market economy, led religious groups to compete for parishioners and encouraged them to adopt new forms of organization and mobilization that made them closely akin to social movements. And we have seen how social movements developed a repertoire of contention that could spill over into institutional and interest group politics without permanently losing their insurgent character. All of these intersections are equally visible in the mixed movement/institutional politics of Western Europe today (Kriesi et al., 1995).

The early and extensive expansion of the ballot produced in America an "excess of democracy" that lured social activism into electoral forms and prevented the "dangers" of democracy that Tocqueville feared from his French experience. In America, as in France, state formation was also a process of movement structuring, much of which Tocqueville missed. American movements *did* respond to a more differentiated and less centralized opportunity structure than Europe's except when – as in the conflict over slavery – there was no way to resolve it except through national conflict. A century later, the same was true, though less lethally, in America's "second reconstruction" (Valelly 2004).

This is not to say that these "American" properties of social movements do not exist elsewhere. Since the 1980s, trans-Atlantic comparative work has been turning up instructive parallels and intersections between European and American movements. But it is interesting that the United States, a country whose politics is so often compared to none other than itself, foreshadowed many of the practices of social movements that have emerged in other advanced capitalist democracies more recently. The joke is on Tocqueville: in its ability to avoid the dangers of democracy, he thought America was unique; but the "very excess of democracy" copied from American movement practice has shown Europeans how to build social movements at the gates of the political process.

4

The French Revolution, War, and State Building

Revolution, war, and state building: three terms that are all part of the broad canvas of contentious politics but have produced largely distinct literatures. This chapter takes its start from the work of Charles Tilly, who gave a great deal of attention to the French Revolution, but also studied war and state building. Yet even Tilly never completely integrated his work on war and state building with his work on revolutions and contentious politics. Using the approach that Tilly pioneered – the systematic disaggregation of historical episodes into mechanisms and processes – this chapter attempts to take Tilly further to provide an analysis of how state building in the presence of war shaped internal contention and the future state during the French Revolution.

Many scholars have seen revolutions as a form of social movement,[1] a term that Tilly used in a more restricted way (Tilly and Wood 2009). In contrast, war has mainly been studied as a subfield of international relations, and sometimes as a contingent side-product of revolution (Walt 1996). State building has been seen as what rulers do in order to wage war more effectively (Tilly 1985; 1990). The only place in which the three regularly come together more than contingently is in the literature on nationalism.

Why such a division of labor, when revolution, war, and state building all foster contention and a great deal of violence? One reason is because wars are generally condemned – even by those who pursue them – while revolutions produce divisions between enthusiasts and opponents, and state building is seen as the inevitable result of war (Tilly 1990), or of men and women trying to live together in comity (Strayer 1970). Another is because of the differences in the historiographies each specialty has produced: from the largely military and diplomatic histories of warfare to the socially and ideologically inflected histories of revolution and macrohistorical models of state building. A third reason is the overspecialization that haunts the contemporary social sciences.

---

[1] Jack Goldstone, in one variant, sees revolutions as a contingent outcome of movements (1998). This chapter draws on my essay, "The French Revolution, War, and State-Building" in *Contention and Trust in Cities and States*, 2011. Edited by Michael Hanagan and Chris Tilly, ch. 6.

Even Tilly, whose *oeuvre* ranged broadly over all three subjects, tended to deal separately with war and state building on one hand and with revolution on the other.[2]

This chapter explores the implicit links between revolution and contentious politics, on the one hand, and war and state building, on the other. I will argue that rulers not only fight wars and build states on their ruins; but also that revolutionaries build states, never more forcefully than when they are simultaneously defending themselves in war. I will use the French Revolution as the canvas on which to examine how efforts to build a new state drove the political process of the revolution and produced many of the outcomes that are more often seen as the result of revolutionary ideology.

Two Determinisms and a Synthesis

When we turn to the literature on the French Revolution, we find that the bulk of the historical writing is divided between social structural and ideological accounts. While a mid-century literature inscribed in a Republican-Marxist tradition focused on the social bases of the revolution (Soboul 1958; Lefebvre 1947), a newer revisionist literature shifted the focus to its cultural and ideological content (Baker 1990; Chartier 1991; Furet 1978, 1992; Hunt 1984). That shift freed the revolution from the rigidities of Marxist determinism, but it substituted for it a new, ideological determinism and left the processes that surrounded the building of a new revolutionary state in the shadows.

In contrast, Tilly saw revolutions as part of the political process, and thus susceptible to examination using the tools he developed as a student of contentious politics (Tilly 1993). But he did not take the final step: linking the political processes within the revolution to his parallel interest in war and state building. This chapter will attempt to explore that linkage. I will argue that the revolutionaries' responses to the crises of the early 1790s were episodes in the construction of a new state. But first, I will briefly summarize the two traditions that Tilly was implicitly writing against in his work on the French Revolution: the Marxist-Republican synthesis and the revisionist work of François Furet and his school of intellectual/cultural interpretations.

The Republican/Marxist Tradition

Too much has been written about the French Revolution's social origins to require much attention here. From the Third Republic on, historians struggled to understand its ambivalent relationship to different social classes. The sociological interpretation of the revolution was never simple, but even scholars

---

[2] Consider the first chapter of his intended final opus: *States, Cities and Trust Networks,* which appears as chapter 1 in Michael Hanagan and Chris Tilly's reader in his honor (2011): while there are four mentions of "war" and three of "warfare," a rapid search for the term "revolution" turns up only one reference, and that one is in the bibliography.

who disagreed about which class had made the revolution were convinced that there *was* a social basis to it. The culmination of the sociological interpretation came in the mid-twentieth century, when intellectual Marxism made its way into the academy, and was employed as a tool to cut through the complexities of the revolutionary decade.

The most controversial of the Marxist historians was Albert Soboul, who deconstructed the class basis of the Parisian *sans-culottes*, and found there a tenuous proletarian presence and a majority of artisans (1958). For Soboul it was the pressures of the *sans-culottes* on the convention that led, in May 1793, to the imposition of a national maximum on the price of grain and thus to the social legislation of the revolution (Gough 1998: 36–37). Sobul was followed by Georges Lefebvre, who periodized the rev-olution according to the prominence of its four most important classes. "The aristocracy, the bourgeoisie, the urban masses and the peasants, each independently and for reasons of its own, initiated revolutionary action," writes R.R. Palmer in the preface to Lefebvre's *The Coming of the French Revolution* (1947: xiv).

However penetrating the analyses of Soboul and Lefebvre, they were bound to lead to a reaction. A partial step away from Marxist orthodoxy came with Theda Skocpol (1979). In the traces of her great teacher, Barrington Moore Jr., she looked at rural class relations as the central cleavage that triggered the revolution but she also looked beyond class at how state structure and fiscal crisis shaped the outbreak of the revolution. William Sewell Jr. took a further step away from class determinism: he saw Soboul as a pioneer in the study of the political culture of the revolution and gave his work a semiconstructivist reading (1994:249).[3] But the fundamental rejection of the Marxist model of the revolution had to await the 1980s, when the decadence of Marxism in the academy was joined by its eclipse in French politics. This takes us to the crucial work of François Furet and his followers.

The Intellectual/Cultural Alternative

It was Alexis de Tocqueville who was the originator of the idea that the revo-lution had intellectual origins (see Chapter 1). When he asked why it spiraled from the relatively liberal phase of 1789 to the dogmatism and violence of the Terror, Tocqueville saw the fault in the intellectuals who were the Regime's *lumières*. These, he proposed, laid the philosophical groundwork for the abstract notions of popular sovereignty that would characterize French revo-lutionary thought and would drive the republic to the practice of terror. This intellectual interpretation was picked up by Daniel Mornet (1989), but his

---

[3] Sewell argued that the *sans-culottes*, whose class composition was heterodox, *believed* that bread prices were the order of the day. "Hunger," Soboul wrote, "was the cement which held together the artisan, the shopkeeper, and the workman, whose common interest united them against the great merchant, the entrepreneur, and the noble or bourgeois speculator" (Soboul 1958: 454, quoted by Sewell 1994: 250).

work was largely forgotten as academic Marxism focused determinedly on the social origins of the revolution.

As Marxism declined in the 1970s and 1980s, both as a secular faith and as a paradigm of history, historian François Furet took up Tocqueville's claims and led an intellectual charge against the sociological model of the revolution. First in his *Penser la Révolution française* (1978), and then, with his collaborator, Mona Ozouf, in a massive compendium of ninety-nine articles (Furet and Ozouf, eds. 1992), Furet made a linkage from the *lumières* to the Jacobins and from there to modern totalitarianism (Furet 1992: 313). For Furet, as for Tocqueville, the revolution was the incarnation of the prerevolutionary philosophical tradition and the Terror was its ultimate expression. But unlike Tocqueville, Furet had before him the lesson of modern totalitarianism, and his condemnation of the Terror had as much to do with his abandonment of his former Communist allegiance as it did with the excesses of the revolution. This became especially clear as the Bicentennial of that revolution approached in 1989 and Furet orchestrated an anticollectivist commemoration and denunciation of the Jacobins, with whom, of course, the French Communists had always identified (Kaplan 1993).

The Tillian Synthesis

Like the Marxists, Furet dismissed the idea of the revolution as the result of mere "circumstances" (1992: 312). But the alternative to structuralism is not mere narrative: history can be divided into a series of processes, each of which consists of a number of interlocking mechanisms. By seeking to identify these mechanisms and their relationship to one another, we can reconstruct the processes of major historical shifts like revolutions. To better understand the particular mix of mechanisms and processes in the French Revolution, we turn first to the work of Tilly on state building and then to his writing on the political process of the revolution.

In his well-known aphorism that "states make war and war makes states," Tilly famously argued that states were the product of war making and of the mechanisms it unleashes.[4] In *Coercion, Capital and European States*, Tilly made three main points about war making and its influence on the formation of modern states:

- first, with respect to capital: from a presence hovering in the background of state building, capital advanced to a partnership role – now stronger, now weaker – with state makers who needed its contributions for war making and state making (1990: 17–19);
- second, depending on the relative concentration and accumulation of capital and coercion, the form of state that emerges will vary substantially (27);

---

[4] The aphorism first appeared in his "War Making and State Making as Organized Crime" in Peter B. Evans, Dietrich Rueschemeyer and Theda Skocpol, eds., *Bringing the State Back In* (1985), and in more systematic form in *Coercion, Capital and European States* (1990).

- third, he begins to elaborate the implications of the theory for citizenship in the modern state.

Where capital was stronger and rulers weaker, he argued, state builders relied on capitalists to rent or purchase military force, and thereby could make war without building large and expanding state structures. The result was the renaissance city-state, the belt of commercially based cities running diagonally from the low countries through western Germany and Switzerland (1990: 143–151). Where coercion was more intensive than capitalist development – as in Brandenburg-Prussia and Russia – rulers squeezed the means of war from their own populations. In fact, in extreme cases, like Tsarist Russia, rulers left few resources for capitalists to accumulate and depended more on foreign loans than they did on domestic capitalists (137–143). It was where capital and coercion grew up in rough balance, as in France and England, that holders of capital and possessors of the means of coercion needed one another, bargained over rights and resources, and produced fully fledged national states (151–160). The relatively greater war-making and state-making capacity of this "capitalized coercion" mode made it more successful than the other two. From the seventeenth century onward the capitalized coercion form proved more effective in war, and therefore provided a compelling model for states that had originated in other combinations of coercion and capital.

Tilly began with the processes of war making, state making, extraction, and protection but eventually deduced from them a number of "civilizing" processes that followed from them: adjudication, distribution, and production:

> From the nineteenth century to the recent past ... all European states involved themselves much more heavily than before in building social infrastructure, in providing services, in regulating economic activity, in controlling population movements, and in assuring citizens' welfare; *all these activities began as by-products of rulers' efforts to acquire revenues and compliance from their subject populations, but took on lives and rationales of their own.* (1990: 31; emphasis added)

"War making," "state making," "extraction," and "protection" eventually produced a bargained relationship between coercion and capital, the mediation by the state of social cleavages, the state's role in guiding the economy, and the diffusion of the citizen army.

But these were long-term processes, sometimes so incremental that they could only be detected in the light of history. But they were linked to short-term contentious mechanisms that transformed the state.

Contention in Revolution

What does any of this have to do with the French Revolution? We can only answer this question after we turn to a second aspect of Tilly's work: his understanding of contentious politics. Tilly argued against the idea that revolutions are a separate species of contention: he applied his concept of contention to episodes ranging from small-scale isolated episodes to protest campaigns, strike waves, revolts, civil wars, and revolutions.

Three observations about the meaning and implications of this broad choice are particularly relevant to the French Revolution:

- first, if contention encompasses episodes of contention ranging from protest campaigns to strike waves, revolts, civil wars, and revolutions, that means that some of the mechanisms that drive "lesser" forms of contention can also be found in revolutions;
- second, and an obvious corollary of the first observation, different forms of contention overlap, intersect, and interact in the same historical periods – including during periods of revolution (Goldstone 1998);
- third, despite the apparently exceptional quality of revolutions, the mechanisms that drive them "chiefly concern the routine operation and transformation of states" (Tilly 1993: 8).

Mechanisms of Revolution

What kind of mechanisms? Tilly argues that a revolutionary situation is triggered by a finite and repetitive series of mechanisms:

- the appearance of contenders, or coalitions of contenders, advancing incompatible claims to control the state;
- commitment to those claims by a significant segment of the citizenry;
- the incapacity or unwillingness of rulers to suppress the alternative coalition and/or commitment to its claims (Ibid.: 10–11).

These intrarevolutionary mechanisms are only different in degree from those that drive other forms of contention – like social movements. Take mobilization: it is the best studied process in the field of social movement studies; or commitment, which social psychologists and sociologists have identified as keys to contention under a variety of different names; or the mechanism that Tilly described in his *From Mobilization to Revolution* as "facilitation" (1978). These mechanisms are found wherever social actors make claims, big or small, on states, and in how states respond to them, including within revolutions.

But such mechanisms are only the starting point for revolutionary *processes*, which are the result of an additional set of mechanisms. Some of these are familiar from the vocabulary of contentious politics: mechanisms like the diffusion of mobilization from early risers to those who identify with them (see Chapter 8); the formation of new or broadened coalitions as the revolutionary process impinges on others' interests and offers new opportunities; the appropriation of existing institutions and organizations for new and bolder purposes; or a shift in scale from the local to the national level or back again.

Other mechanisms come into play as revolutionary gains are contested, modified, and implemented. Revolutionaries who seize and hold onto power for any length of time create new units of state administration and control; when their aims are bold, they have to suppress or co-opt internal countermovements that spring up in response to their reforms; when they are challenged from outside, they build armed forces, levy taxes to pay for these armies, and organize production around their war aims; with all these tasks, they need to provision the armed forces they have conscripted and distribute food to cities they are trying to control. Observe where we have arrived: from a set of short-term mechanisms familiar from the study of contentious politics, we have returned to the longer-term mechanisms that Tilly outlined for the building of states: war making, state building, extraction, production, distribution, and protection. Putting these two sets of mechanisms together gives us an alternative process-based approach to both the structural accounts of the Republican/Marxist synthesis or to the idea-driven account of Furet.

Building a State amid War and Contention: France, 1789–1794

Of course, revolutionaries who seize power differ from the state makers that Tilly studied in *Coercion, Capital and European States,* in the shorter temporal compass of their tasks, their relative inexperience at governing, and the ferocity of their opponents. They also differ in the concentration of political threats and opportunities that their revolution creates and exposes, which other states are quick to exploit (Walt 1996). But because revolutions are liminal events that transform structure in a highly condensed form,[5] their task is not appreciably different from that of the long-term state builders Tilly studied in *Coercion, Capital and European States.* They are not only making a revolution; they are rebuilding state machinery, extracting taxes, conscripting soldiers, organizing production, distributing food, and adjudicating disputes among citizens – all in the context of threats from within and without. The key mechanisms that unrolled during the first half of the revolutionary decade involved the processes of state building, war making, and distribution, inflected with almost constant domestic contention.

State Building
In *The Old Regime and the French Revolution* Tocqueville famously argued that in terms of state building, Napoleon invented little that was new, simply picking up on and refining the centralization he inherited from the old regime (1955: 202).[6] As in many of his other claims, Tocqueville was half right: Napoleon *did* inherit a centralized administrative structure, but it was one that the revolution had invented. The Old Regime state was actually littered with intermediaries: "landlords, seigneurial officials, venal office-holders, clergy and

---

[5] Students of French social history will note that I am extending William Sewell's insightful interpretation of the taking of the Bastille as an event that transformed the structure of French society and the French state. See Sewell 2005 for this analysis.

[6] Tocqueville's memorable phrase is that "since '89 the administrative system has always stood firm amid the debacles of political systems. There might be dynastic changes and alterations in the structure of the state machine, but the course of day-to-day affairs was neither interrupted nor deflected" (*Old Regime* 1955: 202).

sometimes municipal oligarchies as well" (Tilly 1993: 167). As they swept the crazy-quilt of provinces from the map and replaced it with *départements*, districts, cantons, and communes, while sending out *représentants en mission* (168), the revolutionaries applied direct rule for the first time and began to build a centralized state apparatus.

Political scientists have usually described these transformations in administrative terms (Chapman 1955). But they had profound implications for the struggle for power within the provinces and between center and periphery of a rapidly evolving political system. First, they raised the status of some provincial cities while lowering that of significant others, challenging the independence of those who had emerged in the federalist revolts of the early 1790s (Lepetit 1988). Second, they transferred local power from provincial elites to patriot coalitions, drawn mainly from the provincial middle class and then replacing many of these with more reliable administrators. Third, they stripped away the tissue of ancient liberties and exemptions that many localities had enjoyed for centuries (Tilly 1993: 168). Needless to say, these reforms triggered resistance, especially from people and localities that had been exempt from taxation. "Resistance and counter-revolutionary action followed directly from the process by which the new states established direct rule," concludes Tilly (171).

War Making

The revolutionaries were at war almost constantly after Louis XVI's attempted flight. The key turning point came from the Brissotiens and then from the Girondins (Blanning 1986). Wars with Austria, Prussia and, eventually, Great Britain followed in rapid succession. By 1793 France was in a constant state of war that would last, with only brief interludes, for two decades (Lynn 1983). Walt provides evidence on the close relationship between the revolution and war (1996). He focuses on the reasons why external powers were incited by the weakness of the revolutionaries to make gains at France's expense. The urge to go to war was multiplied by other states' perceptions about French intentions and by the French leaders' preoccupation with the danger of counterrevolution – "based on suspicions of treason, rumors of aristocratic plots, and the possibility of foreign interference" (46).

Walt is right that the perception of danger is as powerful a motive for going to war as the danger itself. But he understates the extent to which the revolution really *was* in danger. The revolutionaries were threatened on three fronts – four if one includes the threat from the sea. At one point the British sailed into Toulon Harbor and were welcomed by the locals who were in revolt against Paris (Blanning 1986). It was against the threat of military defeat that the Committee of Public Safety was set up, newspapers critical of the revolution were closed down, political disagreements began to be framed as treason, and volunteerism gave way to conscription (Lynn 1983: ch. 3). More than anything else, the need to protect the revolution from its enemies drove the Republicans toward tighter central control and toward the Terror.

Contentious Politics

Mobilized local elites and opportunistic foreign neighbors were one thing: what pushed the revolutionaries hardest toward the adoption of terror was internal rebellion. In the West, taxation, conscription, and the conflict over church and state produced a massive counterrevolution; in the South and Southwest, federalist rebels occupied Marseilles, Lyon, and Bordeaux; throughout the country, there were pockets of resistance to taxation, conscription, and centralization of control – David Andress identifies at least nine of them in 1793 alone (2005: x). Between them, as Hugh Gough concludes, "war and political conflict ... played a major role in pushing the revolution from crisis to terror" (Gough 1998: 31).

The Vendée Rebellion and its repression were archetypical of this process. As Donald Sutherland writes, "The risings [in the West] revealed an opposition to the revolution that was massive, popular and dangerous" and genuinely counterrevolutionary (Sutherland 1994: 100–101). Back in Paris, faced by the dual threats of war and rebellion, there was "irrefutable proof that the Vendean leaders were negotiating with the British for arms and that they were prepared to attack a port to permit the British to land desperately needed arms and other war materials" (102).

External war and internal rebellion intersected to produce growing fear of collapse and a corresponding ratcheting up of repression by the state. Not only were the rebels known to be dealing with the British; the campaign that the French were planning in Belgium required the rapid transfer of troops that were currently tied down in the West. If the army strove to end the rebellion in the West brutally it was not due to the inherent savagery of the revolutionaries but because "the Republic did not have the resources to continue into 1795" (105). "The impulse to exact revenge, the sense of limitless and ubiquitous betrayal, and military imperatives," writes Sutherland, "combined to drive the terrorists toward a merciless repression" (Ibid.).

The Provisioning Crisis

State building, war, and civil war were the most dramatic sources for the adoption of draconian measures against dissent. But there was also a continuing crisis surrounding the provision and price of food through the half-decade after 1789. The crowd that surged into the convention in September 1993 was calling not only for death to counterrevolutionaries but also for bread (Furet 1992: 293). True, the harvest had improved since the devastating dearth of 1789; but rebellion in the provinces and the provisioning needs of the military reinforced fear of famine in the capital. Grain seizures and fear of plots to provoke famine were endemic in prerevolutionary France (Kaplan 1982); the revolution exacerbated the problem of providing the cities with bread at prices that people could afford. This was one of the demands of the Parisian *sans-culottes* throughout the years 1792–1793 that tipped the scales away from institutional politics. It was the pressures of the *sans-culottes* on the convention that led, in May 1793, to the imposition of a national maximum on the price of grain (Gough 1998: 36–37).

This was not all it produced: in September a mass march of *sans-culottes* erupted into the convention, demanding the creation of a "revolutionary army" to patrol the provinces in search of food and political suspects (Cobb 1987). That "army" fanned out into the countryside, spreading terror and requisitioning grain, while, in Paris, the convention passed the General Maximum to control the price of food (Sewell 1994: 257–258). The combination of *sans-culotte* pressure, Montagnard ability to exploit it, and fear of dearth in Paris combined to produce the atmosphere of crisis that brought the Jacobins to power and launched the Terror.

Interacting Mechanisms

Especially in times of rapid social and political change, mechanisms concatenate (Beissinger 2009). In France in the 1990s, the mechanisms outlined above intersected to produce a high level of tension, repression, and rapid reversals in fortune and direction. The subsistence crisis and its political correlates combined with fear of invasion and with the threat of counterrevolution in the provinces to produce an inexorable pressure toward dictatorship. I cannot do better than quote Sewell's synthesis in its entirety:

> French forces suffered serious reverses in the low countries, leading to the evacuation of French forces from Belgium on 18 March. By then, riots against conscription had broken out in the Vendée and Lyon was in open revolt against the Convention. In an atmosphere of military peril abroad and civil war at home, the Enragés and the sections renewed their demand for price controls and the Montagnards and Jacobins, who were by then involved in a death struggle with the Girondins, hurried to take up the cause. (Sewell 1994: 266)

The basic lesson is not only that revolutionaries face the same problems that confront would-be state builders in "normal times"; they do so in a context that produces rapid mobilization, equally rapid countermobilization, the rapid diffusion of conflict, the repression of some dissenters and cooptation of others, and a host of other mechanisms familiar from the study of contentious politics. These outcomes are familiar to historians; but they need to be related to the process of state building in which the Republicans were engaged. That process was in part cut short with the counterrevolutions of the second half of the decade, but it continued in muted form under Napoleon and his successors. Not only that: it laid the foundation for the machinery of the modern secular state, with its dual implications for democracy and dictatorship. We can see this double outcome in one of the signal innovations of the revolutionary state: the citizen-army.

The Double Meaning of the Citizen-Army[7]

While the revolutionaries created the citizen-army in response to a military threat, that invention was also in a direct line of thought from Republican

---

[7] This section builds on the fundamental work of Meyer Kestnbaum on the origins and construction of conscription-based modern armies. See, in particular, Kestnbaum 2000, 2002, and 2005.

theory. From Renaissance Florence onward, theorists had seen the enlistment of active citizens in the defense of their fatherland as a source of virtue. For example, Leonardo Bruni thought that virtue "requires the fullest participation in the life of the city" and this included participating directly in its defense (Pocock 1975: 86–88). The decline of Florence, in Bruni's view, came from the decision of the citizens to stop bearing arms. "As a result, the effective control of policy fell into the hands of a few, rich enough to possess the resources out of which mercenaries were paid and disposed to employ statecraft rather than arms as the instruments of power" (Ibid.: 89–90). In the same tradition, Machiavelli had urged on the rulers of Florence the development of a civil militia.[8]

Rousseau wrote in a direct line of thought from Bruni and Machiavelli. Military mobilization, for Rousseau, was not only valuable as a way to defend the state; it was a way to create republican citizens (1978: 101–120). He might have been counseling the French revolutionaries on how to respond to the threats on their borders when he wrote that

> As soon as public service ceases to be the main business of the citizens and they prefer to serve with their pocketbooks rather than with their persons, the State is already close to its ruin. Is it necessary to march to battle? They pay the troops and stay home. (1978: 101)

Rousseau was also a source of republican theory about the virtues of the citizen-army. Listen as he counsels the Poles on how to defend themselves against their aggressive neighbors:

> (T)he state's true defenders are its individual citizens, no one of whom should be a professional solider, but each of whom should serve as a soldier as duty requires. That is how they handled the military problem in Rome; that is how they handle it now in Switzerland; and that is how it should be handled in every free state.... A good militia, a genuine, well-trained militia – is the only solution to your problem. (1972: 81)

If Republican theory informed the revolutionaries' pragmatic response to circumstances, it did not determine it. In reality, the revolutionary army combined elements of a new citizen army with the remnants of the Old Regime military. The first response to the threats on the borders was through voluntarism. When that did not work, and the republic was threatened by foreign incursions, the *levée en masse* was decreed in response to *sans-culotte* pressure. But instead of the "spontaneous mobilization" of the street, the convention "declared the entire male population liable for requisition for the war effort, but restricted its practical effects to single men between the ages of 18 and 25" (Gough 1998: 37).

The new recruits brought a revolutionary enthusiasm to the front that was lacking in the Old Regime army, but enthusiasm could not make up for their

---

[8] The classic statement is in *The Prince* (1977: 35–42, 59–63).

lack of experience and discipline. Not only resistance to conscription but defection and malingering were rife. Nor were class cleavages absent from this "citizen"-army – any more than they were absent from French society. While the predominantly middle-class artillerymen stayed with the army, the more aristocratic cavalrymen resigned their commissions. These artillerymen brought with them the use of mobile, massed field artillery they had developed under the Old Regime. Without them, the raw new recruits, mainly of lower class origin, would not have produced the military successes of the revolutionaries or of Napoleon – himself an artilleryman.

The combination of mass voluntarism and conscription began before the height of the Terror. Already in November 1792, the National Convention had set forth a theory of total war through total mobilization. They dreamed that "The women will make tents or serve in the hospitals; the children will shred used linen for bandages; old people will be paraded in public to stimulate the warriors' courage, to preach the hatred of kings and the unity of the Republic" (quoted in Winock 2002: 47). But the Terror shaped both the contraction and expansion of democratic space. As Isser Woloch concludes;

> As initially demanded by popular societies and sans-culotte militants, the mass levy of August 1793 marked the image of an entire nation in arms, throwing itself at its enemies and intimidating them by sheer mass and determination.... The resonance between the army and the home front created a novel and significant democratic space in the era of the Terror. (1994: 316, 317)

The citizen-army thus had a direct role in producing both the modern army and modern national citizenship.

Teachers of French history were once fond of declaring that revolutionary soldiers invaded foreign countries with copies of the Declaration of the Rights of Man on their bayonets. That may not have been quite true but the trope captures the combination of assertive nationalism and citizen mobilization that explains much of the successes of the French military, both in the Revolution and under Napoleon. No less than direct administrative rule over the provinces, the citizen army was a mechanism that tied (male) citizens to the state and to each other through improved education, geographic and social mobility, the integration of new immigrants and, more than anything, the inculcation of a sense of belonging to a common community (Lynn 1983: ch. 6). The obligation for adult males to serve in the military was the counterpart, in the military realm, of the public school and the expansion of the suffrage in the civilian one.

The citizen-army was and remained ideologically polyvalent. If in France it was part of a fundamental democratization of French society that Napoleon called "the career open to talents," in Prussia it was the counterpart of the state-led nationalism that Bismarck used to unify Germany under authoritarian auspices. Even in France the transformation of the citizen army into a professional caste in the second half of the nineteenth century showed the dangers of authoritarian involution.

Not only in France: other new democracies under threat have experienced the combination of social unity, centralization of power, and militant nationalism we see in the French Revolution. Think of the Israeli "people's army," formed when the new state was – like revolutionary France – surrounded by enemies and its leaders attempted to instill a sense of nationhood into a plethora of refugees from Hitler's Europe, the Maghreb, and the Middle East. Like the revolutionaries' *Armée du Nord* in 1791–1794, the IDF became a tool for the socialization of citizens, helping to turn, not peasants into Frenchmen, but immigrants into citizens (Ben-Eliezer 1997). Citizen armies are the classical response of new states to crisis, and as such, they reflect the values and the conditions of these states. How they emerge from that conjunction depends on the enemies they face, the configuration of domestic power, and the guiding ethos of their elites.

Conclusions

History can be seen as the action of structural factors on agents, or as agency transforming inherited structure. In this chapter, I have argued that in the case of the French Revolution, both approaches are defective – the first because it searches for regularity and ignores contingency and the second because it elevates agency to the level of first causes. I have argued that we can only understand revolutions through an attentive unpeeling of the historical narrative into its political process. The process of a revolution – like contention in general – does not boil down to structural determinants; nor does it evaporate into the thin ether of "agency"; it is recoverable only by a careful examination of the mechanisms that constitute the process. That does not mean that all of history is predictable but it does mean that the ambiguities and contradictions that lie buried in history can be uncovered by an analysis of its internal mechanisms.

Think of the institution of the citizen army as it grew out of the French Revolution. It developed as a response to the contentious circumstances the revolutionaries faced. That made it a mechanism, not only for national defense, but for the formation of a centralized state and for socializing its citizens. But it did not take long before that army came to reflect a fundamental characteristic of French society: its highly stratified character. In fact, in contrast to the republican impetus that had infused the army in the early 1790s, the officer corps became an insulated caste, hostile to the republic and to republican values – not to mention to Jews and Germans. In a final irony, the army that electrified Europe in the name of the rights of man and the citizen ended up sending Alfred Dreyfus to Devil's Island. The citizen army was an institutional innovation that contained within it both the germ of democratic citizenship and the source of militant nationalism.

The Jacobin phase of the republic was equally Janus-faced. Just as they were sending suspects to the guillotine, the Jacobins were creating the first hint of the future welfare state, educating citizens, and creating an army that helped to create a national citizenry. This is not to claim that under its ferocious carapace, the Terror was fundamentally democratic; that is no more true than the Furetian conceit that under their democratic costumes, the Republicans of 1793 were Stalinists in training. The revolutionary experience contained both the germ of authoritarian populist-nationalism and the ideal of the virtuous citizen. If that seems contradictory, think of the following parallel: the rag-tag citizen-army that crossed the Delaware with George Washington eventually produced the massacre of My Lai and the abuses of Abu Ghraib. But that, of course, is a different story.

II

MOVEMENTS, PARTIES, AND INSTITUTIONS

5

States, Movements, and Opportunities

In 1991, John McCarthy, David Britt, and Mark Wolfson wrote:

When people come together to pursue collective action in the context of the modern state they enter a complex and multifaceted social, political and economic environment. The elements of the environment have manifold direct and indirect consequences for people's common decisions about how to define their social change goals and how to organize and proceed in pursuing those goals. (1991: 46)

Their observation reflects the findings of a loose archipelago of writings that has developed since the early 1970s under the general rubric of "political opportunity structure." What does this term mean? Since the publication of this influential article, there has been a great deal of debate about the status and importance of this concept, some from those who would like to uproot it from the garden of social movement concepts (Jasper and Goodwin 1998), but much of it from practitioners, like David S. Meyer and William Gamson, whose goal was to prune the plant of unnecessary foliage to help it to flower (1995).

Scholarly debates around contested conflicts are useful but there has been some confusion distinguishing the internal factors that induce people to engage in contentious politics from the external ones that facilitate or obstruct it. There is also the question of how opportunity and threat intersect: scholars have sometimes emphasized opportunity and given less attention to threats. These issues would later be clarified by Jack Goldstone and Charles Tilly, who made a clear distinction between threat (i.e., "the costs that a social group will incur from protest, or that it expects to suffer if it does not take action) and opportunity (i.e., "the probability that social protest actions will lead to success in achieving a desired ourcome"). See Goldstone and Tilly 2001: 182–183). But in the polemics of research, these niceties often go unnoticed.

Two major ways of specifying political structures in relation to collective action are sometimes conflated: opportunities as *cross-sectional and static* and opportunities as *dynamic changes*. This chapter will discuss both specifications but explores in much greater depth why – in my view – "dynamic" opportunities impinge more directly on the decision making of actors than static structures, sometimes permitting actors to create their own opportunities and often creating opportunities for others. I will close by linking the concept of political opportunities to what Gramsci had in mind with his concept of movements engaging the "trenches and fortifications" of civil society (see Chapter 1). But first, we should specify the major elements of opportunity to avoid making the concept of opportunity structure a post-hoc grab-bag of factors that can affect whether and where contention arises.

Elements of Opportunity

By political opportunities, I mean *consistent – but not necessarily formal, permanent, or national signals to social or political actors that either encourage or discourage them to use their internal resources to form social movements.* This broad concept of political opportunity emphasizes not only formal structures like state institutions, but the informal structures that provide resources and oppose constraints external to the group (Kriesi et al. 1995). Unlike money or power, this opens the possibility that even weak and disorganized challengers can take advantage of opportunities created by others to organize against powerful opponents. Conversely, as opportunities narrow, even the strong grow weak, and movements are forced to change their forms of action and their strategies (McAdam 1995).

The most salient kinds of signals are five: the opening up of access to power, shifting alignments, the availability of influential allies, cleavages within and among elites, and the likelihood of repression:

Seizing expanded access. Rational people do not often attack well-fortified opponents when they lack the opportunity to do so. But people with *full* political access may be no more likely to do so. This was what Peter Eisinger found in his analysis of different kinds of municipal structures in the United States (1973). Eisinger argued that the relationship between protest and political opportunity is neither negative nor positive but curvilinear: neither full access nor its absence encourages the greatest amount of protest. He writes that protest is most likely "in systems characterized by a mix of open and closed factors" (p. 15).

The idea that partially opened access to participation encourages protest was supported by the movements for liberation and democratization in the former Soviet Union and Eastern Europe in the late 1980s. As perestroika and glasnost opened new opportunities for political action, protest movements developed that could both take advantage of these new opportunities and go beyond them (Beissinger 2002). Although Mark Beissinger found that violent protest was *not* closely connected with the opening up of opportunities, nonviolent protests were clearly related to opportunity, a finding that dovetailed perfectly with Eisinger's findings, despite the wide differences in the kinds of regimes they studied.

Taking advantage of unstable alignments. A second aspect of opportunity structure is the instability of political alignments, as indicated in liberal democracies by electoral instability. The changing fortunes of government and opposition parties, especially when they signal the emergence of new coalitions, encourage insurgents to try to exercise marginal power and may induce elites to seek their support. In the United States in both the 1930s and 1960s, as Piven and Cloward found in their *Poor People's Movements*, changes in parties' electoral strength encouraged organized labor, the unemployed, African Americans, and other groups and led to changes in the parties' strategies for bringing unrepresented social groups into the electoral arena. Most dramatically, this produced the labor insurgency and unemployed workers' movements of the 1930s and the Civil Rights Movement of the 1960s (1977).

But it is not only electoral instability that encourages collective action, as the record of peasant uprisings in undemocratic systems shows. Peasants have the good sense to only rebel against authorities when windows of opportunity appear in the walls of their subordination. This is what Eric Hobsbawm found when he looked into the history of Peruvian land occupations. The peasants' land grievances were age-old, dating back to barely remembered land usurpations after the Spanish occupation (Hobsbawm 1974). But Hobsbawm found that decisions to take collective action against landlords co-occurred with struggles for power in the capital between elites who, exceptionally, sought support from subaltern classes. The same was true of the southern Italian peasants who seized parts of the *latifondia* in the chaos following the end of fascism. Their land hunger and resentment at landlord abuses were ancient; but it was only when the political system was being realigned that they found the courage to invade large landholdings in southern Italy (Tarrow 1967).

Finding influential allies. A third aspect of political opportunity is the appearance of influential allies, which both William Gamson (1990) and Craig Jenkins and Charles Perrow (1977) found to be crucial in their research on American challenging groups and farm workers. Allies can act as a friend in court, as guarantors against brutal repression, or as acceptable negotiators on behalf of constituencies, which – if left a free hand – might be far more difficult for authorities to deal with. Jenkins and Perrow's (1977) paired comparison of the success or failure of American farm worker groups in the 1940s and 1960s provides a good measure of the importance of allies to collective action. Comparing the farm worker movements of the two periods, they found that the biggest advantage of the latter lay in the presence of three external constituencies: the urban liberals who boycotted lettuce and grapes to support the United Farm Workers' (UFW's) attempts to gain legitimation, the organized labor coalition that supported it in the California legislature, and a new generation of sympathetic administrators in the U.S. Department of Agriculture.

The availability of influential allies took on particular importance in stimulating protest in state socialist regimes in the 1970s and 1980s – for example, in the role that the Catholic Church played in Poland or that of the Protestant churches in East Germany. The example can be extended outside the state: Gorbachev's warning to East European Communist elites that the Red Army could no longer be counted on to defend their regimes was taken as a signal to insurgent groups in these countries that they had in the Soviet General Secretary an unexpected ally.

Taking advantage of divided elites. Conflicts among elites are a fourth factor encouraging unrepresented groups to engage in collective action. Divisions among elites not only provide incentives for resource-poor groups to take the risks of collective action; they also encourage portions of the elite to seize the role of "tribune of the people" in order to increase their own political influence. Comparing different revolutionary moments in Nicaragua and China showed how elite defection in the former affected the incidence and extension of protest (McAdam et al. 2001). Divisions among elites often have the effect of widening the circle of conflict to groups outside the political system and giving them marginal power, while a unified elite leaves less opening for the exercise of such marginal power.

Avoiding repression. Finally, repression is a complex factor in conditioning when and where contention will arise. While some scholars see the likelihood of repression as a factor that deflates mobilization, in other cases – such as the rebellions in North Africa and the Middle East in 2011 – early acts of repression appear to have enraged the population and increased the size and scope of mobilization. It may be that the effects of repression – like opportunities – are curvilinear or that it is the ineffectiveness – and not the degree – of repression that is the major predictor of mobilization.

A Typology of Opportunities

As in any developing paradigm, since the 1970s, when Eisinger first proposed the concept, there has been a healthy and many-sided debate about how to conceptualize political opportunities. Some researchers focused on large-scale structures of opportunity, others on ones that are proximate to particular actors; some have analyzed cross-sectional variations in political opportunity, while others look at how changes in political conflict and shifting alliances trigger, channel, and demobilize movements. What has emerged is an implicit typology of approaches to political opportunities, which appears in Table 5.1.

TABLE 5.1. *A Typology of Approaches to Political Opportunity*

	Temporal Framework	
	Cross-Sectional	Dynamic
Proximate Opportunities	Eisinger (1973)	Amenta (2006)
Scale of Opportunity		
Large-Scale Opportunities	Kriesi et al. (1995)	McAdam (1999[1982])

Proximate Opportunities

Students of what I call "proximate opportunity structure" focus on the signals that groups receive from their immediate policy environment or from changes in their resources and capacities. Not inevitably, but understandably, much of the research in this tradition is intra-national and – as it happens – most of it comes from the United States. Within it, there are two main specifications: policy-specific and group-specific:

Policy-specific opportunities. The focus of most "policy-specific" approaches to opportunity structure is on how the policy and institutional environments channel collective action around particular issues and with what consequences. McCarthy and his collaborators were working in this tradition when they studied how concrete institutions and political processes, like the federal tax code, postal regulations, and state and local fundraising and demonstration regulations shape the collective action decisions of contemporary American movements (1991, 1996). Eisinger did the same when he analyzed how different municipal institutional settings affected urban protest in American cities in the 1960s (1973). Edwin Amenta and Yvonne Zylan did the same when they compared the opportunity structures of different American states (1991).

Group-specific opportunities. In contrast to the policy-specific environment that these authors specified, several scholars have focused on the opportunity structure of specific *groups* and how these change over time. For example, after a long period during which American labor faced legal obstacles to organizing workers, the passage of the Wagner Act in the 1930s facilitated American labor's organizing capability, giving it a new resource to use vis-a-vis business, while the passage of the 1947 Taft-Hartley Act would remove a good deal of this advantage. As long as friendly administrative judges were appointed to it, the National Labor Relations Board (NLRB) favored organized labor, an advantage that would disappear as the courts shifted to an antilabor stance under Ronald Reagan in the 1980s (Goldfield 1982).

Changes in a group's position in society affect its opportunities for collective action as well. For example, in their study of the Civil Rights Movement, Piven and Cloward argued that African Americans benefited from both the postwar rural-to-urban migration patterns that removed them from the worst abuses of Jim Crow, and from the realignment of party politics that followed the breakup of the solid South (1979: ch. 4). Conversely, groups that sprouted from the Civil Rights Movement – like the National Welfare Rights Organization – suffered from constricting opportunities in the political environment of the late 1960s. The changing policy environment affected these groups both positively and negatively.

State-Centered Opportunities

In contrast to approaches that are couched at the subnational or group level, regime-level studies focus on state-centered opportunities. What kind of leverage does political opportunity structure afford insurgent groups? A promising approach to understanding how political institutions and processes structure collective action derives from the "statist" paradigm that became popular in American political science in the 1970s and 1980s.[1] Two complementary approaches, often conflated but actually quite distinct, suggest themselves: cross-sectional and dynamic statism.

Cross-sectional statism. As it developed in the 1970s and 1980s, the statist paradigm was a reaction against earlier approaches in which the state was merely seen as the crossroads of group forces. The advocates of the statist approach now saw the state as "an autonomous, irreducible set of institutions" (Bright and Harding 1984: 3), which shapes political conflict in the interest of its own survival and aggrandizement. More recently, this has been giving way to a more nuanced view of the state as "the arena of routinized political competition in which class, status, and political conflicts ... are played out" (3–4).

Although he didn't use the "statist" label, crossnational statism lay at the heart of Herbert Kitschelt's comparison of the institutional setting of ecological movements in four countries (Kitschelt 1986). In states whose open and closed "input" structures intersect with high and low capacity to implement policies, he argued, the strategies of movements are affected by their institutional policy environments in a variety of ways. For example, the "open" Swedish system, with its high policy capacity, facilitates collective action to the point that ecological movements can operate largely within institutional channels; in contrast, in the "closed" French system, the ecological movement, according to Kitschelt, lacks institutional receptivity and, as a result, uses confrontational strategies (71). The overall structure of the state channels political conflict in determinant ways.[2]

Kitschelt employed his version of crossnational statism to examine a host of documents on the antinuclear movement in France, Germany, Sweden, and the United States; Hanspeter Kriesi and his collaborators framed a massive primary data collection on new social movements in a different set of countries: France, West Germany, the Netherlands, and Switzerland (1995: chs. 1, 2). Their achievement was to pinpoint the impact of different national opportunity structures on a wide variety of social movements over time.

---

[1] Major milestones are Skocpol's well-known book on revolutions (1979) and the theorization of her approach in Evans, Rueschemeyer, and Skocpol 1985. On the United States, see especially Skowronek 1982; Skocpol and Finegold 1982; Bensel 1991; and Vallely 1993 and 2004. For a reflection on and critique of the statist persuasion, see Almond 1988, and the symposium that followed his article in the *American Political Science Review* (1988) under the title "The Return to the State."

[2] Kitschelt's image of collective action around nuclear power in France as extrainstitutional may be influenced by the strategic policy environment of nuclear energy. Nuclear power is, after all, a key arena of national policy for the French state, since it produces power for France's nuclear deterrent as well as for domestic energy needs. It is thus not surprising that the French state should "close" around it. See Scheinman, 1965, on the links between French nuclear energy and nuclear strategy.

Dynamic statism. While both Kitschelt and Kriesi and his collaborators focused on effects of crossnational variations in opportunity structure, other writers focused on how states change and on how these changes produce – or reduce – political opportunities. This perspective argues that – in Bright and Harding's words – "statemaking does not end once stately institutions emerge, but is continuous.... [C]ontentious processes both define the state vis-a-vis other social and economic institutions *and continually remake the state itself"* (1984: 4; emphasis added). This is in many ways the boldest of the four approaches, for its proponents argue that *entire political systems undergo changes that modify the environment of social actors sufficiently to influence the initiation, forms, and outcomes of collective action.*

An example of dynamic statism is found in Richard Vallely's work on the first and second reconstructions in American history (1993, 2004), where he uses changes in state structure and capacity to interpret the failure of the first and the success of the second in empowering African Americans politically. But the boldest attempt to relate changes in states to the political opportunity structure of social movements was Tilly's, in a 2005 book in which he laid out a map of regimes and their influence on the forms of contention that groups employ. Major episodes of contention permanently shape national opportunity structures – especially civil wars and revolutions. But incremental changes in contention – like the growth of industrial conflict in Europe and America in the late nineteenth and early twentieth centuries – also reshape institutions for the reconciliation of competing claims.

In the rest of this chapter, I will focus on the statist perspective on the political opportunities of social movements in both the crossnational and its dynamic specifications. I will argue that while the cross-national approach allows us to link the political opportunities of social movements to a national grid of institutional regularities, the comparisons that follow from it pose a number of problems: from underspecifying subnational and subgroup variations in movement opportunities, to underplaying the dynamic of protest cycles, to excluding transnational influences on social movement activity. In contrast, what I call "dynamic statism" will allow us to specify political opportunity for different actors and sectors, to track changes in opportunity over time, and to place the analysis of social movements in their transnational settings.

National States, Multilevel Movements

Since the eighteenth century, social movements have increasingly directed their activities at the national state, so it was logical that differences in the institutional structures of different states would come to be seen as structuring the emergence and strategies of social movements. Thus, the centralized French state produced movements whose center of gravity rose to the national level; the American federal state produced movements that were more often couched at the state and local levels (see Chapters 3 and 4); the relatively permissive British state encouraged the use of the mass petition and the open-air demonstration; while the repressive Russian state induced opponents to go underground and turn to clandestine organization and the use of terror.

Images of social movements to some extent reflect these differences. Thus, the semiauthoritarian Prussian state influenced the rise of a social democratic movement that was characterized as a "state within a state" while the anarchist and anarchosyndicalist movements of southern Europe were seen as correlatives of the not-very-modern Italian and Spanish states. The French labor movement embraced an associational "vocabulary" that reflected the repressive *Loi Chapelier,* while American movements developed a vocabulary of "rights" that reflected the importance of the law in American institutions and practice.

These crossnational variations in state structure have provided scholars with a useful framework for the interpretation and prediction of national variations in the emergence and structuring of social movements. But three fundamental problems dog the cross-sectional statist perspective: lack of group-specificity, the role of cycles of contention, and transnational diffusion:

- First, the opportunity structures of different movements in the same country cannot be expected to be any more similar than the life chances of the various social actors who constitute them;
- Second, once a major cycle of contention is triggered, in itself it becomes part of the opportunity structure;
- And, third, in a world of movement as global as ours, it seems unlikely that different forms and strategies of social movements would be confined to single types of states; diffusion does not respect the boundaries of national states and societies (Givan, Roberts, and Soule eds. 2010).

These dimensions of movement dynamics – intranational variations, cycles of protest, and transnational collective action – can be illustrated briefly.

Intranational Variations

If social movements simply reflected national institutional contexts, there would be much less *intra*national variation in movements than actually exist, both between movement sectors and within them. Consider the variety of types of mobilizing structures that John McCarthy found between the prolife and prochoice sectors in the United States in the 1980s (1987). In the latter, a sophisticated leadership and an affluent constituency developed an action repertoire that was centered around direct-mail campaigns by formal movement organizations that channeled financial contributions into publicity, education, and lobbying of Congress. In the former, parish-based organizations led a lower-middle-class constituency into direct action campaigns and door-to-door canvassing. Both were equally at home in the "open" political opportunity structure of American public life.

Now consider the variations that are possible within the *same* movement – for example, the environmental movement. In Germany, where the state is federal, Dieter Rucht found a great variety of organizational forms in the environmental movement, extending from "patterns of conventional interest associations and foundations through unconventional associations based on autonomous membership groups and informal networks with specific interests," all the way to the Green Party (Rucht 1989: 73). Perhaps Germany's relatively open political opportunity structure (65–66) helps to explain the movement's heterogeneity, but if so, why did Rucht find the environmental movement to be equally heterogeneous in countries as different – and as centralized – as France and Italy?[3]

Although some national opportunity structures are clearly more "open" than others, state elites are far from neutral between different social actors and movements. Compare the ease with which the nineteenth-century temperance movement was free to operate in the United States with the repression that the labor movement suffered in the same period. The middle-class Protestant women who militated in the former were more cordially received by state elites than the lower-class, immigrant masses who worked the mines and mills of industrializing America (Szymanski 2003). Or compare the warm reception of the Catholic workers' movements by European states in the early part of the twentieth century with the repression suffered by Socialist-led movements in the same times and places (Kalyvas 1996). National opportunity structures may be the basic grids within which movements operate, but that grid is seldom neutral between social actors.

Cyclical Variations

Social movements go through rapidly evolving phases. Thus, comparing even similar movements in different phases of their life cycles can produce a distorted picture (Tsebelis and Sprague 1989). For example, consider the comparative study of revolution: from the start, many students took from the French Revolution an image of fanaticism, bloodshed, and internecine strife. But this was only typical of the Revolution's Jacobin phase. Conversely, most studies of the revolt of the American colonies pass swiftly over the many incidents of bullying, hazing, and outright expulsions of loyalists that marked its early phases (Maier 1972: ch. 2).

Even movements that are less earth-shattering than revolutions go through distinct phases. For example, focusing on the violent clash with the French army when antinuclear protesters marched on Malville in 1977 produced a militant image of French movements that ignored the nonconfrontational nature of other phases of the movement (Rucht 1990: 207–208). Comparing movements across countries can only produce valid comparisons within the framework of

---

[3] Dieter Rucht (1989: 79–80) estimates that the French environmental movement at its peak included about 15,000 different groups with more than 2 million members and a similar degree of organizational heterogeneity to Germany's. On the heterogeneity of the Italian movement, see Diani and Lodi 1988.

these time-series dynamics. Although many after-the-fact observers – no doubt remembering the outrages perpetrated by terrorist groups – characterized the Italian cycle of the 1960s and the early 1970s as "violent," a more detailed analysis showed that organized violence only appeared relatively late in the cycle. At its peak in the late 1960s, Italian movements were far more likely to engage in conventional or confrontational mass collective action than in violence (della Porta and Tarrow 1986).

Transnational Diffusion

From their inception in the eighteenth century, organized social movements diffused across national boundaries: by print media, which carried word of successful revolts to the far corners of the world (Anderson 1991); by immigrants like Tom Paine, who brought the resentment of a disappointed British customs official to the more congenial environment of the New World; and by transnational actors like sailors, who worked in "transatlantic circuits of commodity exchange and capital accumulation" (Linebaugh and Rediker 1990); and most recently by the Internet.

Entire social movements sometimes diffuse across national boundaries and states (Givan et al. 2010). The antislavery movement, which had its origins in Great Britain, made progress by diffusion – through newspapers, agents, and missionaries, and eventually through British policy itself (Drescher 1991; Rice 1982). Later in the century, social democracy diffused the German model to Northern Europe and the Hapsburg Empire. Although its lineaments were only vaguely realized in Italy, Spain, and France, more or less accurate copies of the SPD were established in the Netherlands, Scandinavia, and Austria – not because these countries had opportunity structures similar to Germany's but through transnational contacts between Socialist organizers and because of the growing legitimacy of the German mass party model.

In our era, we not only find a rapid diffusion of models of collective action from one country to another, but a great deal of cross-border collaboration in collective action campaigns (see Chapters 11 and 12). These have been carefully studied in the European peace and environmental movements of the 1980s (Rucht 1990), in the various "social fora" created to counter the institutions of global neoliberalism (della Porta ed. 2007; Smith and Reese 2009), and in the campaign against the Iraq War in 2003 (Rucht and Walgrave eds. 2010). In other cases, movements themselves are organized transnationally – as in the case of Greenpeace (Wapner 1996). In an age of satellite communication, global television, and the Internet, even movements that are independent of one another have almost instant access to information about what others are doing (Rosenau 1990).

In the case of the democratization movements of 1989, we saw a transnational movement that employed similar strategies and rhetoric and in which the latecomers learned from their predecessors in "cascades" of contention (Kuran 1991). The same was the case of the so-called "color revolutions" around the turn of this century, though with more mixed success (Bunce and Wolchik

2011). As for the antiauthoritarian revolutions in the Middle East and North Africa in 2011, the latecomers showed a rapid capacity to learn from early risers, in part through the revolutionary forms of electronic communication that were not yet available to their predecessors in 1989.

If it was ever sufficient to interpret or predict opportunities for mobilization within the walls of the national state, it is less easy to do so today. Because of multiple levels and sectors of movement mobilization, their changing shape in different phases of protest cycles, and their increasingly transnational links, national regularities in state structure must be seen as no more than an initial grid within which movements emerge and operate. To understand how they make their decisions, we must begin with an account of their specific goals and constituencies, the phase of the cycle in which they emerge, and their connection to transnational repertoires of organization, strategy, and collective action.

States and Shifting Opportunities

State building is a secular trend that proceeded inexorably from the fourteenth to the nineteenth and twentieth centuries (Tilly 1992). Movements developed against the depredations of state builders but they did not "rise" in linear fashion; rather, movement mobilization fluctuated broadly, both between social sectors and over time, in widespread strike waves and cycles of protest that responded to the rhythms of economic cycles and to changes in regimes. The increasing frequency of parliamentary targets that Tilly found in England in the years from 1758 to 1834, and the inflection in collective action there from 1789 to 1807 (Tilly 1995; 2008), suggest why: changes in political opportunity affected the likelihood that mass mobilization would be repressed or might succeed and this affected people's collective judgment about whether to protest or to stay at home.

In Britain and elsewhere, once it developed, the social movement form did not go from success to success like Marx's image of the bourgeois revolution.[4] Instead, movements rose and fell, retreated and revived, according to the economic and political conditions of the moment. But what kinds of struggles and which aspects of political opportunity are most likely to provide opportunities for social movement mobilizers? Unless we can specify these better, the concept of political opportunity may remain a grab bag of ad hoc residual categories, adduced whenever "deeper" structural factors cannot be identified. Mobilization into social movements varies as opportunities for collective action open and close, allies appear and disappear, political alignments shift, and elites divide and cohere, and repression varies in its intensity and methods.

---

[4] Marx is worth citing here in detail: "Bourgeois revolutions, like those of the eighteenth century, storm swiftly from success to success; their dramatic effects outdo each other; man and things seem set in sparkling brilliants" (1963: 19).

Short-Term and Long-Term Changes in Opportunity

Although the concept of political opportunity structure developed in its contemporary form only after the wave of movements of the 1960s, looking back through history shows that variations in opportunity were associated with many of the most explosive conflicts in history. And although "opportunity structure" has most often been studied in individual movements in single democratic systems, the concept may be just as useful in showing how globalization translates into different patterns of domestic contention.

Opportunities in Revolutionary France

Consider first the French Revolution of 1789. Although Tocqueville is often accounted the father of political opportunity structure theory (Eisinger 1973), he was actually more interested in portraying the long-term shift in power from the nobility to the crown – and from the provinces to Paris – under the Old Regime than the changes in political opportunity that were occurring on the eve of the revolution. As a result, he failed to observe that it was the aristocratic revival of the 1770s and 1780s and the defection of part of the aristocracy from the crown that launched the revolution. And so obsessed was he with the long-term shift in power to the centralizing monarchy that he failed to notice the shorter-term weakening of the state's capacity for repression. Far from destroying everything in its path, the French state had never overcome the resistance of the nobility, the parliaments, and the municipal office holders to its fiscal demands and was unable to stop the growth of an educated and assertive Third Estate and of an enlightened public opinion. The result was that the short-term decision to open the system to broader participation in July 1788 (i.e., "increased access") unleashed a wave of debate, association, and ultimately revolution (Lefebvre 1947; Schama 1989).

This is not to say that there are no significant long-term shifts in political opportunities and that they make no difference to the incidence and effectiveness of social movements. States change, sometimes profoundly, and these changes produce both opportunities and constraints for social movements. For example, Richard Valelly's study of the impact of the two reconstructions – post-1865 and the 1960s – on Southern politics points to two fundamental changes in the American political system as causes of the failure of the first one and the success of the second: (1) the structure of the party system, and (2) the extent to which the central government controlled coercion within American national territory" (1993, 2004). Where occupying federal troops could not effect the permanent enfranchisement of African Americans in the South after 1865, by 1965, the national state had developed to such a degree that the federal courts could become the guarantors of black voting rights and the National Guard their enforcers. And where the restored Democratic party historically magnified white supremacist influence after the Civil War, by the 1960s, "inclusionists" outweighed "exclusionists" in the American party system.

Global Depressions and Local Opportunities

Global economic changes are sometimes seen as producing broad patterns of resistance across the planet, but in fact, global crises are translated into different forms and degrees of "local" contention. For example, different countries reacted differently to the Great Depression of the 1930s. While workers in Britain languished through most of the period, and German workers were brutally repressed by National Socialism, French and American workers reacted to the crisis with unprecedented levels of collective action and by developing a new type of movement – the factory occupation.

What was the reason for these crossnational differences? There were strike waves in France and the United States and not in Germany or Britain in the 1930s, not because economic distress was greater in France or America, but because of the changes in political opportunities that were offered workers in these two countries. First, reform administrations came to power in Paris and Washington, opening opportunities for access that were not available in either Britain or Germany. Second, there were major electoral realignments in both countries, with a shift to the left and new governing coalitions. Third, the Popular Front in France and the New Deal in the United States offered organized labor influential allies within the state who were willing to innovate in political economic relationships and were unwilling to support the suppression of strikes.

It was the political opportunities opened up by the Popular Front and the New Deal that explained the surge of labor insurgency in France and the United States. We cannot easily explain these similarities by invoking the different nature of the French and the American state, for in both strong-state France and weak-state America, workers responded similarly to similar configurations of strain and opportunity. The obvious conclusion is that we need to interpret political opportunity along axes more dynamic than long-term state continuities or opportunity in general. This is true if for no other reason than that the movements which profit from short-term openings in opportunities frequently lose out when these opportunities disappear or when other actors who are better placed to exploit them enter the arena. Social movements not only seize opportunities; they *make* them, both for themselves and for others who may not share their interests or values.

It is too soon to gauge the effects of the financial crisis of 2008–2011 on contention in different countries, but from Greece, Ireland, Iceland, Portugal, Spain, and the United States in the global North, to Tunisia, Egypt, Libya, Syria, and Yemen in the global South, the crisis took different forms and was processed through different institutional structures. The Greek austerity crisis produced mass protest and violence, while the implosion of the Irish, Icelandic, Portuguese, and Spanish economies produced electoral realignments. Similarly, though there was a commodities crisis throughout the Middle Eastern economies in 2010–2011, the revolts against their governments took radically different forms and had different outcomes, from the partially successful democratizations in Tunisia and Egypt to the civil strife in Libya, Syria, and Yemen to the grudging reforms allowed by the monarchical regimes in the Gulf.

Making Opportunities

Unlike conventional forms of participation, collective action has the unusual property that it demonstrates the possibilities of collective action to others and offers even resource-poor groups opportunities that their structural position alone would not allow them. This occurs when bold new movements make claims on elites that parallel the grievances of those with less daring and less initiative. Moreover, collective action exposes opponents' points of weakness that may not be evident until they are first challenged. It also reveals unsuspected or formerly passive allies both within and outside the system. And, finally, it can pry open institutional barriers through which new demands can pour. Once collective action is launched in part of a system, on behalf of one type of goal, and by a particular group, the encounter between that group and its antagonists provides models of collective action that produce opportunities for others. These can be seen in three general ways.

Expanding a Group's Own Opportunities
A group can experience changes in its opportunity structure as a function of its own actions. For example, protesting groups can increase their opportunities by expanding the repertoire of collective action into new forms. Although, as Tilly writes, people normally use forms of collective action that are culturally known to them (1978), they sometimes innovate, as in the invention of the mass demonstration in early nineteenth-century England (Tilly 1995), or of the sit-in by the U.S. Civil Rights Movement (McAdam 1982). Each new form of collective action finds authorities at first unprepared, and while they are preparing a response, the protesting group can plan an escalation of their forms of collective action (McAdam 1983), creating new opportunities and reaching new publics.

Expanding Opportunities for Others
One of the most remarkable characteristics of collective action is that it expands the opportunities of other challenging groups. Protesting groups put issues on the agenda with which others identify, and demonstrate the utility of collective action that others copy or innovate upon. For example, the American protest movements of the early 1960s – especially the Civil Rights Movement – placed new frames of meaning on the agenda, particularly the extension of the traditional notion of "rights," around which other groups could frame their own grievances. Although this frame extension can occur gradually and in a diffuse manner through the media, educational institutions, and epistemic communities, collective action embodies new claims in dramatic ways that make them visible and available to others in the society.

Creating Opportunities for Opponents and Elites

Protesting groups can unwittingly create political opportunities for their opponents – for example, when a movement threatens another group in a general context of mobilization, leading it to take collective action against the first group; or when the gains made by the first group produce costs, or the impression of costs, to the second (Meyer and Staggenborg 1994, 1998). The competitive ethnic mobilization in the former Soviet Union and Yugoslavia after 1989 were classical examples of this phenomenon (Beissinger 2002). On the one hand, such countermobilization may lead to a sequence of concessions on the part of elites that satisfies competing claims; on the other, it can fuel a destructive spiral of violence such as occurred in Italy in the 1970s (della Porta and Tarrow 1986).

Protesting groups also create political opportunities for groups and elites within the system in a negative sense, when their actions provide grounds for repression; and in a positive sense, when opportunistic political elites seize the opportunity created by challengers to proclaim themselves as tribunes of the people. In fact, the analysis of real-life situations of protest and reform shows that protesters on their own seldom have the clout to affect the policy priorities of elites. This is both because their protests often take an expressive and non-reformist form and because elites are unlikely to be persuaded by challengers outside the system to make policy changes that are not in their interest.

Reform is most likely to result when challengers from outside the polity provide a political incentive for minority elites within it to achieve their own policy goals. Reform often results less from the direct demands of individual protest movements than from subjective or objective coalitions between reformers within the polity and challengers who initiate collective action from outside it. It follows that reformist policies seldom correspond to the claims of the protesting groups; indeed, reforms triggered by their efforts sometimes provide benefits to groups other than themselves, as we will see in Chapter 9. This goes a long way to explaining the radicalization that is often typical after reformist responses to movement claims.

When are parties and interest groups most likely to take advantage of the opportunities created by movements? They appear to do so mainly when a system is broadly challenged by a range of movements, and not when individual movement organizations mount challenges which are easily repressed or isolated. That is to say, reformist outcomes are most likely when civil society produces generalized opportunities to confront elites and authorities with collective action. Since this occurs more easily than the creation of wholly new state institutions, changing opportunities within states are more important to emerging movements than static differences between states.

Conclusions

Underlying the rise of new social movements are socioeconomic cleavages, individual motivations, and group and organizational capacities. But the history of

collective action varies with too much volatility for such slowly evolving structural and motivational factors to fully explain it. This is no more than saying
that we cannot hope to understand the dynamics and the impact of movements
by "placing" them in a static grid of cleavages, conflicts, and state institutions;
we must watch them as a moving target, much as we study ordinary politics.
What I have called "dynamic statism" is one way of doing this. Movements
arise as the result of new or expanded opportunities; they signal the vulnerability of the state to collective action, thereby opening up opportunities for others;
the process leads to state responses which, in one way or another, produce a
new opportunity structure.

But such processes are seldom agent-less shifts of groups and structures
across the chessboard of history. True, there are environmental mechanisms
that create incentives for action: mechanisms like population shift or increase,
resource expansion or depletion, and climate change. These create threats for
some, opportunities for others, and most often combinations of opportunity
and threat (Goldstone and Tilly 2001). But there are also cognitive mechanisms
that induce people to engage in collective action (McAdam et al. 2001: ch. 2),
and relational mechanisms through which they interact with significant others
in society. Movements are often placed at center stage in studies of contentious politics, with parties and interest groups invisible in the wings. The next
chapter argues for a different interpretation: that political parties are often the
phantom at the opera.

6

The Phantom at the Opera

The study of politics has long been marked by a stark disciplinary divide. Forty years ago the study of formal political institutions was seen as the proper province of political science while research on social movements was left to psychologists or "social psychologists whose intellectual tools prepare him to better understand the irrational" (Gamson 1990: 133). Movements were seen as one form of "collective behavior; a category of behavioral forms – including fads, crazes, panics, and crowds – that defined the unusual, the exotic, the irrational in social life."[1] In short, movements weren't seen as a form of politics at all.

Much of that changed with the movements of the 1960s. After the coming of the robust reformist movements of that decade and the "new" social movements of the 1970s, scholars worked hard to link movements to politics. This was particularly true in Western Europe, where scholars like Donatella della Porta (1995), Hanspeter Kriesi and his collaborators (1995), and Dieter Rucht (1989) strove to link the study of these movements to parties and cleavage systems. But among American scholars, there was little attempt to identify the mechanisms that link movements to party politics. The index to *The Blackwell Companion to Social Movements*, arguably the definitive contemporary resource on the subject, illustrates this point: the collection includes exactly two page listings for the term "elections." By contrast "religion" has twenty-one listings, "emotion" boasts thirty two and even "communism" has fifteen (Snow et al. 2004: 717–754).

---

[1] Doug McAdam and Sidney Tarrow "Social Movements and Elections: Toward a Broader Understanding of the Political Context of Contention," Ch. 6 in Jacquelien van Stekelenburg, Conny Roggeband, and Bert Klandermans, eds. *The Changing Dynamics of Contention.* University of Minnesota Press, 2012.

This chapter draws heavily on my article "The Phantom at the Opera: Political Parties and Social Movements in Italy in the 1960s and 1970s." In Russell Dalton and Manfred Kuechler, eds., *Challenging the Political Order.* Yale University Press, 1990, pp. 251–273.

To be fair, elections do figure centrally in a number of empirical accounts of *specific* movements or episodes of contention. But social movement scholars have been slower to recognize the *general theoretical significance* of elections *qua* elections in their work on movement dynamics. Perhaps more tellingly, the initial formulations of the political process perspective failed to make any mention of elections as an important catalyst of movement activity (McAdam 1999[1982]; Tarrow 1983; Tilly 1978). This is an omission that needs to be remedied.

If elections are generally absent from the study of social movements, few analysts of elections touch on the presence or absence of movements at all. The index of the *Oxford Handbook of Comparative Politics* has subject headings for elections and electoral systems; but under neither of these headings do we find cross-references to social movements (2007: 979–980). Not even the article on "Voters and Parties" in that compendium has a reference to social movements (pp. 555–581). The index of *The New Handbook of Political Science* shows a similar absence of cross-referencing between elections and social movements (1996: 808). Of the electoral scholars represented in that volume, only Russell Dalton mentions movements (336–371; also see Dalton 2006). Despite mounting empirical evidence of connections between movements and elections – even in authoritarian systems (Bunce and Wolchik 2011) – these remain largely separate areas of inquiry in both sociology and political science.

In our article "Social Movements and Elections" (2012), Doug McAdam and I called for more attention to "electoral contention." By this term we meant *that set of recurring links between elections and movements that powerfully shape movement dynamics and electoral outcomes.* We distinguished five processes that link movements and parties: elections as a movement tactic, proactive and reactive electoral mobilization by movement groups, the longer-term impact of changes in "electoral regimes" on patterns of movement mobilization and demobilization, and what we called "movement-induced party polarization" in the history of American racial politics (McAdam and Tarrow 2012). In this chapter, I turn more centrally to the movement/party connection in Western Europe during the 1960s and 1970s in Italy, a country in which a new generation of movements emerged from the realignments of the early and mid-1960s. But rather than arising directly as a "new political paradigm" out of the structural development of advanced capitalism, these movements first appeared as an insurgency *within* the party system – a heritage that they never fully transcended. Finally, rather than responding defensively to the new wave of movements, the Italian parties adapted quickly to their challenge by cooptation and preemption.[2] In the overture and the denouement of the drama of the new movements, the party system was neither the villain nor the hero of the piece: it was the phantom at the opera.

---

[2] These are two of the four outcome categories proposed by William Gamson (1990).

Two New Paradigms

In the wake of the student and worker movements of the late 1960s, two models of interpretation arose to explain the period that had just ended. Each had roots in both the collective actors of the period and their academic observers: *The movementist model* was based on the precepts of autonomy from political parties and authorities, on the rejection of hierarchy, and on aggressive confrontational politics. The movementist paradigm in Italy resembled the new social movement school that was simultaneously developing in France and West Germany.[3] What linked the approach in all three countries was its deductive cast and the underlying presumption that the changes of advanced capitalism were creating a new paradigm of interpretive frames, movement organizations, and collective action (Melucci 1980; Offe 1985; Touraine 1971).

The political exchange model developed at the same time among students of industrial sociology who dealt mainly with unions and worker mobilization. Alessandro Pizzorno (1978) and a group of his students and associates (Beccalli 1971; Regalia, Regini, and Reyneri 1978) developed a model in which mass mobilization was seen as the contingent result of enduring conflicts in industrial society. For these scholars, social groups engage in movement activity when the structural balance tilts against them and advantage can be gained by insurgency. Though expressive in form and often in content, the collective action of these groups was seen as part of the ebb and flow of conflict in capitalist society. Unfortunately, their work was largely limited to industrial conflict; hence its relevance to the general cycle of protest that was occurring in Europe remained largely unexplored.[4] This was unfortunate, for they had much to teach scholars of new social movements. Their research showed that the characteristics that the NSM theorists were finding among the new middle class were also prominent in the labor movement. If this was the case, perhaps the new movements were not as "new" as these theorists thought, but were reflecting the genetic "newness" that is found during any new wave of mass mobilization, as American sociologist, Craig Calhoun, would later argue (Calhoun 1995).

New Movements, Old Parties

Five decades later, many of the "new" movements that were spawned in the 1960s are forgotten; others have given way to interest groups; still others – like the Greens – have been institutionalized as parties. Perhaps the breadth of this gap is the result of the theorists' overestimation of the original distance between the new movements and the old party system (Offe 1985)? Or perhaps

---

[3] Readers of this book should be aware that these generalizations do not apply in equal measure to any single theorist. For the review and analysis on which this section is based, see Klandermans, Kriesi, and Tarrow, eds. (1988: introduction).

[4] See Bob Lumley's *States of Emergency* (1990: especially ch. 1), which extends the reach of Pizzorno's theory beyond industrial conflict.

they underestimated the capacity of the parties to adapt to change and took too literally the new movements' rejection of political exchange?

In Italy, as in France and Germany, the party system was often cast in the role of villain in the scenario of the movementist model. But a look at several aspects of the relationship between the parties of the Left in Italy and the new movements that appeared in that period suggests that parties are more usefully seen as creative prompters in the origins, dynamics, and ultimate institutionalization of new social movements than as old actors cast offstage by their movement detractors. In order to understand this reciprocal dynamic, we need to go behind the 1968 period to see where and when the roots of the new movements emerged.

In an important article, Mayer Zald and Michael Berger (1987) pointed out that new movements frequently do not arise directly out of the structural changes of advanced capitalism but from insurgencies within existing organizations. In Italy, at least, even those Italian movements that rejected the party system deeply reflected the alignments, the interpretive themes, and the repertoire of actions of the existing parties of the Left. To understand how this occurred we must first briefly summarize the role that the party system played in the postwar settlement and in the years preceding 1968. The New Left did not arise in the mid-1960s because the curtain had gone up on a new act of capitalist society, but because a political realignment in progress provided it with political space in which to act and with the script on which to construct a new scenario.

The Postwar Settlement

The major characteristics of the postwar settlement in Italy are usually seen as: the reproduction within its domestic politics of the international Cold War; a domestic cleavage structure that pitted a Communist-led working-class bloc against a Christian Democratic-led conservative one; and weak and inefficient political institutions. Each of these is true enough as a starting point, but each was modified in the course of the 1950s and early 1960s.

The bipolar alignment: The postwar Italian settlement was similar to Germany's in every respect but in the most important one: the United States and its domestic allies never succeeded in delegitimizing the Communist-led opposition. This not only broadened the political arena to include a historic bloc which – in West Germany – could be artificially identified with the hated East; it also produced a competitive dialectic *within* the Left that helped keep alive ideological themes that were rapidly sublimated in West German political culture.

Left and right subcultures: The Italian settlement did resemble the German one in one important respect: rather than being governed by an intransigent probusiness Right, the governmental coalition was built around a *centrist* position in which religion had a deeper foundation than capitalism. Of course, just like the CDU/CSU, the governing *Democrazia Cristiana* (DC) had close ties to business. But it was never the party *of* business, both because Italian businessmen had learned to have a healthy disrespect for the profession of politics and because, from the first de Gasperi government on, the DC understood that it needed to govern from the center to remain in power.

Nor was the Left ever as proletarian or as militant as it was often portrayed. The Italian Communist Party (PCI) organized thousands of farmers and agricultural workers, influenced the *petit bourgeoisie* in many regions, and had a strong basis among intellectuals. Despite the polarized pluralism of the country's political party space (Sartori 1966), Italy developed a species of the open and occasional partisanship characteristic of liberal democracy (Parisi and Pasquino 1980; Tarrow 1974).

In fact, there was a symbiosis between the two ideological monoliths that took some time to become apparent. Although neither the DC nor the PCI ever became a "catch-all" party, in the jargon of the 1960s (Kirchheimer 1966), both were trying to "catch more" support than in the past, to some extent from among the same electorate. The long-run effect of this competition for the political center was to moderate their competition and create a need in the governing party to extend its coalition toward the Left. That opening appeared in the early 1960s when the DC succeeded in wooing the Socialist Party (PSI) away from the left-wing opposition bloc. Bringing the Socialists into the governing coalition had the intended effect of splitting the left but it also placed a party determined not to lose its progressive credentials within the governing circle.

Weak institutions, strong parties: The weakness of Italian governmental institutions is infamous. But Italy's frail executive was not a sign of weakness, but a desired outcome of the 1948 constitutional settlement. Its counterpart was the strengthening of the parties in parliament. In fact, the real institutional success story of the postwar settlement was the tremendous increase – *vis-a-vis* its pre-Fascist past – in the strength of the party system, both in parliament and in the country. Although elections soon lost the "Christ versus Communism" militancy of the immediate postwar years, the two main parties did retain a kind of monopoly – over mobilization (Galli and Prandi 1970). Outside the party system representation was stifled, and it was increasingly difficult for new issues to be placed on the agenda or for new groups to gain a hearing except by granting a political party a mandate for representation. Even much of the press was party-controlled or party-influenced, and many associations – for example, farmers and Catholic Action – gained their benefits through a family relationship *(parentela)* with their party sponsors (LaPalombara 1964).

The parties' monopoly of representation began to collapse in the early 1960s, as interest associations asserted their independence and new social groups began to clamor for representation. The most important source of this change was the new salaried middle class of the cities, which doubled in size as a proportion of the active population between 1951 and 1971 (Sylos-Labini 1975). Another was the southern immigrants in the cities of the North. Lacking a "culture of work" and the party loyalty of the traditional northern working class, from 1962 on they showed that they were available for "wild" forms of industrial action (Sabel 1982).

The same period revealed a profound secularization of Italian society, especially in the metropolitan areas of the North, where church attendance was declining, family ties were being loosened, and citizens were forming nonparty-linked associations. The partisan subcultures that had structured people's lives since the Liberation – as well as their voting behavior – were actually in profound decline as scholars were crystallizing them into formulas like "polarized pluralism" (Sartori 1966) or "imperfect bipartyism" (Galli and Prandi 1970). Secularization also produced new demands for civic modernization, for increased access to services and education, and for a government that could attack the problems of an advanced industrial society.

The Realignment of the 1960s

These changes in the postwar settlement produced a change in the quality and intensity of political debate, preparing the ground for a new generation of political movements by identifying overarching issues, establishing a mutual awareness among diverse social and political actors, and creating new political space. Across the political spectrum, there was a widespread debate over the transition to mature capitalism and its costs and promises. In governmental circles, the debate focused on economic planning, on the technical needs of a modern society, and on the defects of the existing industrial relations system. On the Left a lively debate opened on the tendencies in modern capitalism. In governing circles, the debate on the economy was stimulated by a small group of liberal thinkers in and around the small but influential Republican Party, led by Ugo la Malfa, who would be budget minister in the first center-Left government. But the ferment also had expressions in Catholic circles, particularly among a group of younger economists who had come out of Catholic Action and were active in the Interministerial Commission for the South and in the semipublic SVIMEZ (Association for the Development of the South).

On the Left, the debate took on a more ideological tone, but was no less portentous. The Communists, through their Gramsci Institute in Rome, held an important conference on "Tendencies in Italian Capitalism," which put them ten years ahead of their French comrades in recognizing the effects of economic change (Gramsci Institute 1962). A strategic debate on the role of new social actors began in the party at the same time. Sensing the decline of its traditional rural supporters, the party began to look for new electoral allies in the expanding parts of the new middle sectors, long before the "new" social movements of the 1970s were ever imagined.

As for the Socialists, they were more concerned with readying themselves for a future role in government than in understanding the future of Italian capitalism. But political opportunism has strange effects: the prospect of joining the government led the PSI to put reforms on the government's agenda – education, planning, pension reform – which would later become rallying points for mass protest. Ironically, but not for the first time in history, the themes of future protest movements were popularized by the very people who would eventually be the object of attack for the positions they took on them.

The Center-Left Government

Such was the atmosphere in which the DC brought the Socialists into government in 1963–1964. The "Opening to the Left" was neither the first nor the last stratagem the Christian Democrats used to hold on to power. The DC had always been willing to share resources with other political groups, first with the (conservative) Liberal Party and then with the moderate Social Democrats and Republicans. But when coalition politics were extended to the PSI, it became a much more risky undertaking. First, the PSI was too large to relegate to subaltern status like the Republicans or Social Democrats; and second, its shift from opposition to government provided political opportunities to others outside the governing circles that stimulated mobilization. The inclusion of the Socialists in the coalition also exposed the PSI to public criticism in a way that made plain how divided the government was and how strong were the forces on either side of the debate.

Some of these issues revealed the conflicts in the center-Left without touching the mass public or stimulating a broad debate: for example, the compensation of the stockholders of the electric companies that were nationalized in 1962; the shape and extent of the economic planning apparatus; the implementation of the regions ordained by the Constitution (Gourevitch 1980). But other issues – such as pension reform and the divorce issue – triggered a wider circle of conflict. Most important in this respect was educational reform, for it gave the PCI a popular parliamentary platform from which to appeal to middle-class concerns and provided the student Left with a ready-made theme around which to organize (Tarrow 1989, ch. 6).

The center-Left also encouraged mobilization because of its more tolerant attitude to dissent, for the Socialists could ill afford to be identified with repression. Neither the old recessionary solution to wage increases, nor unleasing the forces of order against demonstrators, nor the use of political anti-Communism were possible with the PSI attempting to preserve its claim to a share of working-class votes and gain support from the new middle class. For example, when striking workers were killed by police in Avola and Battipaglia in 1968, the PSI called for an investigation and joined the Communists in a call to disarm the police. The Center-Left, rather than depolarizing the political conflict structure, led to a widening cycle of conflict.

The Widening Cycle of Conflict

The debates that followed the center-Left experience in Italy were similar in many ways to debates about the New Deal in the United States: both revolved around the academic issue of whether they were progressive or system-preserving. But like the New Deal, the center-Left government placed issues on the agenda that it could not resolve and – by its own internal divergences – gave groups outside the coalition the chance to intervene in debates that had begun within it. This was true both for the Communists and for the extreme Left.

The Communist Party

Although the center-Left government challenged the PCI, driving it out of many municipalities that it had governed jointly with the PSI, it also left the party with a predominant position in the unions and induced it to adopt more aggressive policy postures to expose the PSI's betrayal and protect its remaining bastions of working-class support. That the Communists did not lose electorally after the beginning of the center-Left experiment assured them in their conviction that the country might still have a left-wing future. When the protest cycle broke out in the late 1960s, they were therefore encouraged to adopt more radical positions at their Congress of 1969. But the Communists had their ear to the ground even earlier than the 1969 period of mass labor protests. For example, in the debate over pension reform in early 1968, they quickly sensed a pressure for change that had not been evident a few years before. Thus the party was far more open to worker and student militancy than the French Communists, and more sensitive to the new currents than the unions.

The New Left within the Old Left

As for the *non*-Communist Left, its appearance dates, not from 1968, but from the early 1960s, when the debate on the center-Left government began. For as one traditional party of the Old Left – the PSI – was preparing to turn to enter the government and the other – the PCI – was seeking support from the new middle class, new actors were preparing to challenge both for political space on the Left. They did so both *within* the structures of the Old Left and outside of them, through a combination of old and new themes of mobilization and by using both conventional and confrontational forms of action.

Soon after the effective start of the center-Left experiment, conflict began to stir within the party system. Splits in the Socialist and Republican Parties in 1963 and 1964 were followed by an attempted merger between the Socialists and Social Democrats in 1966 and by talk of forming a unified party of labor by the moderate wing of the PCI. The most important split created a new left-wing socialist party, the PSIUP, from the radical wing of the PSI, after that party decided to join the government in 1963. Drawing its membership from the Socialist Party's most radical cadres, the *socialproletari* sought to occupy political space to the left of the PSI; but the hegemony of the Communists led them to attempt to outflank the PCI as well. Many of the "extraparliamentari" of the future New Left would cut their teeth in the PSIUP.

The new party soon became active in the cities and universities in which the PCI was strongest, challenging it for supporters among new groups of workers and students. It was not uncommon for demonstrations to be jointly organized by *socialproletari* and Maoists or for PSIUP members to militate within outright extraparliamentary groups. The PSIUP goaded young Communists to adopt more radical positions within their party and urged them to participate in joint demonstrations that older PCI leaders frowned upon.[5] For many young intellectuals, the PSIUP was a bridge from the institutional political arena to the new movements forming outside the polity.

Insurgent currents also developed within the PCI. For example, an engaged communist intellectual wrote in an anonymous pamphlet that the Communist Party "attracts a generic adherence among the working class, but fails to seek a more engaged participation ... Why should anyone want to militate in a party that doesn't get you any further than Parliament? It is enough to vote for it" (Accornero 1967: 10). Another insurgent group was the one around Lucio Magri, Luigi Pintor, and Rossana Rossanda, the leaders of the future "Manifesto" group, who would eventually be expelled from the party.

Catholic Leftists

Even in the Catholic camp there were defections and insurgencies against the orthodoxy of the Church and the Christian Democratic Party. The ACLI, the association of Catholic workers, split between left-wing and right-wing factions in this period. Catholic Action, a traditional bastion of anti-communism, lost thousands of members (Cattaneo Institute 1968). Many future student radicals received their first political socialization in Catholic student associations like *Intesa Universitaria* and *Gioventù Studentesca* (GS). When a revolt broke out among students at the Catholic University of the Sacred Heart in Milan in 1967, the leaders were all former Catholic Action or GS militants.

Even before Vatican II liberalized the church, new Catholic journals began to give a sympathetic hearing to radical doctrines. In the devout Veneto region, the journal *Questitalia* sympathetically followed the development of the student and workers' movements, while in Tuscany, *Testimonianze* was in touch with Florentine marxists and gave a sympathetic hearing to the "theology of terrestrial realities" (see Tarrow 1988). Here and there, religious "base communities" began to preach the gospel of the poor, using the parish structures of the most conservative institution in the country to mount an insurgency against it (Sciubba and Pace 1976).

It is no accident that these new currents in the universities, the church and the institutional Left began to stir just as the party system was undergoing its most delicate realignment since 1947. More surprising in a country that observers still saw divided into air-tight political subcultures, people were beginning to cross the once-unassailable chasm between the Marxist and Catholic subcultures. Insurgents were not only distancing themselves from the moderates who controlled their respective political organizations; they were beginning to find one other across the traditional political divide between the nation's subcultures within new movements outside institutional politics.

[5] For examples, see Tarrow 1989: chs. 3 and 7.

Strangers at the Gates

Outside the party system, new political groups were appearing and mobilization was beginning to escape traditional channels well before the magic year 1968. This was first apparent in a generation of "little" reviews of both the secular and Catholic Lefts that developed in the early 1960s (Becchelloni 1973; Lumley 1990). Each of these represented less a journal than a cadre of militants who hoped to use the press to create an alternative to the existing party system. These reviews circulated even to small towns and distant regions through the mails and by way of students returning home on vacation, and were passed around from hand to hand.

The best known of the "little" reviews was *Quaderni Rossi,* published in Turin. Although it was founded by a dissident Socialist, Raniero Panzieri, it also attracted support from among Communists, unionists and independent leftists. It built on a traditional leftist theme – worker centrality – and attacked both the PCI and the PSI for deflecting the workers from their revolutionary tradition (Magna 1978: 315). Unionists who would play an important role in consolidating the future factory councils were attracted to Panzieri's teaching no less than future extraparliamentary leftists like Adriano Sofri, a founder of *Lotta Continua,* and Michele Salvati, who would become an influential political economist. Splits within the *Quaderni Rossi* group soon created two new workerist reviews, *Quaderni Piacentini* and *Classe Operaia.*

Some of these young leftist groups limited themselves to making propaganda, but QR began a tradition of "intervention" in the factory that ranged from involving workers in surveys of factory conditions to fomenting strikes and insurgency against the unions. Particularly aggressive were various "workers' power" groups that formed around the country in the mid-1960s (Tarrow 1989, ch. 5). But worker insurgency could only be stimulated during peak periods of contract negotiation; this put the new radical groups in the untenable position of having to wait for union initiatives against management to attack the hegemony of the unions over the workers. Although they had scattered successes, these waves of militancy quickly evaporated between contract negotiation periods.

The New Student Movement

It was in the university that a mass base was available with which to outflank the party system. But even there, mobilization was not generated spontaneously: the student movement arose out of revolts within the party-affiliated student associations, and was generated by the latters' own agitation against the government's plan for educational reform. The student movement illustrates better than any other how issues placed on the agenda by the "old" party system provided the tools for insurgents to mobilize a new mass base.

The campaign against the government's educational reform plans began with a coalition between the PCI- and PSI-led student association, the *Unione*

Goliardica, and the DC-affiliated *Intesa Universitaria*. Many Catholic and leftist student militants came to know each other, and moved together to more radical positions, through this intrainstitutional debate. When both party-led associations resisted attempts to radicalize their positions, the militants joined with external activists to form a new mass movement. The culmination came at an occupation of the administrative building of the University of Pisa in 1967 against the government's reform plans, when the insurgents outflanked the old student movement by adopting a radical workerist set of theses (Lumley 1990).

The old student associations were soon scored with conflicts that turned the debates of the national student assembly, the UNURI, into heated ideological conflicts (Pero 1967). The radicals were proposing that all the traditional student associations merge into a single national student union in which the parties would lose their tutelary role. At a congress in Rimini in the spring of 1967, they purposely presented a motion that the majority refused to accept (Cazzaniga 1967). It was soon after this that the traditional associations collapsed.

The proposal to form a unified student union with a workerist ideology illustrates how New Left activists constructed new themes within a traditional leftist matrix to use against the Old Left. The PCI had long put forward a broad strategy of alliances (Hellman 1975); the idea of a single national organization, which would express the students' solidarity and autonomy, was perfectly compatible with its proposals and in fact first appeared within the Communist-led *Unione Goliardica*. The PCI could not easily oppose a single national student union. Yet such an innovation had the potential to give the radical students a forum in which to challenge party control. The party's reformist wing was hoisted by its own petard of alliance building.

Instrumental and Expressive Claims

New expressive elements were more prominent in the university student protests than in any other part of the social movement sector. However, they first developed around political, instrumental, and policy-oriented demands. The policy-oriented nature of the demands of the student movement can be seen in a statistical breakdown of its demand structure calculated from daily Italian newspaper data.[6] Table 6.1 compares the various types of demands made in the university protests to those found in all the protest events analyzed from a national newspaper-based archive collected between 1966 and 1973 (Tarrow 1989). The table shows that in over 60 percent of the university disputes, the students put forward claims for new rights, for substantive benefits, or for or against policies of the government. In 17 percent of the disputes, the protests were simply expressive, affirming the students' identity, showing their sympathy

---

[6] The data were gathered from a daily reading and enumeration of all striker, civil protests, and violent collective action reported in Italy's major newspaper of record, *Corriere della Sera*. For a description of how the data were collected and analyzed, see Tarrow 1989, Appendix B.

TABLE 6.1. *Italian University Students' Protests Compared to All Protest Events: Types of Demands*

Demand Type	Student Events	All Events
Substantive protests		
Getting rights	17.3	3.5
Getting more	28.1	42.0
Policy demands	18.0	13.3
Expressive protests		
Identity or solidarity	11.5	10.8
Opposing others	5.0	25.8
Getting out	0.7	0.9
Mixed types		
Substantive and expressive	19.5	3.7
Total	100.1	100.1
(N)	(139)	(4,296)

Source: Author's data.

for others, opposing other groups, or demanding the overthrow of the system. But the newspaper data also underscore the uniqueness of the university students' movement and its links to the new social movements of the 1970s.

This can be seen in three ways: first, the students demanded new rights of participation. The theme that underlay most of these protests was that of autonomy, sometimes expressed as a struggle against academic authoritarianism, sometimes against the party-led student associations, and sometimes extending to a demand for a student-run university (Grazioli 1979: 30–35, 186–191). The students sought the right to assemble, to influence curriculum and teaching procedures, and in some cases to reorganize the university. They wanted to be able to publish freely, to criticize professors within and outside the classroom, and to take exams when they pleased.[7]

Second, Table 6.1 shows that the university students were more interested in general policy issues than most other social actors. They made their own policy demands or tried to stop government actions of which they disapproved. This concern with general policy was most evident in the area of university reform, but students also demonstrated against the war in Vietnam, in favor of pension reform, and against fascism and police violence. Their policy proposals were radical and were sometimes put forward in a spirit of play, but they were far more likely than other social groups to make demands that went beyond their "hard"' material interests.[8]

---

[7] This theme of "autonomia" was later appropriated by extreme left workerist groups in the 1970s, some of whom eventually passed into armed struggle. For a source on the evolution of the theme of "autonomia" see Tarrow 1989: ch. 8.

[8] For additional evidence that the students were more likely to "mind other people's business" than other social actors, see Tarrow 1989: ch. 5.

TABLE 6.2. *University Protests and All Protest Events,*
Italy, 1966–1973: Forms of Action

	University Student Events	All Events
Conventional	40.7	56.1
Confrontational	37.4	18.9
Violent forms	18.5	23.1
Other forms	3.4	2.1
Total	100.0	100.2
(N)	(356)	(9,006)

Source: Author's data.

Third, far more than other social actors, the university students' demands collapsed "the wall between the instrumental and the expressive" (Zolberg 1972: 183). Some new social movement theorists have argued that movements have an underlying "logic" that is either instrumental or expressive (Rucht 1988). But the Italian students used expressive means to advance instrumental goals – as in their use of workerist symbolism to demand a unified national student union. Rather than following either a straightforward instrumental or an expressive strategy, like many new social movements, they were "radically pragmatic" (Lumley 1990). This takes us to their repertoire of contention.

Convention and Contention

From the very beginning, many of the Italian students' protests were built around confrontations with authorities. Table 6.2 compares the use of conventional, confrontational, and violent actions by students in the universities to the incidence of these types of action in the protest events as a whole.[9] The students used confrontational forms twice as often as other social actors did. In the first half of 1968 alone, of the university-based protests for which we have detailed information, confrontational forms of action were used in 90 percent of the cases.[10] The main form of contentious action that the students developed was the occupation of university faculties.

The occupation was no new creation. It had been a traditional action form of the Italian Left since 1919–1921, when the plants of the sprawling Fiat empire in Turin were occupied by the workers (Spriano 1964). It reappeared in 1943–1945 as workers took control of their factories from managers who had worked hand-in-glove with the corporate state. The traditional Left continued to use the occupation during the postwar period as a means of expressing its

[9] For a discussion of these three main repertoires, see Tarrow 1989: ch. 3. The concept of the repertoire of contention is developed by Tilly 1978 and 1986 and especially in 2008.

[10] Excluding protest events outside the universities which appeared to include students, there were twenty-nine protests about educational issues recorded in *Corriere della Sera* in the first half of 1968. This is the operational indicator of "university-based protests."

policy demands and gaining publicity. In 1965, for example, the Communists symbolically occupied the municipalities of Pisa and Genoa to embarrass the Socialists, who were negotiating for the formation of new municipal governments with the DC. In an ironic incident in Pisa, they "instructed" the student militants of the *Unione Goliardica* in how to use the occupation (cited in Tarrow 1989, ch. 10).

But the leaders of the student movement used the occupation tactic not only as a dramatic and disruptive form of action but also as a "practice of the objective" of direct democracy to create social and educational space for themselves. Occupations quickly became a basis for other actions in which solidarity reigned, social constraints were relaxed, and group activities were organized. Teams of enthusiastic students printed newsletters and produced wall posters; courses were organized and debates were carried on; activists formed new networks crossing previously established political lines. Occupations were crucibles for the release of new energy and the production of new social networks.

The carefully crafted documents produced by these occupations were designed both to express the movement's goals and, more pragmatically, to bridge the differences between groups of varying ideological derivation. The same was true for the other forms of direct action invented by student activists in these years: they were less a spontaneous expression of the "life-space concerns" of the activists than instruments developed out of the process of confrontation to form new collective actors. For example, until they were turned out into the street by the authorities, left-wing Catholic activists routinely occupied churches to express their demands. Turning defeat into victory, they "invented" the performance of the mass in the piazza which had the advantage of attracting both nonpracticing Catholics and the irreligious into their movement (Tarrow 1988).

In summary, in the student movement, activists opposing the old party system radicalized debates that had begun within that system. They developed a language of utopia and confrontation that was designed to outflank the Old Left, hold the movement together, and appeal to new supporters. If the old parties were often a target of the movement, it was less because they opposed its aims than because they were a necessary target against which to build new identities. But the Old Left was also the foundation upon which the new movement was built. As two observers of the French scene in 1968 (Schnapp and Vidal-Naquet 1971, n. 17) wrote:

> In France and Italy the very fact that there exist large workers' parties which are revolutionary in speech, if not in practice allows the student movement to present itself as the University detachment of a revolutionary workers' party that does not exist.

After Mobilization

If the party system was a participant in the overture of Italy's protest cycle it also took part in its denouement. Many observers emphasize the violence that follows protest cycles, but another school of interpretation stresses the institutionalization of social movements. As Theodore Lowi (1971: 54) writes:

> When movements act on the government or any of its parts, there tends to be action with very little interaction – that is, very little bargaining. But this is not violence ... The effect of the movement is of another sort altogether: *the demands and activities of a movement tend to activate the mechanisms of formal decision-making.*

How does such institutionalization occur? Through the decline of mass mobilization and the attempt of movement leaders to keep their organizations alive by providing members with selective incentives? Through the cooptation of leaders into established institutions and the transformation of militancy into compliance? Or through the efforts of political parties and interest groups to adapt to insurgency and to absorb the energies of the movements? All three processes could be observed in Italy in the mid-1970s.

Movement-Party Competition

The movementist model left us with an image of the political parties as "old gardeners" who attempted to prune the fertile wild flowers of the new movements that arose in the 1960s. This is certainly part of the picture – especially in cases like that of the French Communists, who were particularly resistant to the message of liberation that the new movements bore. But the PCF is a poor example of party response, for its antimovement tactics were a recipe for failure. Indeed, it was in part the Communists' hostility to the new movements that provided a social base on which the resurgent *Parti Socialiste* could build in France.

The Italian Communists' adaptation to the new movements represented a more flexible response than that of their French comrades. Unwilling to encourage movement organizations that it did not control, the party competed with them for support among new social actors. Unlike the French Communist leaders, the PCI began to question inherited dogmas and seek support from the new middle class before the new movements of the 1960s and 1970s arose (Blackmer and Tarrow 1975; Hellman 1975). But because the party assumed that it could count on the support of the working class, its efforts aimed at not offending the old and the new middle class, whose support it was increasingly seeking, leaving a strategic opening for its competitors among radical elements of the workers.

This competition had its brutal side. For example, the PCI would sometimes send tough factory militants as a *servizio d'ordine* to "protect" its youth demonstrations from being broken up by the radicals. But it also had a more pragmatic aspect, as the party, the unions, and the movements bid for support of new social actors like urban slum dwellers, ecologists and women, with competing programs and broad mass forms of action. The only area in which the party refused to follow the new movements was the realm of "vanguard violence," which it roundly condemned, both among its own militants and in the extreme Left. [11]

Across the Frontiers of the Polity

Social movement theorists often conceive of the institutionalization of movements taking place through the cooptation of their leaders or the preemption of their policy goals by elites (Gamson 1990: ch. 1) However, rather than suffering debilitating preemption or corrupting cooptation, movements often act in uneasy coalition with elements in the old party system. The outcome of their struggle is often reform – partial, disappointing, but incremental reform (see Chapter 9). If we only visualize new social movements growing up outside of and against politics, it is difficult to see these composite effects. But seen in combination with changes in ordinary politics, we find objective – and sometimes self-conscious – coalitions forming between political parties and interest groups that sometimes, under some conditions, achieve some of the goals of the movements.

The Radical Flank Effect

The main function of the the radical new social movements for reform in Italy was a "radical flank effect" – radicalizing and publicizing issues that had already appeared on the public agenda and making alliances with groups within the frontiers of the polity. An example can be found in the case of the Women's Movement. An independent Italian women's movement was virtually nonexistent before 1968, with most women's organizing dominated by the Catholic CID *(Centro Italiano della Donna)* and the Communist-Socialist UDI *(Unione Donne Italiane)*. In the reflux against the New Left of the early 1970s, women organized in the unions and extraparliamentary parties and in a plethora of collectives, consciousness-raising groups, and in *ad hoc* mobilization campaigns (J. Hellman 1987). This led, among other things, to pressure for a new abortion law outside the parliamentary parties.

The years 1975–1977 were full of reports of demonstrations in favor of abortion by independent feminist groups, institutional interest groups like the UDI, and radical extraparliamentary groups attempting to overcome their well-deserved macho image. These were not concerted efforts, and many of the groups had conflicting goals. Sometimes there was a common front attempted between challengers and members of the policy elite. But, more commonly, such groups operated independently of one another, each in complete awareness of

---

[11] The tenants' movement is a good example of the interorganizational competition that developed among movements, parties, and trade unions. From the beginning, it was not a homogeneous radical movement but a cross section of the social movement sector, with institutional, semiinstitutional, and antiinstitutional elements competing for support (Daniele 1978). It would thus not be fair to say that the movement was institutionalized only as the cycle wound down; like the student movement, at least a part of it was linked to the Old Left from the start. For example, Perlmutter (1988) cites figures that show that PCI militants were active in a large number of "spontaneous" neighborhood groups in Turin from the start.

what the others were doing. The net effect was to force abortion on to the policy agenda and to force the institutional parties to deal with it.

The demonstrations of the new feminist groups had vivid expressive elements: organizers might dress up as witches, sport pink armbands, and refuse admission to men marchers. But we cannot understand their impact if we look only at this "expressive logic." For the new feminists forced the question of abortion onto the policy agenda and combined with developments within the party system to revoke the old Fascist-era family legislation and produce a moderate abortion law. The bill that resulted, and passed in 1978, did not grant women the right to "open, assisted, and free abortion" that the feminists had demanded. But its moderate language made it possible for the DC to abstain from the parliamentary vote, for the PCI to combine with the Socialists and the lay center parties in support of a compromise, and for abortion to become legal in a country in which the Vatican was still a powerful political force (Ergas 1982).

Movements into Parties

In his provocative book about cycles, Albert Hirschman observed that political involvement is characterized by "oscillation between periods of intense preoccupation with public issues and [periods] of almost total concentration on individual improvement and private welfare goals" (1982: 3). For Hirschman, "Western societies appear to be condemned to long periods of privatization ... followed by spasmodic outbursts of 'publicness' that are hardly likely to be constructive" (132).

However we judge its impact, the wave of mobilizations of the 1960s cannot be said to have led only to privatization. On the contrary, it had major impacts on public life, not only through the triggering of a series of new movements – like the ecological, antinuclear, peace, and women's movements – but also upon cultural life, interpersonal relations and attitudes toward authority (Tarrow 2011: ch. 11). Most important in the long run, the new movements and the new value orientations they fostered significantly affected the institutional settings against which, but also *within* which, the new movements arose.

For example, the Communist Party, which was the target of much of the insurgency of student and worker militants in the 1960s, was also the beneficiary of much of the residual activism at the end of the period.[12] For as mobilization waned in the early 1970s and some activists entered new movements, while others accepted positions in the unions and a few took up the desperate cause of armed struggle, a significant number of those socialized into politics in the 1960s became militants in the Communist Party. Between 1969 and 1978,

---

[12] The data summarized here come from a jointly written article (Lange, Tarrow, and Irvin 1989) based on data provided to use by CESPe of Rome. I am grateful to my collaborators for their willingness to allow me to refer here to our joint work and to the CESPe for the use of their data. For a more extensive analysis of the CESPe survey, see Accornero, Mannheimer, and Saraceno (1983).

TABLE 6.3. *PCI Delegates to 1979 Provincial Party Congresses: Generation of Entry by Pathways of Recruitment*

Background	1921–1946	1947–1956	1957–1966	1967–1969	1970–1973	1974–1976	1977–1979	Total
Traditional								
Young Communists	24.1	56.8	50.1	37.9	21.8	17.5	27.5	29.5
PCI family	35.3	9.4	12.4	10.8	7.6	0.5	6.2	10.8
Union	1.7	5.9	10.1	14.8	20.5	21.3	15.0	15.3
Other party	3.4	2.3	1.8	1.9	2.5	1.1	0.7	1.9
New Movement	2.1	1.0	1.9	0.9	10.0	11.3	8.0	7.3
Mix of traditional and new	4.9	12.6	12.4	16.0	25.0	25.8	27.3	20.0
Multiple Backgrounds	0.6	1.7	1.3	1.8	4.9	4.8	5.6	3.5
None	28.1	10.3	10.1	9.9	8.3	11.6	9.6	11.7
Total	100.2	100.0	100.1	94.0	100.6	93.9	99.9	100.0
Row percentage	9.4	7.9	13.1	8.7	23.6	25.7	11.4	99.8

Source: Author's data.

in fact, party membership rose by one-quarter, from just over 1,500,000 to just under 1,900,000 (Barbagli and Corbetta 1978; Lange, Tarrow, and Irwin 1989).[13] A survey of the delegates to a party congress allows us to at least see how rapidly they moved into its grassroots decision-making level. Table 6.3 summarizes data drawn from the CESPe survey of 1979 provincial congress delegates, showing both the generational breakdown of the congress delegates and their paths of recruitment.

Reading along the bottom row of the table, we can see how the generational composition of the congress delegates bulges with those who were recruited into the party after 1969 and before 1977. Although one would normally expect a traditional mass party to be staffed at the grassroots level by militants who had been in the party for many years, by the late 1970s, the new PCI activists were overwhelmingly drawn from among those who were socialized into politics within the decade after the student-worker movements of 1967–1969.

Reading along the top four rows of the table shows how people from the traditional sources of PCI recruitment (the FGCI, the Young Communist Federation, and Communist family backgrounds) were giving way to those with union or other political backgrounds. And reading along the lower rows

[13] Marzio Barbagli and Piergiorgio Corbetta (1978), basing their conclusions largely on correlations between the strike rate and party membership at the subprovincial and provincial levels, concluded that it was from central and southern Italy that the party recruited the largest numbers of its new members. Stephen Hellman (1980), using more disaggregated data from Turin, found a positive correlation between strikes and increases in party membership.

in the table shows that recruitment from movement backgrounds or a mix of traditional and movement background increased dramatically after 1966. If one disaggregates the data still further, the curious amalgam of those with a background in both the Communist Youth Federation and in a social movement mushrooms after 1966: while tiny proportions of the militants recruited into the party before 1967 had such a mixed background, they rose to 7.5 percent of those recruited in 1967–1969, all the way to 13 percent of those recruited between 1977 and 1979 (data not shown in table). Socialization into politics through new movement activity became an important source of old party recruitment.

Conclusions

Beneath the surface stereotypes of a rigid opposition between the wild, spontaneous, and antipartisan new movements of the 1960s and 1970s, and the staid, tired, conservative institutions of the Italian party system, there was a more complex and interpenetrating set of relations than what the "movementist" model would predict:

First, the mobilization of the 1960s was triggered by the realignment of the party system, which produced the policy issues, the political space, and some of the militants who later formed a new generation of new social movements.

Second, these movements were formed partially against, but also partially within associations run by the party system, the unions, and even the Catholic Church. The new movements have rightly been pictured as having an antiinstitutional vocation; it has far less often been observed that they had sources and communication channels within the traditional institutions of Italian democracy and used these as resources with which to build a following.

Third, political change occurred, not through the dramatic clash between institutional and antiinstitutional armies, old and new political paradigms but through the competition between parties, unions, interest groups and movements, through reform coalitions, and through the absorption of at least a part of the "people of 1968" within the party system after mobilization ended.

In their writings, new social movement theorists cast the old parties as critics of the creative dramas of the 1960s and 1970s. But rather than the villain of the piece, these parties were the phantom behind the operatic performances of the New Left (LaPalombara 1987). They sketched the themes that the new movements would adopt and orchestrate; they trained some of the actors who then walked alone onto the stage as insurgents; they developed a repertoire of actions upon which the movements – like a jazz ensemble – would improvise and radicalize; and after the show was over, they welcomed many of them into the party fold.

But this was no mere *opera buffa*. It had aspects of both tragedy and drama. As one veteran of these movements, Adriano Sofri, reflected on the history of the new movements founded in the 1960s,

The tragedy is that the words that we inherited [from the Old Left] were never contested, but were simply accompanied by other words. We took the nouns and instead of proving them false ... we added adjectives to them, an incredible quantity of adjectives. (Sofri 1985)

Even this veteran of the 1960s, who sits inside an Italian prison today, recognized how far within the gates of the Italian polity he and his "extraparliamentary" comrades were.[14]

---

[14] Sofri, who offered these reflections, was one of the main leaders of the extraparliamentary group, *Lotta Continua,* and was accused of having organized the murder of Guido Calabresi, a policeman who was accused of responsibility for the death of an anarchist in police custody after an infamous bombing of a bank in Milan. For a brief biography, go to en.wikipedia.org/wiki/Adriano_Sofri.

III

EVENTS, EPISODES, AND CYCLES

7

From Eventful History to Cycles of Contention

Social movements engage in action and action can be broken down into events. But what do students of contention mean by events? And how do events relate to the broader concepts of episodes, campaigns, and cycles of contention? The *Oxford English Dictionary* (Compact Edition 1971: 338) gives us the following as its main definition of the term "event":

> The (actual or contemplated) fact of anything happening; the occurrence of. Now chiefly in phrase In the event of: in the case (something specified) should occur.

A second meaning of the term for the *OED* is "anything that happens ... an incident or occurrence; a third is "that which follows upon a course of proceedings"; a fourth is "what becomes of or befalls (a person or thing" (339); and a fifth is a combination of meanings two and three. A lot of meanings these!

Historians have been no more univocal than the *OED* about the meaning of events. Fernand Braudel looked down his nose at events as "surface disturbances, crests of foam that the tides of history carry on their strong backs" (1972: 21). Olivier Dumoulin tried to retrieve the event from its Braudelian exile, calling it "the historical fact that leaves a unique and singular trace, one that marks history by its particular and inimitable consequences" (1986: 271). Across the channel, Philip Abrams gave the concept theoretical power when he wrote that an event

> is a transformation device between past and future.... It is not just a happening there to be narrated but a happening to which cultural significance has successfully been assigned.... Events, indeed, are our principal points of access to the structuring of social action in time. (Abrams 1982: 191)

This chapter draws on two related papers: "Studying Contentious Politics: From Eventful History to Cycles of Collective Action." Published in Dieter Rucht, Ruud Koopmans, and Friedhelm Neidhart, eds., *Acts of Dissent: New Developments in the Study of Protest*. Berlin: Sigma, 1998, pp. 33–64 and "Charles Tilly and the Practice of Contentious Politics." *Social Movement Studies* 7: 225–246.

In recent years, there has been an "eventful turn" in the social sciences too, approaching something like Abrams' apotheosis of the event. Drawing on the "cultural turn" in history, authors like Marshall Sahlins and William Sewell Jr. trained analytical lenses on the concept of events. At the other end of the qualitative/quantitative spectrum, other social scientists have been using events as their main data points as they employ systematic empirical methods to analyze population ecologies, social conflicts, and political struggles. Taking their cue from the work of Alexander George and Andrew Bennett (2005), Henry Brady and David Collier have dignified the systematic study of political processes under the term "causal process observations," which they distinguish from the more familiar strategy of "data-set observations" (2004: 253). Events have returned to the center of social scientific and historical scholarship.

But there are contentious issues as well. How do we recognize and analyze the *key* event in a historical sequence of events? How far can we go in construing history as a series of events (what will be called, in this chapter, "event histories")? And how can we relate these "Big Events" to others and to institutions and political processes? Finally, how can we relate events – whether the Great Events of narrative history or the sequential ones of event histories – to broader episodes of contentious politics, to cycles of protest, and to revolts and revolutions?

This chapter will begin such an effort. Rather than attack the subject deductively, or summarize vast bodies of empirical research, I will use examples from the work of three major scholars who have been employing events in historically based collective action research. I call these approaches:

- *event-ful histories*, adopting that term from Sewell's concept of the theorized narrative;
- *event histories*, as the term has been developed in the organizational ecology tradition of American sociology by Susan Olzak and her students;
- *events-in-history*, the approach developed by Charles Tilly, beginning with his 1964 study, *The Vendée* and culminating in his last book, *Contentious Performances* (2008).

Each approach has advantages and defects, but each one – if pursued single-mindedly – holds the risk of driving event-based historical research into diverging channels, to the detriment of our knowledge of the dynamic processes of collective action. Moreover, each approach offers a different answer to a key question for social movement scholars: "how can collective events be used to trace the presence, the dynamics and the outcomes of contentious politics?"

The Return to Eventful History

The return to eventful history (though for many British and American historians there never was a departure) dates from Lawrence Stone's polemical charge against quantitative social historians in the 1970s (1979; but see Stone 1982). "Forced into a choice between *a priori* statistical models of human behavior, and understanding based on observation, experience, judgment and intuition," he wrote, some of the new historians, he hoped, "are now tending to drift back towards the latter mode of interpreting the past" (1979: 19). Stone's polemical attack on statistical history gave pause to a whole generation of students, but it did not lead to a research program.

More subtle, and thus more effective, was the influence of Clifford Geertz, whose pellucid prose and dramatic portrayal of ritual-laden events convinced many younger scholars that "thick" description could unpeel layers of meaning even from things that had happened centuries ago (1973). Thus, Robert Darnton interpreted the sporadic killing of cats in late eighteenth century France as a cultural ritual pregnant with implications for the revolution that was about to occur (1984); Carlo Ginzburg reinterpreted the changing meaning of witchcraft in Friuli in the light of the cultural pressures of the Inquisition on popular culture (1984); Lynn Hunt interpreted a dispute about statuary among French revolutionaries as a symbolic struggle over the meaning of the revolution (1984). In another part of the world, Marshall Sahlins wrote that, "what makes an act or incident an event is precisely its contrast to the going order of things, its disruption of that order" (Sahlins 1991: 45; also see Sahlins 1985). For these scholars, events were singular, pregnant with meaning, and occasions for enlisting their cultural sensitivities in interpretive efforts.

In the meantime, historical sociology was taking a different route than the caricature that Stone had airily dismissed. One strand was using historical demography to understand the social dynamics of the past.[1] Another used macrohistorical comparisons between whole states and societies (Skocpol 1994). A third, represented here by the work of William Sewell Jr., took the big historical event as its focus.

Sewell and the Culturation of Narrative

Along with Sahlins, Sewell is the foremost exponent of this big event approach in the social sciences. In three sharply polemical but historically informed papers, eventually collected in his *Logics of History*, Sewell proposed that historical sociology be rebuilt around the analysis of events (2005). He took his own advice with an in-depth analysis of an event that was to mark the entire French Revolution and much else besides: the publication of the Abbé Sieyes' *Qu'est que c'est le tiers état?* (1994) and with another – the taking of the Bastille by a Parisian crowd on July 14, 1789 (2005: ch. 8). And he engaged distinguished macrohistorical sociologists like Skocpol, Tilly, and Immanual Wallerstein in the name of a more narrativized history than what their general structuralism produced (2005: ch. 3).

But as if the various dictionary meanings of the term "event" surveyed at the outset of this chapter were not enough, Sewell proposed another, more

---

[1] For example, see the ingenious use made of military recruitment data by Roderick Floud to understand class differences in nutrition in *Height, Health and History* (2006). Also noteworthy was Jack Goldstone's *Rebellion and Revolution in the Early Modern World* (1991).

cultural and sociological meaning. "Events," he writes, "should be conceived of as sequences of occurrences that result in transformation of structures. Such sequences begin with a rupture of some kind – that is, a surprising break with routine practice" (2005: 227). Sewell has been moving away from quantitative social history and toward an emphasis on the particularity of great historical events for some time (Ibid.: ch. 2). In his *Logics of History*, he offers the taking of the Bastille as an archetypical example: it was not the raw *facts* of milling crowds, reluctant defenders, the dramatic charge on the fortress, the forced entry, the freeing of the few miserable prisoners and the beheading of the unfortunate governor that rendered the invasion a noteworthy event. These would have been lost under the unfolding series of *journées* that followed, had they not been given political impact by the multiple insecurities that the occurrence produced, which in turn gave rise to a process of "collective creativity" (Ibid.: 250). The sequence of occurrences that followed the taking of the Bastille was sensational, but its ultimate importance was that it linked two modes of activity previously thought to be unconnected: political and philosophical claims about a nation's "sovereign will" and acts of popular violence (255). It was because it gained "authoritative sanction" that the taking of the Bastille became "the establishing act of a *revolution* in the modern sense" (257–259).

From Structure to Events

The importance of Sewell's project goes well beyond French historiography. In his theoretical work over the past two decades, he developed a structurally related, causally heterogeneous, path-dependent, and contingent concept of events that grew out of his critique of other historical sociologists and from an increasingly constructivist reading of history. In an earlier paper in the series, he had argued that most historical sociologists mistakenly limit themselves to two conventional notions of time – what he called "teleological" and "experimental" temporality (2005: ch. 3). He argued that both of these are deficient – even fallacious – forms of temporality and that historical sociology needs to adopt a much more subversive eventful notion of temporality – which sees the course of history as determined by a succession of largely contingent events. Much of history, writes Sewell, is made up of mere happenings, most of which only reproduce social and cultural structures without significant changes. These, for him, are not events. Events are that relatively rare subclass of happenings that significantly transform structures. An eventful conception of temporality, hence, is one that takes into account the transformation of structures by events. But happenings only become events amid the uncertainty of structural change (2005: 229).

Sewell was seizing a moment when the major modern structuralist metanarrative – Marxism – was collapsing. In its place, he brought the event as a central theoretical category. He should be praised for his effort to relate events to structure. But was he as wise to limit his concept of events to ruptures of normal causality? This was a move that led him to exclude from his concept of events occurrences that were not *seen* to produce ruptures, as well as those whose effects on history were incremental. For example, in work published contemporaneously with Sewell's book, Wolfgang Streeck and Kathleen Thelen identified three types of incremental change – drift, layering, and conversion (2005). These would not qualify as events in Sewell's ontology, but they have major implications for historical change. The danger of Sewell's method – if followed mechanically – is to downplay event-poor yet structurally rich processes that can have a profound effect on history.

To write history is to choose, but if the choice of great events for an eventful history leaves out both occurrences that are not seen to bring about rupture and noneventful processes, doesn't Sewell's proposal return us to a more traditional form of narrative history? Might it not produce, in the words of one of Sewell's favorite targets, "the temptation to let a few spectacular and well-documented conflicts dominate interpretations of change" (Tilly 1995: 65)? There is an alternative approach, one which begins with *populations of events* and relates them both to one another and to noneventful phenomena through statistical elaborations: events within history.

Events within History

As Stone, Sewell, and others[2] were rethinking and theorizing narrativity at the qualitative end of social history, a loose archipelago of historical sociologists and political scientists were applying advances in computational technology to the systematic analysis of contentious events. The first in this line of event analysts were, of course, students of strikes, who had ready-made official series of comparable events available to them with detectable properties and outcomes.[3] Was a union present in the strike? How long did it last? What proportion of the workers participated? Did the strike succeed or fail? By merging their data on strikes with aggregate data, they were also able to tell us much about the relationship between strikes and economic trends and ferret out changes in the structure of the strike over long time periods. But they did not contribute especially well to our understanding of other forms of contention – protests, demonstrations, riots, and rebellions. For that an adaptation of their methods would be necessary.

---

[2] Mention should be made of the stimulating rethinking of narrativity by Margaret Somers, especially her 1992 and 1993 essays. Somers focuses on the formation of collective identities and their relationship to conceptions of citizenship. Thinking more broadly, we might also consult the anthropological work of Sally Falk Moore (1987), of the historians David William Cohen (1994), Christopher Lloyd (1993), and Pierre Nora (1994), not to mention the sociologists Andrew Abbott (1988, 1992), Ron Aminzade (1992), and Larry Isaac and Larry Griffin (1989).

[3] This tradition dates to the econometric analyses of Orley Ashenfelter and John Pencavel in the United States in 1969. For France, see Perrot 1987 and Shorter and Tilly 1974. For Italy, see Franzosi 1995.

Protest Event Counts

Most strike analysts were economists or economic sociologists, but in the 1960s, the methods they used began to be applied to other forms of collective action – protests, demonstrations, riots, and violence in general. As statistically trained political scientists and sociologists turned their attention to contentious politics, the once-dominant tradition of focusing on cases of social movement campaigns was joined by the systematic study of contentious events in which social movements might – or might not – participate (more on this below). The major stimuli in this scholarly trend were "the riots" of the American urban ghettos, but scholars soon began to study violence cross-culturally too (Gurr 1970). And as the older concept of the crowd as a wild and anarchic gathering gave way to more down-to-earth conceptions of groups contending over interests and ideals, historians and social scientists turned to the systematic analysis of more pacific forms of contention.

But there were problems, both of data and conceptualization. First, because of their lack of institutional structuring, the forms of contention these scholars studied could less easily be related to outcomes than was the case for strike research (see Chapter 9). Second, because protests produced few reliable official sources of statistics, analysts had to turn instead to the aggregation of quantitative indicators from narrative sources (Favre et al., 1990; Gamson 1975), police sources (Fillieule 1994, 1995), and especially from newspaper records (Jenkins 1985; McAdam 1982; Tarrow 1989). Third, although some analysts attempted to encompass all forms of contentious politics (Tilly 1995) or all types of protest events (Tarrow 1989), most were drawn to specific series of events, like violent ones (Gurr 1970, 1987), civil rights protests (McAdam 1982) communal and ethnic conflicts (Gurr 1993) or particular forms of contention like the barricade (Traugott 2010) or the demonstration (Tartakowsky 2004).

A fourth problem was conceptual: although the systematic study of events was based on an "event sweeping" strategy which turned up events carried out by a wide variety of actors, most of the researchers in this tradition coded their results as if there were a one-to-one relationship between protest events and social movements (Kriesi et al. 1995). But what of protests carried out by political parties, interest groups, or temporary aggregates of aggrieved people? If all of these were "social movements," there was a misfit between most scholars' definitions of movements and the data that were seen as their empirical expressions. Either some kind of triage needed to be used to separate movement-based events from others, or events would need to be seen as evidence of contentious politics in general (McAdam et al. 2001).

These problems were not fatal: since the tradition of event counting and analysis began in the 1960s, there has been increasing methodological sophistication in how event-based statistical work on contentious politics is carried out. Where early analysts employed armies of assistants to pore over dusty archives and yellowing newspaper files and were usually content to portray their findings graphically or in tabular form, more recently there have been two major methodological developments:

First, researchers are turning experimentally to the enumeration of events by machine coding from on-line newspaper or press agency records (Bond and Bond 1995; Franzosi 1987; Imig and Tarrow 2001). This procedure risks losses in accuracy and detail while offering immense reduction of time and expense over manual coding procedures. While still critically in need of validation and elaboration through more sensitive computer programs, machine coding holds promise for scanning large datasets over long periods of time where general trends or broad comparisons are more important than subtle changes.

At the same time, some sociologists have begun to employ a family of data analysis methods first developed in population ecology called "event history" methods (Allison 1982; Tuma and Hannan 1979). These have been applied to collective violence and protest by a number of scholars (see the review in Olzak 1989). They have been applied to the births and deaths of movement organizations by Debra Minkoff (1995), and to discrete sequences of linked events like Sarah Soule's analyses of the "shantytown" protests against apartheid in South Africa (1997, 1999). Susan Olzak's study of American ethnic conflict can serve as a microcosm of the strengths and difficulties of newspaper-based, statistically-organized series of protest events.

Olzak and the Practice of Event History
Moving from William Sewell's sonorous prose to Susan Olzak's statistical elaborations in her *Dynamics of Ethnic Competition and Conflict* (1992) leaves the reader feeling like a time traveller. While Sewell is intent on interpreting meaning, Olzak is interested in describing her data. The result is a much less exciting read, albeit a marvelously well-documented and well-organized one that focuses on one form of social conflict – ethnic conflict – measured through the techniques of event history analysis. Olzak's book is a superb example of the systematic enumeration of contentious events and an analysis of their relations with broader social and economic processes – immigration, business cycles, employment opportunities, and ethnic competition – exactly the kinds of processes that Sewell's focus on great events made it difficult for him to tap into.

Olzak's work is familiar in some ways and path-breaking in others. It is familiar in her strategy of studying a standardized set of collective activities for the same set of spatial units over the same time period. In this respect, her book is reminiscent of the tradition of statistical research on strikes. However, her procedure differs from this tradition – which is usually based on official statistics – in her almost complete reliance on newspaper sources. Olzak believes – and I think she is right – that the sacrifice in numerical exhaustiveness that she incurs in avoiding official statistics is more than compensated for by the greater richness of detail and interpretation that she found in the newspaper sources.

Using newspaper sources so plentifully lends to Olzak's work a resemblance to some of the social movement research on the 1960s carried out in the United States (Burstein 1986; Jenkins 1986; McAdam 1982). But she departs from this

tradition both in confronting a much longer timespan and in basing her enumeration and coding of the newspaper sources on entire articles, rather than
on headlines or newspaper indexes (1992: 234–235). Olzak's book also differs
from these studies in a number of other ways. First, where many "protest event"
scholars are catholic in the kinds of collective action they study, Olzak restricts
her attention to only one type – *ethnic* collective action – and, within that category, to two subtypes – ethnic conflict and ethnic protest. Second, where many
scholars use one or another sampling technique, Olzak enumerates her events
from a daily set of records. Third, she does not draw on secondary sources
systematically, but relies principally on the statistical record provided by her
primary dataset and on covariates from other statistical sources.

We can use Olzak's study to question the more general properties of "event
history" approaches. First, there is little attempt in this tradition to theorize
about the meaning of events. When we try to glean what Olzak means by
events we find that the concept lacks the theorized structural and cultural
prominence given it by Sewell or Sahlins. She defines her conflict events as
"nonroutine, collective and public acts that involve claims on behalf of a larger
collective" (53).

Second, Olzak's criteria for compiling "event histories" are nominal, where
Sewell's was purpose-built. As she describes the technique, it begins with recording exact information on the timing of a series of events and on their locales. She
then uses this information to estimate the rates of transition between discrete
events, making the procedure extremely sensitive to the bunching of events that
are typical of cycles of protest, and relates their density to structural covariates, like changes in the rate of immigration. In Olzak's words, "event-history
analysis can use information on the timing of events in a series of localities to
estimate models that take both unit-specific characteristics and the timing of
events [into account]" (63, 232).

Third, Olzak's analysis of her data is relentlessly statistical, using the entire
period of the study as her evidentiary basis and paying little attention to the
great events that would preoccupy Sewell, or to the historical contexts in which
they occur. In fact, Olzak's sharpest contrast with Sewell is her relative indifference to the connections between events and institutional or policy changes.

Probably as a result of its statistical sophistication and its lack of attention to general social and institutional change, Olzak's book has been largely
ignored by most historians. This is a great pity, because beneath its statistical
crust, the book is a goldmine of variously demonstrated associations between
different forms of ethnic collective action and structural processes that may be
typical of other racially-plural or immigration-drawing societies. For example,
Olzak finds that the causes of attacks on different ethnic groups appear to be
remarkably similar – they are led by macrolevel processes of immigration, economic contraction, and growth of the labor movement (211). But their effects
on different groups in American society differed dramatically, with attacks
on African Americans and Chinese immigrants far more sensitive to business
cycles than attacks on white immigrants. In fact, black Americans paid a high

price not only for their own attempts to struggle out of poverty, but from those of white immigrants as well (224).

The Hazards of Event History

Olzak's book is a major study, but it has a fundamental weakness that is the result of her single-minded devotion to event history methods. In specifying the variables to be examined within a linear time-series model, it is insensitive to key tipping points in history that are not directly reflected in her data. Thus, crucial Supreme Court cases – such as *Plessy v. Ferguson* (164 U.S. 537), which upheld the constitutionality of racially segregated facilities – find no place in her event analyses. Taken to an extreme, this can be a major problem. Consider the implications from another sector of American social history – the changes in the strike. From a decentralized act of rebellion in the early nineteenth century, by the 1930s, it had become part of a planned campaign of putting pressure on employers. This shift resulted from the incremental process of unionization, but also from the legalization of collective action which resulted from a rapid sequence of judicial decisions between the 1840s and the 1870s. Once the courts had admitted the legality of strikes, the nature of the strike changed, its use spread to previously unorganized sectors, and its correlation with various structural properties of industry shifted. Without looking at institutional shifts like the judicial legitimation of collective action, we would have difficulty understanding the changing pattern of strikes in America.[4]

How can the qualitative richness of a Sewell and the quantitative rigor of an Olzak be combined? Or are quantitative and qualitative historical studies of collective action doomed to follow diverging and mutually-indifferent paths? I don't think so: for the most successful effort to combine the richness of historical interpretation with the rigor of historical time series, we can turn to what I call "events-in-history," an approach we find in the work of its foremost exemplar, Charles Tilly.

Events in History

For many years," Tilly wrote,

> Investigators sought to do one of two things with those collections [of events]: either to explain place to place variation in the intensity of conflict or to analyze fluctuations over time. For those purposes, simple counts of whole events served reasonably well. They served well, that is, so long as investigators could agree on what counted as an individual event. (2008b: 10)

---

4 Olzak was aware of the historiographic gaps in her research. She writes, in closing her book, that "because the primary theoretical focus of this volume has been political and economic competition, this study has left unexplored the active role of legislation and government agencies" (222). But all she offers in compensation is the addendum that it seems plausible that the actions of powerful and legitimate authorities, such as the local government, police, the state militia, and other organizations affect the rate of contemporary ethnic and racial violence (222).

While eventful histories, like Sewell's, were built around great events, Tilly complained that what he called "event-counters" were bound by the thick-N, thin-data character of the catalogs they constructed and tended to adopt newspaper writers' definition of events. Tilly was looking for a middle ground, "where logical rigor meets the nuances of human interaction," between Sewell's embedding of events in thick history and the thin but broad sweep of event historians like Olzak.

Tilly's first move was to discard the conventional practice of transforming the words he found in textual sources into pre-coded numerical data for purposes of analysis. For each event that he and his coders uncovered, they assembled numerous "codesheets," compared and reconciled sources, added verbal material where it was available, and paid particular attention to how contention was organized, who organized it, and who or what were its targets. In his first effort in this direction, *Contentious Politics in Great Britain* (1995), Tilly recorded all the major subjects, verbs, and objects of each act of contention that his sweep of contentious gatherings from print sources turned up.

From these experiences, Tilly drew three lessons:

- First, it is practically feasible to record and analyze the internal dynamics of contentious episodes instead of settling for classified counts of entire events.
- Second, linking the verbs in published accounts of contentious gatherings with the objects of their challenges makes it possible to move from flat analyses of events to treatments of the connections among contentious actors (27). If it is collective interaction that we are interested in, our focus should be on the action verbs that characterize the performances that link claims-makers to their objects and targets. Rather than characterize each event or episode as an expression of a single action (e.g., "workers struck," students sat-in," "terrorists bombed") his subject/action/object triplets allowed him to find out how actors and their actions combined in complex episodes.
- Third, recording particular verbs rather than general characterization of the action is critical for understanding the internal dynamics of episodes of contention. The central lesson was this third one. This laborious procedure permitted Tilly to detect and analyze changes in the processes of British contention from the middle of the eighteenth century to the reform period of the 1830s. This takes us to the concepts at the heart of *Contentious Performances:* episodes, performances, and repertoires of contention.

Episodes, Performances, and Repertoires

What we see when we examine long streams of contention are not discrete events but more complex *episodes* in which these events are embedded. For Tilly, episodes are "Bounded sequences of continuous interaction, usually produced by an investigator's chopping up longer streams of contention into segments for purposes of systematic observation, comparison, and explanation" (2008:10). Episodes can be reconstructed from participants' recollections, where these are accessible; from reporting media's conventions; or by "letting observed interactions and their interruptions delimit episodes, for example, by regrouping available accounts into one-day segments of interaction" (Ibid.) Tilly chose the interactionist solution. By examining streams of contention, the inner connections within them, and the responses to them of authorities, he strove to delimit the boundaries of episodes of contention, within which particular performances combine.

The distinction Tilly made between events and episodes is important, because while the former are often defined as independent happenings by media sources that generally detect them only when they erupt on the public scene, using episodes as his unit of analysis permitted Tilly to do two things: first to see to what extent the same combination of performances – for example, the march ending in a public meeting; the peaceful demonstration leading to police repression, in turn leading to violent ripostes – appear repeatedly in the same sequences of events. Secondly, it permitted him to see how repertoires evolve over longer time periods: for example, when and why the ceremonial march ended in street battles, as it did in the competitive parades between Catholics and Protestants in Northern Ireland in the nineteenth century (172). The episode became the unit of observation within which different performances could be observed or inferred and different repertoires of contention developed. Here are Tilly's two key analytical terms:

Performances are "learned and historically grounded" ways of making claims on other people which, "in the short run ... strongly limit the choices available to would-be makers of claims" (4–5). "People make claims," he continued,

> with such words as condemn, oppose, resist, demand, beseech, support, and reward. They also make claims with actions such as attacking, expelling, defacing, cursing, cheering, throwing flowers, singing songs, and carrying heroes on their shoulders." (Ibid: 5)

Tilly immediately added two qualifiers: one of which narrowed the range of the contentious performances and the other which broadened it:

- He narrowed the contentious performances he studied to those involving governments, not because he thought "governments must figure as the makers or receivers of contentious claims" but because, at a minimum, governments monitor, regulate and prepare to step in "if claim-making gets unruly" (Ibid: 7);
- But he broadened the range of his inquiries to go well beyond social movements, which he defined as "a very-limited range of claim-making performances" (Ibid).

The second qualifier was the more important one. Tilly insisted that social movements are a particular, historically discrete form of organizing contention and not the be-all and end-all of contentious politics (2004b). He broadened the range of inquiry to all kinds of contentious events, in order to study rebellions, strike waves, revolutions, nationalist episodes, democratization, and terrorism. He also wished to focus on the dynamic relations between these different forms of contention: the protest that grows into a social movement; the movement that triggers a revolution; the repression that escalates into a coup. Only by recognizing these different types of contention and their relationships could Tilly discover whether and when there were fundamental shifts from forms that dominated contention in one period to those that replaced them: changes in repertoires.

Repertoires Tilly defined as "claim-making routines that apply to the same claimant-object pairs: bosses and workers, peasants and landlords. Rival nationalist factions, and many more" (2008:14). This theatrical metaphor calls attention to the clustered, learned, yet improvisational character of people's interactions as they make and receive each other's claims." In his most evocative simile, Tilly wrote:

> Claim-making resembles jazz and commedia dell'arte rather than ritual reading of scripture. Like a jazz trio or an improvising theater group, people who participate in contentious politics normally have several pieces they can play, but not an infinity.... Within that limited array, the players choose which pieces they will perform here and now, and in what order. (Ibid.)

Variations in repertoires occur for three main reasons:

- first, some kinds of regimes permit some performances, forbid others, and tolerate still others; that constrains actors to shy away from some performances, choose others, and innovate between the two.
- second, the history of contention constrains peoples' choices (16). You are more likely to call an episode revolutionary if your country has experienced one in the past than if it never experienced one.
- and third, changes in political opportunity structure encourage some actions, discourage others, and give people the opportunity to innovate on known scripts.

This model of innovation around known scripts and opportunities led Tilly to one of his more controversial claims: that "contentious performances change incrementally as a result of accumulating experience and external constraints" and not as a result of the "great events" that Sewell and others have studied (5). But what of the French Revolution? The suicide bomb? The sit-ins in the American Civil Rights Movement? The wave of antineoliberalism around the turn of the new century? Are there no epochal shifts in the repertoire of contention? Tilly's answer was: "very seldom." Instead, he saw the combination of opportunity, constraint, and innovation producing two rhythms in national profiles of contention: the short-term rhythms within particular episodes and campaigns that could produce flare-ups of innovation; and the longer-term rhythms of secular changes in national repertoires, like the one that Tilly found between mid-eighteenth- and early-nineteenth-century Britain.

Two Repertoires

Tilly saw two rough poles of contentious politics in Britain during this period, each of which was an adaptation to a different type of society.. He writes

> The first is parochial, bifurcated and particular: It was *parochial* because most often the interests and interaction involved concentrated in a single community ... *bifurcated* because when ordinary people addressed local issues and nearby objects they took impressively direct action to achieve their ends, but when it came to national issues and objects they recurrently addressed their demands to a local patron or authority, who might represent their interest, redress their grievance, fulfill his own obligation, or at least authorize them to act ... *particular* because the detailed routines of action varied greatly from group to group, issue to issue, locality to locality. (1995: 45)

The second set of events were cosmopolitan, modular, and autonomous:

> They are *cosmopolitan* in often referring to interests and issues that spanned many localities or affected centers of power whose actions touched many localities ... *modular* in being easily transferable from one setting or circumstance to another ... *autonomous* in beginning on the claimants' own initiative. (1995: 46)

These secular changes in British collective action did not appear randomly in British history; they correlated roughly with the growing centralization of the state and the capitalization of the economy. With respect to the first set of changes, Tilly's analyses showed how the partial democratization and extensive increase in capacity of the British regime between the 1750s and the 1830s affected the tenor and the extent of contention over that period. He wrote:

> A bigger and higher-capacity state intervened more aggressively in local life, taxed more heavily, exerted more control over the food supply, and regulated workers' organizations more closely. Parliamentarization shifted power away from the crown, the nobility and their patron-client networks. It also increased the impact of the legislators' actions on local affairs. These changes gradually undermined the effectiveness of claim-making performances in the eighteenth-century mode: particular, parochial, and bifurcated. In their place, cosmopolitan, modular, and autonomous performances gained leverage. Social movements came into their own. (2008: 159–160)

But the second set of changes summed up in the Industrial Revolution are harder to link to the changes in repertoires that Tilly's analyses expose. In fact, the reader will look in vain for statistical correlations between shifts in the nature of contentious politics and changes in capitalism. Tilly did not include strikes in his enumeration through an explicit choice: "For thirty years," he noted, in a personal comment to the author, "capitalism has dominated the discussion and I want to redress the balance." The cost is that capitalism hovers offstage in his account, but it is seldom glimpsed in the actual analyses of contentious politics.

From Events to Cycles

One implication of studying "events-in-history" hinted at by Tilly's work on Great Britain was to facilitate our understanding of "cycles of contention."[5] Less momentous than revolutions, more connected than contingent chains of events, the concept of cycles, studied through the systematic gathering of events data during "short rhythms" of ten- to twenty-year periods, is a bounded way of studying the connections among events, between them and noneventful processes and in the light of major political changes, helping to interpret history as an interactive progression between structure and action.

The analysis of such dense collections of events can help to study the processes of diffusion of new repertoires within cycles (see Chapter 8). It can also help us to trace the construction and diffusion of new frames of meaning (Snow and Benford 1992) and new collective identities within sequences of collective action (Pizzorno 1979). It can help to explain why formerly inert mass publics suddenly emerge in cascades of collective action (Lohmann 1993, Kuran 1991). It holds promise of moving from the cataloguing of contentious events to a *relational* analysis of the interactions between contenting actors, their allies and enemies, and the state. Cycles of contention are also related to what Mark Beissinger called "waves" that diffuse across broad territories, like the "color revolutions" that spread across the former state socialist world around the turn of the century (2009).

Cycles of contention may be related to changes in repertoires. First, within a given cycle, themes, symbols, and tactical innovations of individual actions and groups influence one another, as when American students borrowed the sit–in and other collective action frames from civil rights activists during the 1960s. Second, the intense interaction of a cycle generates opportunities and incentives to innovate that appear much more rarely and with greater risk outside such cycles. Third, the shift within a cycle from an expansive to a contracting phase alters the strategic situations of participants, thereby changing the relative attractiveness of different forms of interaction, not to mention the relative salience of other actors as models, enemies, rivals, or allies (McAdam 1995). Fourth, forms of action associated with successful garnering of support, gaining of publicity, or pressing of demands tend to generalize and become long-term additions to collective-action repertoires, while those associated repeatedly and visibly with failure tend to disappear.

Cycles also produce changes in the organizational dynamics of movements (Minkoff 1996). As movements crystallize into organizations, the most successful forms may be imitated and diffused across sectors and even across national boundaries (McAdam and Rucht 1993). They may also produce changes in the alignments of institutional actors, interest groups and parties, as elites

---

[5] This is a concept I first called, more narrowly, "cycles of protest" (Tarrow 1989), and broadened to "cycles of contention" in reaction to Tilly's bolder and broader framework. For other work that has used the concept of cyclicity fruitfully, see Koopmans 1993 and 2004.

jockey for position to respond to the actions of mass publics (Burstein and Freudenburg 1978). They can also produce a split between institutional collective action and the organized violence that often arrives at the end of a wave of protest (Koopmans 1993; Tarrow 2011: ch. 10). Finally, the interactions between contentious actors and authorities can be traced through the dynamics of the course of a cycle. There is some evidence from Central America, for example, that repression varies in intensity according to the phase of the cycle in which it is used (Brockett 1995).

Revolutionary Cycles

These relational aspects of cycles suggest parallels to revolutions. A revolution is a rapid, forcible, durable shift in collective control over a state that includes a passage through openly contested sovereignty (Tilly 1993). Tilly distinguishes between revolutionary situations (moments of deep fragmentation in state power) and revolutionary outcomes (transfers of state power to new actors), designating as a full-fledged revolution any extensive combination of the two.

Revolutionary situations resemble extreme cases of social-movement cycles: as the split within a polity widens, all rights and identities come to be contested, the possibility of remaining neutral disappears, and the state's vulnerability becomes more visible to all parties. Just as successful mobilization of one social-movement contender stimulates claim making among both rivals and allies, revolutionary claimants on state power incite offensive or defensive mobilizations by previously inactive groups. One group's actual seizure of some portion of state power, furthermore, immediately alters the prospects for laggard actors, who must immediately choose among alliance, assault, self-defense, flight, and demobilization. Consequently, rivalries, coalition making, demand making, and defensive action all spiral rapidly upward. By analyzing aggregates of contentious events within revolutions and relating the latter to the political processes and structural conditions surrounding them, we may learn more about both types of historical configurations.

Conclusions

Is there an Occam's razorlike choice between Sewell's call for thick description of temporally ordered, contingent, and structurally ruptural events, Olzak's rigorous statistical modelling, and Tilly's combination of performances, episodes, and repertoires, and between the "short rhythms" of cycles and revolutions and the "long rhythms" of historical changes in repertoires? In the rapidly changing state of research on contentious politics it is too soon to tell, and there is probably no reason to choose. The search for optimal methods too often descends into "right way" tests of orthodoxy, a descent of which we have seen far too much in recent scholarly fads and which is destructive of real intellectual dialogue. More promising – if less neat – is the "analytical eclecticism" proposed by Rudra Sil and Peter Katzenstein in a notable 2010 article. "Analytical eclecticism," they write, "is an intellectual stance that supports efforts to complement, engage, and selectively utilize theoretical constructs embedded in contending research traditions to build complex arguments that bear on substantive problems of interest to both scholars and practitioners" (Sil and Katzenstein 2010: 411).

"Eventful history," "event-history" methods, and "events-in-history" all hold promise for replicable, comparative and cumulative research on collective action in modern societies. The danger is that each of the approaches will drive those who adopt them into such different methods and perspectives that each group of specialists will proceed in blissful indifference to the contributions of the others – or worse, to reject them as epistemologically "wrong" or – even worse – old-fashioned! The optimal result of the current proliferation of approaches to event-based collective action would be the triangulation of narrative case studies, event histories, and events in history, attentive to the dynamics of the cycles of political struggle within which they occur. But given the fate of past history of attempts at scholarly synthesis, that process may be as contentious as the subject on which it focuses.

8

From "Moments of Madness" to Waves of Contention

In turbulent periods of history, writes Aristide Zolberg, "the wall between the instrumental and the expressive collapses." "Politics bursts its bounds to invade all of life" and "political animals somehow transcend their fate" (1972: 183). Such moments are unsettling and often leave participants – not to mention elites and political authorities – unhappy. But they may be "necessary for the political transformation of societies," writes Zolberg, for they are the source of the new actors, the audiences and the force to break through the crust of convention (1972: 206). These moments – which are close to what William Sewell Jr. meant by "historical ruptures" (Sewell 2005: ch. 8) – are what Zolberg calls "moments of madness."

Zolberg was not the first to notice the condensed intensity of such moments. With Tocqueville, look at the 1848 revolution, when "a thousand strange systems issued impetuously from the minds of innovators and spread through the troubled mind of the crowd. Everything was still standing except the monarchy and parliament, and yet it appeared as if society itself had crumbled into dust under the shock of revolution" (1942; quoted in Zolberg 1972: 195). Or with Edgar Morin, look at May 1968 in France, which "was carried away by 'the great festival of youthful solidarity,' the 'permanent game' which was also a serious strategy, in which revolutionary incantations achieved a 'genuine socialization'" (1968; quoted in Zolberg 1972: 184). In such moments, the impossible becomes real – at least in the minds of participants.

An important question about such moments is often overlooked: their relationship to the long-term development of the repertoire of contention. Some observers think such moments are totally new, creating new forms of collective life (Lefebvre 1965) and producing new collective identities (Pizzorno 1978). But when we confront the creative aspects of "moments of madness" with the historical development of the repertoire of collective action, we find a puzzle.

This chapter draws on "Cycles of Collective Action: Between Moments of Madness and the Repertoire of Contention." Published in *Social Science History*. 17 (1993): 281–307. (Reprinted in M. Traugott, ed., *Cycles and Repertoires of Collective Action*. Duke University Press, 1995.)

For as Tilly has argued, the repertoire developed slowly and haltingly and no faster than the development of states and capitalism. If moments of madness produce a tapestry of collective action, as Lefebvre, Pizzorno, and Zolberg think, why has the repertoire developed as slowly as it has? Is it because the forms of contention that explode during such exceptional moments are not as exceptional as they seem at the time? Or because – precisely because they are so exceptional – they are rejected and repressed when order returns? Or rather, is the incremental pace of the repertoire's change due to the fact that the absorption of new forms of contention is mediated by more institutional processes? The question can be posed in more analytical terms if we return to the concept of the repertoire as it was developed by Charles Tilly (see Chapter 7).

Tilly saw the repertoire of contention as the whole set of means that a group has for making claims of different kinds on different individuals or groups (1986: 4). Because different groups in similar circumstances have similar repertoires, he speaks more loosely of a general repertoire available to the population as a whole. At any point in time, he writes, the repertoire available to a given population is limited, despite the abstract possibility of using virtually any form of contention against any opponent. The repertoire is therefore not only what people *do* when they make a claim; it is what they *know how to do* and what society has come to *expect them to do* from within a culturally sanctioned and empirically limited set of options (Tilly 1978: 151).

It follows from this definition that the repertoire of contention changes slowly, constrained by institutional resistance and the slow pace of cultural change. As Arthur L. Stinchcombe writes in a perceptive review of Tilly's *The Contentious French*:

> The elements of the repertoire are ... simultaneously the skills of population members and the cultural forms of the population.... Only rarely is a new type of collective action invented in the heat of the moment. Repertoires instead change by long-run evolutionary processes. The viability of one of the elements of a repertoire depends on what sorts of things work in a given social or political structure, on what forms of protest have been invented and disseminated in a population and on what grievances a given form is appropriate to express. (1987: 1248, 1249)

But if Tilly and Stinchcombe are right, then do Zolberg's "moments of madness" – in which men and women not only "choose their parts from the available repertoire" but "forge new ones in an act of creation" – have no effect (1972: 196)? Are the newly forged acts of resistance no more than momentary explosions in the slowly evolving history of contention, doomed to disappear as participants tire, supporters melt away, and the forces of order regroup and repress their challengers? Or are they related to longer-term changes in collective action? How do history's "moments of madness" relate to the long, slow progress of the repertoire of contention?

This chapter proposes a solution to that problem through the concept of systemic cycles of contention. I will argue that moments of madness do not transform the repertoire of contention all at once, but contribute to its evolution through the evolution of larger cycles in which innovations in collective action are diffused, tested, and refined in adumbrated form and sometimes become part of the accepted repertoire. It is within these larger cycles that new performances combine with old ones; the expressive encounters the instrumental; traditional, social actors adopt tactics from new arrivals; and newly invented forms of collective action become modular. Cycles of contention are the crucibles in which moments of madness are tempered into the permanent tools of a society's repertoire of contention.

Cycles of Contention

Although protest waves do not have a regular frequency or extend uniformly to entire populations, a number of features have characterized such waves in recent history. These features include heightened conflict, broad sectoral and geographic extension, the appearance of new organizations and the appropriation of old ones, the creation of new "master frames" of meaning, and the invention of new forms of collective action. Because these elements provide the skeleton for the rest of this analysis, I will briefly outline them here.

- *Heightened conflict:* Protest cycles are characterized by heightened conflict across the social system: not only in industrial relations, but in the streets, the villages and the schools.

For example, in their time-series data on France, Shorter and Tilly correlated the rate of violence per year with other forms of collective action. They reported that "since the 1890s, the times of extensive collective violence in France have also been the times of hostile demonstrations, mass meetings, explicitly political strikes and calls for revolution" (1974: 81). Similar findings emerged from my study on the Italian wave of protest in the late 1960s and early 1970s. It is this co-occurrence of turbulence across the social sector that brings it to the attention of elites and sets in motion a process of institutional adaptation, repression, or collapse (Tarrow 1989: ch. 3).

- *Geographic and sectoral diffusion:* Cycles of protest also have traceable paths of diffusion from center to periphery.

This was discovered by George Rudé in the grain seizures he studied in France from the 1770s; by Edward Shorter and Tilly in the nineteenth- and twentieth-century French strikes that they analyzed; and by Bianca Beccalli in her study of Italian strikes. Such cycles also spread from heavy industrial areas to adjacent areas of light industry and farming. Particular groups recur with regularity in the vanguard of waves of social protest (e.g., miners, students), but they are frequently joined during the peak of the cycle by groups that are not generally known for their insurgent tendencies (e.g., peasants, workers in small industry, white-collar workers).

- *Social movement organizations:* Protest cycles are often touched off by unpredictable events, and they almost never are under the control of a single movement organization.

The high point of the wave is often marked by the appearance of supposedly spontaneous collective action, but in fact both previous traditions of organization and new forms of organization structure their strategies and outcomes. Nor do existing organizations necessarily give way to new movements in the course of the wave. From the wave of industrial unrest in Western Europe in the 1968–1972 period we have evidence that – while organized groups were taken by surprise – many of them quickly recouped their positions and adapted to the new forms of collective action created at the peak of the strike wave (Dubois 1978: 5; Klandermans 1990).

- *New frames of meaning:* Protest cycles characteristically produce new or transformed symbols, frames of meaning, and ideologies that justify and dignify collective action and around which a following can be mobilized.

Such new frames typically arise among insurgent groups and spread outward, which is how the traditional concept of "rights" expanded in the United States in the 1960s. The rights frame eventually spread to women, gays, Native Americans, and advocates of the rights of children, animals, and even the unborn (Snow and Benford 1988). These new cultural constructs are born, tested, and refined within the cycle and may then enter the political culture in more diffuse and less militant forms, serving as a source of the symbols mobilized by future movement entrepreneurs.

- *Expanding repertoires of contention:* A final characteristic of protest cycles is perhaps their most distinctive trait: they are crucibles within which new weapons of social protest are fashioned.

The barricades in the French revolutions of the nineteenth century; the factory occupations of 1919–1920; the sit-down strikes of the French Popular Front period; the direct actions of the 1968–1972 period in Italy – new forms of collective action develop within the experimental context of cycles of protest. The most successful – and the most transferable – become part of the future repertoire of collective action during quieter times.

To summarize: a cycle of protest will be operationalized in this chapter as an increasing and then decreasing wave of interrelated collective actions and reactions to them whose aggregate frequency, intensity, and forms increase and then decline in rough chronological proximity. This leads to three related questions:

- First, what is the balance within a cycle between the institutionalized forms of collective action from the inherited repertoire and the less institutionalized ones that reflect something like Zolberg's "moments of madness"?
- Second, what kinds of activities does the moment of madness contain? Is it predominantly made up of violence? Of conventional forms of action used

in greater magnitude than usual? Or of a combination of violent, confrontational, and conventional forms of participation?

- Third, how do these forms of collective action translate into permanent changes in the repertoire of contention?

These questions will be examined in the case of a ten-year period of mass mobilization and protest in Italy from 1965 through 1974.

Assumptions and Data

A few simplifying assumptions will have to be accepted in order to fit Zolberg's intuitive concept of moments of madness into an empirical and historical framework. I will translate his concept of "moments of madness" into the sudden onset of collective action near the beginning of a protest cycle. I operationalize new social and ideological actors with the presence and frequency of unorganized protest. And I will reduce Zolberg's complex question of "lasting political accomplishments" to the character of collective action observable at the close of the cycle.

The data that will be used to illustrate the incidence and impact of moments of madness come from both machine-readable and qualitative newspaper data collected in Italy for the 1965–1974 period from a daily coding of *Corriere della Sera* (Tarrow 1989: app. A). For each protest event identified, information was recorded on the forms of action used, the participants involved, groups targeted, claims made, and outcomes that could be observed. The newspaper data were supplemented by archival research, interviews with former participants, and documentary sources. Secondary data from other studies supplemented the primary data.

The Italian Cycle

Historical memory tends to foreshorten the rhythms of contention into long, shallow valleys and short, pointed peaks. But when we reconstruct cycles of contention from the newspaper record, we see that the peaks that leave the most indelible impressions in public consciousness are really parts of broader swells of mobilization that rise and fall more gradually than popular memory remembers. The subtitle of Todd Gitlin's important book tells it all: *Years of Hope, Days of Rage* (1987). In Italy, the public record shows years of contentious collective action that began in the early 1960s and continued to produce mass action through the 1970s.[1] Figure 8.1 presents the events enumerated from the *Corriere* for each half year from the beginning of 1965 though the end of 1974. The curves are based on the total number of conflictual events in the newspaper, from petitions and delegations, through strikes, public marches and demonstrations, all the way to violent clashes and organized

---

[1] The late 1970s began a second, more violent period of conflict. On this change, see della Porta 1995 and della Porta and Tarrow 1986.

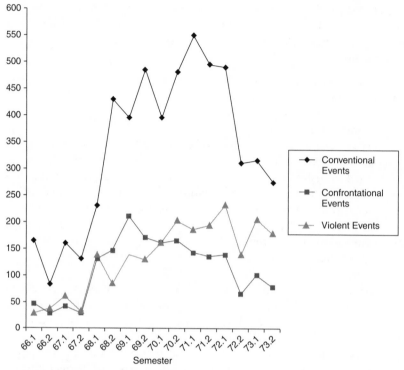

FIGURE 8.1. Italian Contention, 1965–1972.
Source: Author's data.

attacks. From the mid-1960s on, Italy entered a long period of social and political conflict.

There is a puzzle in Figure 8.1 that can help us to understand the relationship between the cycle's "moment of madness" in 1968 and its long-term dynamic: the evidence shows that the number of collective actions continued to rise until after the turn of the decade – two years after the period that Italians remember as *il sessantotto*. Was 1968 a false spring, a mere reflection of what was happening across the Alps, or did it have special characteristics that distinguish it from the quantitive peak of collective action later on? Unraveling the puzzle will require us to turn from counting the events to the changing character of contention in the course of the cycle. We can do so first by distinguishing the institutional from the noninstitutional aspects of collective action and then by looking at the appearance of new social actors.

Convention and Contention
In each period of history some forms of collective action are sanctioned by habit, expectations, and legality, while others are unfamiliar, unexpected, and are rejected as illegitimate by elites and the mass public. Consider the strike. As

late as the 1870s it was barely known, poorly understood, and widely rejected as a legitimate form of collective action. By the 1960s, however, the strike had become an accepted part of collective bargaining practice.

Looking at the Italian data from the 1960s and 1970s, we find high levels of routine and conventional forms, like strikes, alongside confrontational and violent ones. Figure 8.1 operationalizes as "confrontational" forms such as occupations, obstructions, forced entries, and radical strikes, and attacks on property, antagonists and authorities, and clashes with police as "violence." "Conventional" forms contain petitions, audiences, legal actions,[2] marches and public meetings, and strikes and assemblies. The relative frequency of the conventional forms of collective action, as opposed to the use of both confrontation and violence, can serve as a measure for the inherited repertoire.

Figure 8.1 shows that just as confrontational and violent forms of collective action were rising during the period, so were routine and conventional ones. At the peak of their protest cycle, Italians were fighting, raiding, obstructing, and occupying premises far more often than they had in the recent past; but they were also – and predominantly, in quantitative terms – engaging in well-known routines of collective action inherited from the conventional repertoire. The most common forms of collective action found in the newspaper data between 1966 and 1974 were strikes, marches, and public meetings. Just behind these were the confrontational forms of occupations and obstructions, with assemblies and petitions close behind them. Only then do we find the four main forms of violent conflict.[3] When movement organizers think of how best to mobilize large numbers of people against superior forces, they most naturally turn to the inherited repertoire. What is most interesting is that, even during "moments of madness" like 1968, institutional, confrontational, and violent forms of collective action cooccurred.

But note the differences over time in the employment of the different types of collective action. As Figure 8.1 shows, while all three major types increased during the upward slope of the cycle, their respective curves differed. While violent forms of attack increased mainly toward the end of the cycle (see della Porta and Tarrow 1986 and della Porta 1995), the much higher conventional curve peaked in 1971. As for confrontational forms of collective action, these reached their height in 1968–1969 – the years celebrated in popular memory as the peak of contestation. This contrast between the peaks of conventional and confrontational collective action can help us to understand the internal dynamic of the cycle and the role of the "moment of madness" of 1968–1969 within it.

---

[2] The study focused only on contentious collective action, operationalized as actions that disrupted the lives of someone else. It did not enumerate "audiences" or legal actions. These appear in the data only when they accompany at least one form of disruptive action. Thus, conventional forms are understated, which makes their numerical preponderance in the data even more striking.

[3] The table calculates the forms that were used as a proportion of the total forms of collective action, producing an "N" larger than the total number of events, because several forms of action often combined in the same event.

The "Moment of Madness"

1968–1969 brought a wave of confrontational collective action to Italy that placed workers and students in unprecedented confrontations with authorities and others. This can be seen not only in the number of confrontational actions during these years, but in their level of tactical flexibility, in the radicalization of the strike, and in the occupation of university premises. In these three ways, there was evidence of a "longer May" (e.g., *maggio strisciante*) than what was experienced across the Alps at the same time (see Chapter 9).

Tactical Flexibility

As protest intensified, there was a decline in the presence of known organizations. Did this decline produce a loss in tactical ability? Quite the contrary: during this period the degree of tactical flexibility increased, as evidenced by the increase in the average number of forms of action used in each protest event. We can see this in the use of nonstrike forms of action by strikers in the data in Table 8.1. If the ability to array a variety of forms of collective action is a sign of a "moment of madness," then Italy in the years from 1967 was going through just such a period.

Radicalizing the Strike

Many of the nonstrike forms of action in Table 8.1 were conventional – assemblies, routine actions, and public displays. And strikers almost always put forward instrumental demands, as can be seen in the rhythm of the strike rate during periods of national contract renewal. These conflicts often followed an almost ritualistic sequence. First, the unions would hold conferences at which platforms were elaborated and voted on; then brief strikes would be called in key firms or industries – usually those in which the unions were strongest; then, building on the momentum that had been demonstrated in these strongholds,

TABLE 8.1. *Strikers' Use of Nonstrike Forms of Action, by Year*

Form of Action	1966	1967	1968	1969	1970	1971	1972	1973
Public display	31	28	78	107	97	–	78	74
Assembly	10	15	40	69	84	59	43	33
Routine action	13	15	37	59	88	77	87	14
Confrontation	32	15	52	118	72	70	31	33
Violent clash	20	5	33	18	23	34	16	15
Attack on property	12	4	13	28	19	12	3	8
Attack on persons	2	3	4	19	9	10	4	6
Total other forms 120	85	257	418	392	372	262	183	

Source: Author's data. Reported in detail in Tarrow (1995:297).

national strikes would be called; finally, contract negotiations would begin (Golden 1988). Nothing could be more predictable or more institutionalized.

But as Table 8.1 also shows, many of the forms of action developed by strikers were confrontational or violent, especially in the three-year period 1967–1969. Toward the end of the 1960s a new phase was added; plant committees began to regard contract agreements reached at the national level, not as a ceiling, but as a floor on which to demand more ambitious plant-level agreements. This meant that industrial conflict extended beyond contract renewal periods and that the center of gravity of the strike fell from the national level to the plant or local level, where radical actions were more likely to explode. There was a sharp proportional increase in local strikes from the middle of 1968, when the first plant-level wildcat strikes broke out (Tarrow 1995: 296).

The extension of the strike to the plant level was more than quantitative; it reflected a flowering of new strike forms, some inherited from past cycles of industrial conflict, but others invented on the spot (Dubois 1978). A whole new vocabulary of strike forms developed, from the *sciopero bianco* (go-slow) to the *sciopero a singhiozzo* (literally, hiccup strikes) to the *sciopero a scacchiera* (chessboard strikes) to the *corteo interno* (marches around the factory grounds to carry along undecided workers) to the *presidio al cancello* (blocking factory gates to prevent goods from entering or leaving the plant). The logic of these innovations in the strike repertoire was to produce the maximum amount of disruption with the minimum expenditure of resources. In addition to these permutations within the strike, workers learned to combine different forms of collective action with the strike. Within the factories, occupations, obstructions, and forced entries challenged assembly-line rhythms and the authority of foremen; outside the factories, workers adopted public forms of display, expressive forms of action, and traffic blockages to publicize their demands. These public demonstrations often contained symbolic military elements (e.g., mechanics would frequently bang on milk cans with pipes as they marched), but they also contained important elements of play and theater and bore a resemblance to the traditional carnival.[4] During their "moment of madness," workers were simultaneously going public and intensifying disruption in the workplace.

The Occupation as Collective Life

As in the United States during the 1960s, occupying institutional premises was the form of collective action most frequently used by Italian students (Tilly and Tarrow 2007: 18–20) and owed much to the American example. At first, such occupations were enthusiastic and joyful activities, especially in the takeovers of university faculties carried out during the 1967–1968 academic year (Ortoleva 1988). But although some faculties were almost continuously occupied from early in the 1967–1968 academic year until the spring of 1969, the

---

[4] The best evocation of the carnevalesque aspects of these events will be found in Bob Lumley's *States of Emergency* (1990).

magic of shared participation and achievement could not endure. Not only did vacations and ever more frequent roustings by the police prevent the occupants from creating "free spaces" in the universities; such actions became institution-alized and factional groupings formed their own organizations that attempted to gain control of the various assemblies and commissions. By 1969–1970 occupations had taken on a ritualistic character, with standard banners and posters that reflected the ideological line of this or that movement organiza-tion, a *servizio d'ordine* of security guards – some of whom would later appear as the military cadres of the extraparliamentary groups – and regular police roustings and counterdemonstrations.

Diffusion and Modularization

The most innovative and confrontational forms of collective action declined in use after 1969. By 1970s, the unions – never absent from the factory – had regained control of the strike movement. In the universities, the increasingly organized extraparliamentary groups turned student protests into set-piece productions that soon took on a routinized character. When participation flagged, these groups shifted their activities to the secondary schools. In those instances where the police moved in, clashes ensued, providing an opportu-nity for the groups' armed *servizi d'ordine* to gain prominence and inducing much of the mass base to vanish.[5] There was also widespread weariness with what came to be called "assemblearismo" – the habit of calling an assembly to deal with every question. By the mid-1970s, academic friends who had been enthusiastic supporters of the movements of the late 1960s had become jaded and disillusioned. Especially as violence emerged in the workplace and on the streets, there was a widespread growth of privatization (Hirschman 1982).

What was the impact of the "moment of madness" on Italian society and on the repertoire of contention? To answer that question, we will have to ask which parts of the new repertoire survived the collapse of the movements of 1968–1969. As we saw in Figure 8.1 and Table 8.1, while the greatest increases in tactical innovation occurred in 1968 and 1969, conventional collective action continued to grow in magnitude until 1971. That such mobilization increased after tactical creativity declined – and even in the face of growing violence in the streets – suggests that protest may have been spreading to sectors of Italian society that otherwise would not have engaged in it. Social groups and regions that had not participated in the first wave of mobilization began to strike, demonstrate, and – in a few cases – to loot and burn.[6] Collective action

---

[5] The appearance of violence seems to have been an important motive for the disappearance of many young women from the movement. For a particularly significant episode see Tarrow 1989: 327–328.

[6] The so-called revolt of Reggio Calabria, which left the southern city occupied by state police for months, was a prime example of this outbreak of violence. See Tarrow 1989: ch. 9 for this episode.

frames that the students developed in the context of university occupations – such as the theme of *autonomia* – became a key slogan (albeit with different implications) outside the universities during the early 1970s. And forms of protest that were first experimented with in university faculties and the large factories of the north became general models for collective action in other settings and regions – for example, the practice of "*autoriduzione*," the self-reduction of work, payments, or taxes.

Autoriduzione

Institutional routines do not have to be attacked by straightforward striking; they can be disrupted by simple noncooperation, as was the case for the *autoriduzione* campaigns that began in the Pirelli factory near Milan in 1968. The skilled Pirelli workers sensed that the increase in factory orders in the context of a labor shortage gave them an unusual degree of leverage vis-a-vis management. As the practice of "self-reduction" spread, workers would simply decide on their production rate, ignoring piecework schedules in coordinated campaigns of passive resistance. Observers of the period thought they saw spontaneity here; but it took enormous coordination for a technically advanced productive process to be deliberately slowed down in a self-reduction campaign.

By the early 1970s the technique had been extended to urban movements by well-organized national extraparliamentary organizations like *Lotta Continua* – for example in the group's campaigns for the self-reduction of rents in public housing projects and in mass refusals to pay gas and electricity bills and transit fares (Perlmutter 1987; 1988).

By the mid-1970s, *autoriduzione* had became modular – that is, a model of collective action that was diffused across a wide range of social and territorial space and adapted to a variety of social and political conflicts. And as it was diffused, the practice became more routinized, with professional movement organizers teaching their supporters how it was done – much as the sit-in was diffused to a variety of protest groups in the United States.

But repetition and modularization had another effect: unlike its first employment at Pirelli, where it caught management off-guard, elites and authorities soon learned how to respond to it. If workers could self-reduce their assembly lines, piecework rates could be adjusted to penalize them for it; if rate-payers refused to pay their utility bills, their gas or electricity could be cut off; and if commuters failed to pay their bus or tram fares, the fare itself could be canceled, as occurred in one Italian city, with the cost transferred to general revenue collection. Modularization of the new forms of collective action made them easier to diffuse to new sectors and social actors, but also facilitated social control.

The Assembly in the Workplace

Not all of the innovations in collective action that first appeared in the moment of madness were as easily managed as *autoriduzione*. Before 1969, union organizers had been unable to gain access to factories to meet with workers and were forced to waylay them at the factory gates after a day's work or organize meetings after hours. Some of the most dramatic moments in the hot autumn of 1969 occurred when insurgent workers triumphantly carried their leaders onto factory grounds, where tumultuous assemblies were organized and strike votes taken. As the cycle wound down and the unions reasserted their control, workers returned to more conventional and institutionalized forms of collective action (Regalia 1985). But the assembly in the place of work remained a permanent conquest for the workers and an institutionalized accretion to the future repertoire of collective action.

In summary, even though the radicalization of the strike, the occupation, and other radical innovations declined as the cycle of contention moved beyond its "moment of madness," there was a normalization of the new forms of acton, much as the sit-in was normalized in the United States. Through concepts like *autonomia* and practices like *autoriduzione*, and through the expansion of the practice of the assembly in the workplace, Italy's "moment of madness" had a permanent impact on the country's repertoire of contention.

There were other changes as well – like the organized violence that developed towards the end of our period and fed into the "armed struggle" of groups like the Red Brigades (della Porta 1995; della Porta and Tarrow 1986). Organized violence put the greatest stress on the political system but it had a long-term effect on institutionalization too: it drove the Communist Party, which had equivocated on the question of where it stood with respect to protest, to effectively cast off its revolutionary origins and place itself alongside the centrist Christian Democracy as an enemy of terrorism.

Movements and Cycles of Contention

In his intuitive and perceptive article, Zolberg concludes that moments of madness bring about significant transformations in three distinct ways:

- First of all, the "torrent of words" that the cycle fosters produces an intensive learning experience whereby new ideas, formulated initially in coteries, sects, and so on, emerge as widely shared beliefs among much larger publics....
- Second, these new beliefs expressed in new language become anchored in new networks of relationships which are rapidly constituted during such periods of intense activity....
- Third, from the point of view of policy ... "these instant formulations become irreversible goals which are often institutionalized in the not-very-distant future" (206).

Each of Zolberg's three themes implies an indirect and a mediated – rather than a direct and unmediated – effect on the future repertoire of contention:

With respect to Zolberg's first theme – the "torrent of words" typical of the moment of madness – just as new ideas filter down from their originators to those who vulgarize and domesticate them, the new forms of collective action invented in the enthusiasm of the moment of madness become modular. Think of the practice of *autoriduzione,* as it spread from the Pirelli plant to other factories, then to urban protests for rent and rate reductions, and finally (in its most farcical version) as teenagers' justification for breaking into rock concerts without paying for a ticket. Not the new invention itself, but its distilled, refined, and routinized products become part of a more lasting practice of collective action.

With respect to his second theme – the embedding of these new concepts and new language in new networks – moments of madness diffuse new ideas, spread out across society, and provide opportunities to others to take up tactics that have proven successful. College students who go home for the weekend teach younger brothers and sisters how to organize an occupation; arrested militants who are shifted from troublesome urban prisons to more remote ones teach common criminals how to politicize their discontent; radicalized workers who become union organizers bring their militant practice to smaller and less politicized factories.

It is with respect to changes in public policy and institutions that society absorbs a portion of the message of moments of madness. For example, think of the factory councils that became the grass-roots institutions of the Italian trade unions after being created in shop floor conflicts; or of *assemblearismo* that affected life in Italian universities for years to come; or of the women's health clinics that were the result of the women's movement of the 1970s: none of these were what the militants of 1968 dreamed of, but none of them would have been likely in the absence of the cycle of contention out of which they arose. Such mediated effects imply an intervening and dynamic process connecting the utopian dreams, the intoxicating solidarity, and the violent rhetoric of the moment of madness to the glacially changing, culturally constrained, and socially resisted pace of change.

Cycles and Waves of Contention

I have used the term "cycles" to refer to the rise and fall of contention within particular countries. But such cycles often diffuse into *transnational waves of contention.* This is not the place to examine such widespread patterns of diffusion (Beissinger 2009): scholars like Mark Beissinger (2002) for the 1989 revolutions; Valerie Bunce and Sharon Wolchik (2006) for the "color revolutions"; and Kurt Weyland (2009) for the 1848 revolutions have all dealt with the dynamics of transnational waves of diffusion. What should be emphasized is that, even more than in domestic cycles of contention, transnational "waves" are far from homogeneous. The liberal sentiments that triggered the 1848 revolution in France had given way to ethnic nationalism by the time the revolution reached the Balkans; and the democratic impulse that initiated the fall of Communism opened the way for ethnic separatism by the early 1990s (Beissinger 2002). Those who force open the gates of oppression in the name of freedom are often swept aside by more powerful antidemocratic forces who mobilize using the tools and opportunities created by democratic early risers.

Few people dare to break the crust of convention. When they do so during moments of madness, they create opportunities and provide models of collective action for others. Moments of madness – seldom widely shared, usually rapidly suppressed, and soon condemned even by former participants – appear as sharp peaks on the long curve of history. Within them, new forms of contention flare up briefly and then disappear, and their rate of absorption into the ongoing repertoire is slow, partial and uneven.

Although it is too soon to assess the outcomes of the recent revolutions in the Middle East and North Africa, there is already evidence that the "moment of madness" in the winter and spring of 2011 is resulting, in part, in violence (think of Libya!) and in part in normalization. Cycles of contention last much longer and have broader influence than the moments of madness we see reported in newspaper headlines and on the Internet; they are, in Zolberg's words, "like a flood tide which loosens up much of the soil but leaves alluvial deposits in its wake" (206).

IV

OUTCOMES OF CONTENTION

9

Social Protest and Policy Breakthroughs

May 1968 and After

The politics of reform has usually been viewed as an incremental process – which indeed it is, under most circumstances. The model for this mode of analysis is found in Aaron Wildavsky's work on the budgetary process. The best predictor of the size of a public budget in year n, Wildavsky found, was the size of the budget in year $n - 1$ (1974). But from time to time, waves of policy innovation emerge above the gentle plain of ordinary politics. For understanding these breakthroughs, incremental models of policy making are not nearly as helpful as models based on changes in contentious politics. Major electoral realignments, political crises, the ends of wars or military threats, leadership succession, the emergence of new social coalitions: such nonincremental changes frequently trigger periods of reform. What Valerie Bunce writes of political succession in the former Soviet Union can be extended to a number of different types of political systems: "Major changes," she writes, "if they occurred at all, tended to be introduced in conjunction with the rise of new chief executives" (Bunce 1981: 225).

But what of the effect of contentious challenges on policy reform? Despite generations of work on the subject we have very little clear idea of the impact of such episodes on reform. One of the reasons for this gap is that reform has often been conceived of as a top-down extension of citizenship (Marshall 1964), either through incorporation (Rokkan 1970) or through elite policy diffusion (Heclo 1970). A second reason is that social activism often coincides with political changes of a more conventional type, making it difficult to sort out the responsibility for a particular policy change (Burstein and Freudenberg 1979). A third is that scholars most often focus on movement *emergence*, giving less attention to the slower, less dramatic processes of policy elaboration, negotiation, and implementation. And a fourth is that most serious challenges to the polity emerge as parts of cycles of contention, in which elites are

Parts of this chapter first appeared in "Social Protest and Policy Reform: May 1968 and the Loi d'Orientation." *Comparative Political Studies.* 25 (1993): 579–607 and were reprinted in Marco Giugni et al., *From Contention to Democracy.* Rowman and Littlefield, 1999.

responding less to any single challenger than to generalized threats to their power (see Chapter 8).

While it is possible to correlate outcomes with the timing of movements' efforts, it is not as easy to identify particular movement actions as the causes of specific policy outcomes. The relationship between movements and outcomes becomes even more complicated when we recognize that the *targets* of contention – elites, authorities, other groups – respond in different ways to similar opportunities. The relative weight of different factors in producing movement outcomes has been a bone of contention. While Paul Burstein and April Linton (2002), have seen public opinion washing out the influence of movements in producing outcomes, others, like Katrin Uba (2009), do not find support for their hypothesis. And while some scholars think movements have a direct effect on outcomes, others see these effects as indirect, while still others see "joint effects" of movement actions, favorable political opinion, and the presence of influential allies (Amenta 2006; Giugni 2001; Giugni and Yamasaki 2009; Kolb 2007).

May 1968: A Window for Reform

We do have a near-laboratory case for studying the political impact of a major wave of protest on policy innovation – May 1968 in France. As two of that period's most acute historians observe: "despite the retreat of the movement and its rejection in the ballot box, the Events were the carriers of potentialities that, by one means or another, durably mortgaged the French political scene in a way that had to be immediately faced" (Capdeveille and Mouriaux 1988: 219, author's translation). But here is a puzzle: how could the May crisis "durably mortgage the French political scene," when it produced few coherent policy proposals, left a disorganized and almost-collapsed movement in its wake, and led to an enlarged conservative majority and a dispirited and divided opposition?

The answer we give to this question depends on how we think social movements influence reform – either directly, through the power of the people, or indirectly, through changes in the structure of political opportunities they trigger. If we proceed from a pure "protest leads to reform" model, we will have difficulty explaining why *any* reforms should have followed the May movement, for that movement was soundly defeated. But if we understand policy innovation to be mediated by changes in the political opportunity structure – for elites as well as for the mass public – it is less surprising that a wave of protest was followed by a major reform. This, at least, is the consensus that has been emerging among students of the policy outcomes of social movements.[1]

---

[1] For two major groups of studies on movement policy outcomes, see Amenta 2005 and 2006, Amenta and Zylan 1991, and Amenta, Halfmann, and Young 1999, on one side of the Atlantic, and Giugni 1998 and 2001 and Giugni and Yamasaki 2009 on the other. This emerging consensus dovetails with the "political opportunity" model that has been put forward by this author and others, though not always explicitly.

In the months following the June 1968 electoral triumph of the Gaullist Party, the government – not without internal dissent – selected from the jumble of demands for change that had erupted during May a project for educational reform – the *loi d'orientation* of Minister Edgar Faure. The movement of May had spread far beyond the universities – especially into the working class; but the policy response directly addressed the universities, where the events had begun and which the Gaullists saw as a potential flashpoint for future disturbances. They did not ignore the working class, but after conceding major wage increases, the government devalued the franc, thereby reducing many of the gains that the workers had made as the result of their general strike in May (Salvati 1981).

The educational reform law that resulted was intended to restructure the university system around three broad goals: autonomy, pluridisciplinarity, and participation (Chalendar 1970: pts. 2 and 3; Fomerand 1974: ch. 5). It replaced the old faculties with departments (U.E.R.'s); it broke up the massive University of Paris into twelve different "campuses"; and it provided the machinery for all the French universities to elect governing councils and create their own internal statutes.[2] It would be difficult to imagine so major a change being introduced into the sclerotic structure of French education without the impulse of a major political earthquake.

What is the implication of this story for the theory of the relations between social movements and policy innovation? In what follows, it will be clear that an exceptional electoral mandate and a threatening political crisis opened a window for policy innovation. But the brevity of the crisis and the factionalization of the movement of May left the initiative for reform to elites, allowing the reform to become ensnared in the mechanisms of parliamentary and academic politics. As the political struggle moved from the streets to the halls of Parliament and to the cabinets of ministers, it was institutional politics that decided its future. As I will argue in the conclusions, this has implications for the relations between protest and reform that go beyond the case at hand.

Readers of this book and those familiar with the "political process" approach to social movements will recognize this argument as a version of the theory of political opportunity structure (see Chapter 1). This is ironic in a way, for few of the *enragés* of May were interested in reform. What this suggests is that, as Chapter 5 argued, opportunities shift in the course of a cycle of contention, from challengers to the polity to their allies and opponents within it, and from radicals to moderates within the movement. It also reaffirms, as Doug McAdam argued from his work on the civil rights movement, that the nature of opportunities shift as the energies in protest cycles move from early risers to latecomers

---

[2] Jacques F. Fomerand's PhD thesis, "Policy-Formulation and Change in Gaullist France: The 1968 Orientation Act of Higher Education" (1974) is the best existing analysis of the policy process surrounding the Orientation Act and its policy outcomes. Fomerand also includes a basic chronology of the policy process (6–7) and the full text of the law (342–355). Also see Fomerand (1975) for a summary of his most important findings.

(1995). The determinants of the outcomes of a cycle of contention do not result directly from the forces of production, from power imbalances, or even from the initial grievances that trigger its emergence; instead, as Mark Beissinger has shown for a very different set of movements (2009), they result from factors internal to the cycle and from the interactions that result from the reactions of elites to the early risers whose importance declines as the cycle shifts from its "moment of madness" to its processing by political elites (Zolberg 1972).

The Opportunity for Reformism

In the summer of 1968, the movement of May hardly seemed to have produced reasons to expect a season for reform. In the public, there had been a rejection of the utopian dreams of the May movement; in the government, reformers were licking their wounds; on the institutional Left, the parties that had, reluctantly, tried to step into the breach opened by the students had been soundly defeated; while in the loose archipelago of leftist groups that emerged from May, small *groupuscules* were moving towards armed struggle and most of the protesters had gone home. But three major factors facilitated the reformers' task in the summer and fall of 1968: first, an informed debate about higher education that predated May by several years; second, the very suddenness and brevity of the May-June crisis; and, third, the strength of the Gaullist electoral mandate. Taken together, these factors gave the government a fertile political opportunity and gave the educational reform an unusually smooth beginning.

The Reformist Background

In thinking back to the conflagration of May 1968, it is easy to forget that the 1960s were a decade of discussions, debates, and attempts at educational reform – in France as elsewhere. From the reform projects of the Resistance, which had culminated in the never-implemented Langevin-Wallon report of 1947, through two important *colloques* of Caen in 1956 and 1966, to the passage of the Fouchet Reform of 1965, the "modernization" of the universities had become a major issue in key sectors of education, in modernist industrial circles and among certain groups in the world of politics and the administration (Bourricaud 1982: 37).

Groups of reformers, including some of the most distinguished names in French academia, had called at one time or another for most of the reforms that would later appear – admittedly in different form – in the *loi d'orientation*. Summarizing these proposals from François Bourricaud's extensive treatment, they included, notably: increased support for research, the opening of the university to society; the modernization of teaching; the replacement of the faculties with something approaching the American department; the removal of barriers between universities; a degree of autonomy in the financing of research outside the state's annual educational budget; the elimination of certain chairs; and even – in one version – the limited participation of students in university governance (Bourricaud 1982: 38–45). The reformers had an interest group – the

Association for the Development of Scientific Research – and maintained close ties with important officials in the Education Ministry, even succeeding "in enlisting the support of a number of politicians" (37). This coalition for reform was partly responsible for placing – and for keeping – educational reform on the policy agenda during the 1960s.

But the reformers did not attack all the defects of the system with equal vigor. Claude Grignon's and Jean-Claude Passeron's summary of the major reforms that were implemented between 1954 and 1967 shows that the significant reforms were mainly concerned with the organization of degrees. They left out the problem of the structure of the faculties or universities, archaic methods of teaching, and the relation between teaching and research. Although the faculties of law and medicine implemented significant reforms under government prodding, where the arts and sciences were concerned, the "new system ... [did] not necessarily imply a break with the old teaching organization and still less with the system of traditional attitudes" (Grignon and Passeron 1970: 32). But by 1968, a cadre of educational reformers could be identified as an elite support base for reform.

A Short and Abrupt Crisis

The May crisis was also quite short, which strengthened the reformers' hand, both against those whose instinctive response was for greater law and order and against their enemies on the Left. Even adopting the kind of broad definition used by Alain Schnapp and Pierre Vidal-Naquet (1988), the French May was over very quickly, compared, for example, to its Italian counterpart (see Chapter 8). In fact, the sudden beginning, the rapid diffusion, and the complete collapse of the May-June events were its most visible characteristics. By the *rentrée* to the universities in the fall, solidarity had so broken down among student groups and between the students and their supporters that they posed no real threat. It was this lassitude, against the general fear of the renewal of contestation, that gave the reformers the space they needed to shift the center of gravity from the streets to the political arena.[3]

The Crisis and the Mandate

As the movement of May ended, there was uncertainty about what the students would do at the *rentrée* and how their actions would affect the workers

---

[3] The May events largely exhausted the capacity for collective action of the other major sectors of French society too. Although groups as different as cadres (Groux 1988), white collar workers, public employees, farmers, Catholics (Hervieu-Leger 1988), parents' associations (Vernus 1988), and even football players (Wahl 1988) had been swept into the movement of May, their attitudes to the crisis were sharply divided. Statistics provided by the French Ministry of Labor show that the number of days lost to strikes in the years following the May outbreak was actually lower in 1969 and 1970 than it had been in 1966 and 1967 (Capdeveille and Mouriaux 1988: 107). Although there were signs of continued worker militancy after May – for example in a greater willingness to occupy plants during strikes (108) – the accords of Grenelle effectively closed the industrial relations crisis.

and others who had joined them in May. With the virtues of hindsight, we can see that there was little prospect for a renewed revolt in the fall of 1968. But in July, when the new reformist minister of education, Edgar Faure, was appointed, no one really knew whether the movement was dead. The fact that the summer vacation brought a deadly quiet to the educational establishment might have meant that the movement was over or it could have meant that its leaders were regrouping for the next round of contention.[4] Faure's appointment was a response to this fear and he was quick to take advantage of it (Chalendar 1970; Fomerand 1974, 1975).

It was not only the Gaullist electoral victory that explains Faure's mandate but the humiliation the general had suffered in May, when his political space was constricted by the refusal of his allies to organize the referendum he wanted (Charlot 1989). By putting a reformer like Faure in charge of the Education Ministry and giving him a sweeping mandate for reform, de Gaulle could hope to strengthen his position vis à vis his party. A former radical who had never been central to the Gaullist coalition, he was suspect to many in the Gaullist Party because of his identification with many of the Fourth Republic's excesses. But he was far more palatable to de Gaulle, whose previous efforts at educational reform had been undermined by leaders of his party.[5]

Scale Shift and Factionalization

Given the conflicts surrounding higher education in May, it might be supposed that a reform like the one Faure proposed would stimulate opposition mainly from the activists of May. But movements arise quickly, rapidly shift their focus, and seldom focus on the details of reform. In addition, *this* movement had rapidly left educational issues behind as it shifted in scale to a focus on national politics. The dynamics of the cycle also exposed fractionalization that was so severe as to reduce its capacity to return to the issue of university reform. Both of these features of the movement of May gave Faure a relatively free hand to elaborate a major project of reform.

---

[4] In a personal interview, Michel Alliot, who was part of Faure's ministerial cabinet in 1968–1969, recalled that, when visitors would complain to General de Gaulle of the damage that the Faure reform might do to higher education, he would remind them of the collapse of the system in May. Interview April 2, 1990.

[5] Faure's appointment can best be understood in the coalitional terms used by Peter Gourevitch to understand de Gaulle's resignation after he lost the referendum of 1969 (1978). The Gaullist coalition had never been limited to loyalists and conservatives; it had from the beginning appealed to "modernizers" who wanted to make France into an advanced industrial nation. In the fall of 1968, de Gaulle saw the educational reform of 1968 as a way to regain the support of the modernists, short-circuit the power of the conservatives in his party, and reestablish his personal links with the electorate (Gourevitch 1978). An educational reform under the leadership of a "modernizer" like Faure seemed to fit the bill.

Scale Shift

If the May movement began in the universities, once it had evolved from the terrain of student demands to that of political power, there was no turning back. Encouraged by the overreaction of the then-minister of education in clearing out the courtyard of the Sorbonne in May, and by the police brutality which followed, the students quickly focused their energies on politics. As Passeron writes, "The united front against the traditional university exploded as soon as the disdained institution was no longer available to bring together its attackers and paper over their opposing criticisms" (Passeron 1986: 382, author's translation).

Scanning the documents that have been assembled by Schnapp and Vidal-Naquet (1988: pts. 2 and 3), one cannot help but be struck by how quickly a great number of student groups shifted their attention from the university to politics. The result was that the greatest student mass movement in the country's history lacked an educational counter-program at precisely the moment when a strengthened Gaullist majority put forward a major program of university reform.

Factionalization

Nor was there any such thing as a unified movement for university reform in French society. Had Faure and his collaborators wished to reflect movement opinion in the law they proposed to Parliament in October, they could not have found a coherent representative of these views among the student organizations, the teacher's unions, or the universities in general. This was as true of students and teachers as it was of the relations between various student groups and of various levels of the educational establishment.

- *Students and teachers:* the most obvious conflict was between students and their professors. The mythology of May '68 has left the impression that the students enjoyed considerable faculty support. This is in part the result of a few, highly publicized translations of books by progressive university professors and in part due to a confusion between the "heroic," national phase of the movement – when the stakes were the installation of a new kind of regime – and the more prosaic concerns of students and teachers. In terms of the latter issue, there was a deep cleavage between the radical student groups which emerged from May and the bulk of University professors – even those on the historic Left.
- *Conflicts among students:* if there were cleavages between teachers and students, the ideological differences among the student groups were even sharper. Before May, some of these groups had been reformist; others had reformist tendencies within them; while others rejected the university as a relevant arena for change from the beginning.[6]

---

[6] Before May, for example, the Union des Etudiants Communistes were "divided among "orthodoxies," "italiens," and several varieties of extremists (Schnapp and Vidal-Naquet 1988: 16).

- *Conflicts among teachers:* the bulk of the French professoriat had never been enthusiastic about a movement that some of its members saw as juvenile, while others feared what they saw as its subversive dangers. Divisions among the teachers' organizations that had participated in the May movement were almost as broad as those within the student movement.

The best example was the FEN (Fédération de l'Education Nationale), which was constitutionally only a federation of teachers' unions, but which had increased its importance during May. Even at the height of the movement, FEN's internal constituencies were divided. While the organization of teachers of higher education (SNeSup), was under *gauchiste* control, and joined the students in their movement in the university, the secondary school union, SNES, controlled by the Communists, opposed *contestation* and tried to brake the movement in the lycées. These divisions may well have been partly responsible for the Federation's incapacity to put forward a viable alternative to the Faure reform when, in October 1968, it held its "Etats Généraux de l'Université Nouvelle" (FEN 1969). The constituent unions divided at the conference on mainly sectoral lines. Remarkably, this national conference failed to discuss the forthcoming university reform altogether (pp. 207–208).

Thus, in the highly politicized crucible of tendencies and organizations that emerged from the movement of May, there was no unified movement for university reform. Had Faure and his collaborators wished to reflect the movement's views in the law they proposed to Parliament in October, they could not have found a coherent representative of these views among the student organizations, in the teacher's unions, or in the universities in general. The absence of such a coherent movement made it easy for Faure to maneuver, but, as we shall see, the collapse of the movement and its internal divisions after the *rentrée* removed the radical flank that was the major incentive for reform.

Reform in the Political Process

Faure's strategy was to build a coalition for reform out of some elements of the former movement, some educational modernizers, and Gaullist loyalists. He wasted no time in making contact with modernists who wanted to build a university in tune with the modern world, and with radicals who wanted to see the Napoleonic system dismantled. Distrusted by the conservatives, he nevertheless made contact with representatives of the Catholic educational hierarchy and met secretly with leftist student leaders in the evening. Faure's first formal move was to set up a number of study commissions and to make contact with many of the *instances de fait* that had organized spontaneously in the effervescence of the spring, and began a series of meetings with interested groups – some of them *sub rosa*. He drew the FEN into his plans and met privately with CGT leader Georges Seguy, convincing him – and through him his PCF comrades in the teaching profession – not to oppose the reform. In the months following his appointment, Faure diverted attention from the much-feared renewal of mobilization in the streets by creating a "bouillonnement au sommet" around himself and his cabinet.

Faure sounded very like a progressive in the fall of 1968, but his true strategy was to take advantage of the potential threat of a disorganized, but still potentially dangerous movement and a strengthened Gaullist majority. He built a political and ideological coalition based on the conservatives' hope to preserve social peace, the modernists' desire to create universities that would be adequate for a modern society, and progressives' hopes for real student participation in university decision making. In legislative terms, the coalition-building exercise was a success; by November 7th, only four months after he took office, the reform passed both houses of Parliament with overwhelming majorities (Fomerand 1974: ch. 4).

But Faure's coalition depended on fear of a renewed May, the disorganization of the opposition, and de Gaulle's personal support. It also failed to take account of the institutional power of the professorate to turn the reform to its advantage – a capacity that the reform actually increased. As fall gave way to winter and winter to the following spring, with the reform's implementation and de Gaulle's sudden resignation after the failure of the 1969 referendum, the cracks in the reformist coalition became deep fissures.

The Weaknesses of the Reform

Seldom had so many sweeping changes been proposed in such haste or had to be implemented in such a short time.[7] In fact, at the end of the legislative process, even the idea for taking a year to put the system into gear was scrapped. By December 31, 1968 – within two months of the law's passage – some 600 provisional new departments (UERs) had been created. By April, elections for new joint councils had been held for students and faculty all over the country. The new universities almost immediately elected their presidents and submitted draft statutes to a commission of the Conseil d'État. By the 1970 *rentrée*, even the thorny problem of dividing the University of Paris into thirteen new universities had been largely completed.

A number of unfortunate results followed from this haste. The greatest problem had to do with the creation of the UERs and their integration into the newly created universities. For rather than following the educationally rational course of creating the new universities first and then allowing them to define their internal structures, Faure's cabinet created a "provisional" list of UERs very rapidly – by December 1968 – and only then moved to the broader step of aggregating them into universities. The result was that the provisional UER's – some of them no more than new names for old faculties and institutes – gained an institutional base from which they could defend their interests and shape the new universities. Though the fear in governing circles was that radical students would take over the provisional UERs, the real danger was that the

---

[7] The haste was not accidental. Alliot was of the opinion that "in France, the only decisions that are taken are taken quickly." Interview April 2, 1990.

professorate could use them to consolidate its position and prevent real innovation from being carried out (Chalendar: 177).

The problem was reinforced by the reluctance of the prime minister's cabinet to see the law implemented in the frenzied atmosphere of *l'après-mai*. Although Faure and his staff proceeded almost immediately to the designation of the new universities – naming seventeen of them by March 1969 and thirty-seven more by June (Chalendar, p. 192) – the prime minister's office was not happy over the plans to apply the law to the *grandes écoles,* France's elite universities (189). "Under different pretexts," his staff found reasons for delay and "the signature of the Matignon [i.e., the prime minister's office] was held back until Faure's departure as Minister" (193). There was an even longer delay in the case of the Paris universities, but this related more to the need to find a solution to feuds and political differences within the old Sorbonne than to the dictates of high politics. And while the government delayed, academic mandarins who had no enthusiasm for reform had time to regroup.

The Revenge of the Mandarins: Faure and his cabinet expected the newly created UERs to be provisional, and this for two reasons: "The Minister could himself complete or modify [the plan], and the councils of the new universities, once elected, could equally question them in creating their statutes" (175). But they calculated without taking into account two important factors: first, it would require a continued commitment to reform in the political system for the spirit of the reform to survive; and second, they took insufficient account of the power of the academic establishment to delay or reshape the reform.

In principle, there was no reason why this could not have been done on an educationally rational basis. But professors wanted to join their friends, their political allies, and those whose votes they could count on. Those who favored genuine reform found their way to experimental universities like Vincennes or to Paris VII; others created solutions of convenience, like Paris I; while those who dreaded change could remain in the old faculties – like law and medicine in Paris, which remained virtually unchanged. The reformers' urgency in beginning the reform with the UERs, while the government delayed in creating authoritative university institutions, left the reform hostage to the revenge of the mandarins.

Business as Usual: No doubt, had an actively reformist Education Ministry remained in place, led by a minister with the political will to defend his reform, provisional arrangements based on hasty decisions or on poor educational policy could have been revised. But the season for reforms, like the season of protest, was short. After less than one year in power, and as the result of de Gaulle's ill-considered referendum and resignation, Faure was removed from power by the new government of Georges Pompidou and his cabinet was dispersed. Pompidou replaced Faure with Olivier Guichard, a Gaullist loyalist who administered the law without personal conviction or political imagination. And Guichard's tenure coincided with a series of administrative and management changes that left little time or energy for reform. This merry-go-round of ministers and their cabinets that followed did little good for the newly formed universities.

The Narrowing Window for Reform

But if the reform failed in its boldest aspirations, it was not primarily because of the power of the educational establishment or because Faure lost his position when de Gaulle resigned. The reform passed so swiftly because Faure and his collaborators had built a coalition on the fear that of the danger of mobilization in the streets. When that threat failed to materialize, the impulse for reform declined. The industrial and educational *rentrée* provided evidence that – except for small groups of isolated agitators – the movement of the previous spring was dead.

This can be seen in the sharp decline in collective action in general – and of confrontational protest in particular – at the *rentrée*. As the estimate of student demonstrations, public marches, and violence from July 1968 through June 1969 in Figure 9.1 shows, it was mainly *after* the reform was passed, and during the election of the new student councils, that contestation was renewed. In fact, the reform helped bring student protest back to where it had started. In contrast to West Germany and Italy, where the same period saw a move out of the universities, the election campaign for the new student councils brought the student movement back to the campus, where both violent and nonviolent collective action accompanied the campaign. While the press featured the most violent encounters when radical groups attempted to stop students from voting, in fact, most of the collective action surrounding these elections was

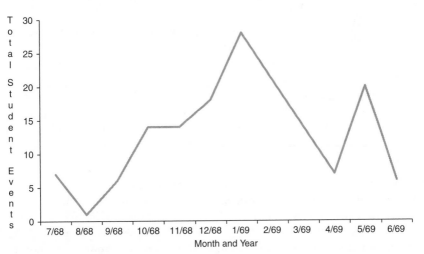

FIGURE 9.1. Student Events in France, July 1968–June 1969.
Source: Author's data.

peaceful and the sixty percent quorum of participation was not always reached (Fomerand 1974: 240).

The first evidence of the declining enthusiasm for reform appeared in Parliament. Each step of the legislative process led to a whittling down of the liberality of the initial reform plan. Many of the amendments were inspired by the academic establishment, either working through the prime minister's office or through individual members of Parliament. As a result, in the final text and in the implementation of the law, each of the bill's original principles was compromised. In the electoral colleges, the weight of the more liberal maîtres-assistants and assistants was reduced from Faure's generous proposal of August (Chalendar 1970:117), and that of the students was made dependent on their level of electoral participation (149 ff.). As for the cherished goal of opening up the university to the outside, little was said about it in the final text of the law, but external groups held a statutory proportion of seats on the university councils. Not even the regional councils foreseen by Faure to coordinate educational policy were created, for after de Gaulle's ill-fated referendum on the regions, there was little enthusiasm for decentralization in the government that succeeded him.

Conclusions

The major implications of the failure of the *loi d'orientation* are three:

First, like critical elections and major crises, protest waves like that of May 1968 do not simply take advantage of an existing political opportunity structure but become an important component of that structure and, through it, provide opportunities for others – including reformists within the elite, like Faure;

second, while they may help to unleash a reform process, protest waves are not sufficient to produce significant reforms – they also require the presence and entrepreneurship of well-placed reformists who can turn the impetus for change into concrete proposals and pilot them through the political process;

and *third,* waves of mobilization can produce a temporary coalition for reform, but they are often too brief, too divided, and too multivoiced to supply reformers with sustained support when the fear of disorder evaporates.

This is not to claim that protest and reform are unconnected: May 1968 was unusual for the rapid spread of mobilization, for the threat it posed to the Gaullist-led government, and for its rejection by public opinion in the elections that followed. But other periods – like the Popular Front in France, the New Deal and Great Society in the United States, and the 1968–1972 period in Italy – saw a similar cooccurrence of protest and reform. As the Tillys concluded from their study of a century of conflict in Europe:

No major political rights came into being without readiness of some portions of those [protesting] groups to overcome the resistance of the government and other groups, consequently without considerable involvement of those groups in collective violence. (1975: 184)

In all these cases, it was not mobilization that produced reform, but a realignment in the governing coalition triggered by that mobilization and exploited by skillful political entrepreneurs.

In analytical terms, much of the variance in the outcomes was explained not by the independent but by intervening causal mechanisms. "Protest," to paraphrase the work of Rufus Browning and his collaborators in the United States, was "not enough" to produce reformist outcomes for minority groups without the intervening influence of elections, political realignments, and leaders able to take advantage of a widening political opportunity structure (Browning, Marshall, and Tabb 1984). This suggests that the study of social movements will remain fatally incomplete unless scholars become more sensitive to the relations between contentious and institutional politics.

What are the scope conditions of these observations? Turning, on the one hand, to periods of ordinary politics, it is axiomatic that the processes of convention will dominate processes of contention. But the same, I will argue, is also true for periods of revolutionary change. Think of the revolutions of 1848 that Kurt Weyland has written about in a stimulating comparative analysis (2009): while the "early risers" in that "springtime of freedom" rapidly dethroned established rulers and their success diffused across the continent (Soule and Tarrow 1991), by 1849 frightened liberals and military intervention had pushed them aside. Even in the heartland of the revolution – France – by 1851 the republic was dead.

Does this mean that all waves of contention are bound to ultimate defeat and reaction? That is not the message of this chapter. For although the insurgents of May 1968 squandered much of their political capital in a torrent of words, some reforms – for better or for worse – *did* emerge from the period of protest: not only in the universities but in the primary and secondary schools; not only in the educational system but in the factories and the welfare system. The message of this chapter is not that contention inevitably leads to its opposite but that its ultimate effects must be understood as they wend their way through the political process through the interaction between strangers and insiders at the gates of the polity.

10

"What's in a Word?"

How Contention Shapes Contentious Language

Words are polysemic. This is especially true for the words used for contentious politics. To the extent that they survive, their meaning changes in response to social change, political realignments, and cultural developments. But another reason why meaning changes is that words diffuse to different locales, where they are adopted by different agents for different purposes. Think of how the term *terrorism* diffused from France to Russia and ultimately to the rest of the world. Here is the first meaning of the term in the *Oxford Educational Dictionary*:

> *Terrorism:* 1. Government by intimidation as directed and carried out by the party in power in France during the Revolution of 1789–94. (*OED Compact Edition, II,* 1971, p. 216)

This definition that might well have been proposed by the French Republicans who invented *Le Terreur* two centuries earlier. In September 1793, under the control of the Jacobin Party, the National Convention declared that "the government of the Terror is on the order of the day." For many years afterward, the terms *terror, terrorism,* and *reign of terror* all referred to state terrorism.

But by the second half of the nineteenth century, a second usage was invented, when the Russian populist group, Narodnaya Volya, assassinated Tsar Alexander in 1881:

> 2. A policy intended to strike with terror those against whom it is adopted; the employment of methods of intimidation; the fact of terrorizing or the condition of being terrorized. (Ibid.)

An earlier version of this chapter was presented to the conference on Social Movement Outcomes at the Wissenschaftszentrum Berlin, June 2011. I am especially grateful for the contributions of Philip Ayoub, Breno Bringel, Wayles Brown, Bonnie Buettner, Valerie Bunce, Anne Costain, Nicole Doerr, Berk Esen, Bela Greskovits, Ulrike Liebert, Dieter Rucht, Bogdan Vasi, and Kathrin Zippel to my detective work on the language of contention in their countries. Miriam Brody, John Meyer, Conny Roggeband, Sarah Soule, David Strang, and Bogdan Vasi offered helpful comments on earlier versions of the chapter.

From then on, with the notable exception of the Stalinist practice of indis-
criminate purges, the use of the term *terrorism* meant the actions of nonstate
actors against states or other actors. Although occasionally, the American, the
Israeli, or other governments are accused of *state terrorism*, it is this second
usage – the employment of methods of violence by nonstate actors to strike
terror amongst their opponents – that has become dominant.[1]

What's in a Word?

What's in a word? As the example of *terrorism* suggests, terms for contention
change as they diffuse to different locales, where they are adopted by different
agents and for different purposes. Think of Mark Traugott's work on the barricade. We now know that the origin of the term was the rows of barrels (i.e., *bar-
riques*) that were rolled across Parisian streets to protect neighborhoods from
thieves. But by the nineteenth century, they were turned into instruments of
revolution, as street fighters confronted the forces of order by building piles of
rubble, paving stones, and whatever else came to hand (Traugott 1995; 2010).
We also know from Roger Gould's work how the barricade transformed from
a form of neighborhood defense to an all-Parisian instrument of insurrection
(Gould 1995). And we know from the 1848 and other revolutions that the barricade diffused across Europe and came to be identified with revolution.

Thanks to the work of Traugott, Gould, and others, we know a great deal
about how the barricade diffused across the map of Europe and beyond. But we
know much less about why some other contentious terms disappear in the mists
of history while still others survive and diffused. Think of the critical juncture
of the Solidarnosc period in Poland in 1980–1981: in that period, the "reappro-
priation of language by the people and exercising freely the new nonmandatory
speech were at the very heart of what was happening," writes Elzbieta Matynia.
But as Matynia also writes, "in the rush by outside observers to cover the news –
the protest strikes, marches, negotiations, Soviet troop movements – this verbal
dimension of our experience was simply too subtle, too personal, too invisible,
to be captured by the press, much less by television (Matynia 2009: 3).

Inspired, in part, by the "cultural turn" in social movement studies and,
in part, by my own efforts to specify the concept of repertoires of contention
(see Chapter 8), this chapter focuses on the invention of new terms and new
concepts for contentious action and their diffusion over time and across space.
I will argue that new terms for contentious repertoires arise out of critical junctures (Collier and Collier 1991). I will then argue that *symbolic resonance* is
in part responsible for the survival and diffusion of some terms, while others,
less symbolically resonant, disappear. By this term I mean *the degree to which
a particular term resonates with culturally familiar concepts in a particular
culture* (Snow and Benford 1988). But symbolic resonance is not sufficient

---

[1] Even more striking: the shift was almost identical among the French – who gave the term its original meaning – and the United States, the target of the terrorist attacks on September 11, 2001.

TABLE 10.1. *A Typology of the "Diffusability" of Terms in Contentious Politics*

	Strategic Adaptability	
	Low	High
Low Symbolic Resonance	*Shantytowns*	*Boycott*
High	*Male Chauvinism*	*The Strike & La Grève*

to insure the survival and diffusion of a concept: contentious language that survives and diffuses must enjoy what I call *strategic modularity*: that is, *the degree to which terms that emerge in one strategic context can be transferred to others without losing the strategic advantages they originally possessed.*

It goes without saying that the least diffusible innovations will lack both symbolic resonance and strategic modularity, and that the most successful ones will possess both qualities. I will use Sarah Soule's research on the anti-Apartheid tactic of building "shantytowns" in the United States in the 1980s to illustrate when and why a new concept reaches a dead end. At the other extreme, the diffusion of the term "strike" for the withdrawal of labor from England, and *grève* from France for the same behaviors shows how symbolic resonance and strategic modularity work together, even against official resistance.

Two intermediate examples that will be examined in this chapter are the terms *boycott*, which lacked symbolic resonance when it was first invented in Ireland in the early nineteenth century, but could be adapted strategically to a wide variety of settings, and the term *male chauvinist*, which had great symbolic resonance when it was invented in the American women's movement in the 1970s, but declined as an arm of that movement because it lacked strategic modularity.

Table 10.1 lays out the structure of the argument. In each of the next four sections, I will refer indifferently to both the durability and the "diffusability" of the four terms I will examine. Based on the pioneering work of Gwendolyn Mink, Conny Roggeband, and Kathrin Zippel, in the fifth section, I will use the diffusion of the concept of "sexual harassment" from the United States to Western Europe to show how concepts diffuse and how they change as they are adapted to different cultural and political settings. In concluding, I will raise several questions about how the study of language can be added to the repertoire of concepts in the study of contentious politics.

The Etiology of a Failed Innovation

Some contentious terms do not last much longer than the critical junctures that produce them. The "shantytown" protest – memorialized by Sarah Soule in her

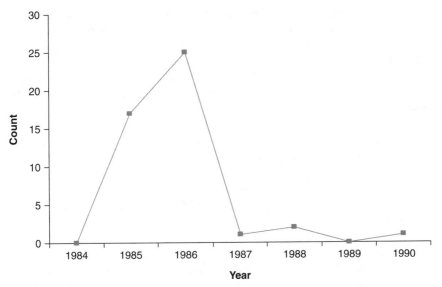

FIGURE 10.1. "Shantytown" Protests for Divestment, U.S. College Campuses, 1984–1990.
Source: Data kindly provided by Sarah Soule.

research on campus anti-Apartheid protests (1995, 1997, 1999) – spread rapidly across American college campuses in the mid-1980s. But by 1990, the term had virtually disappeared. Figure 10.1 tracks the number of "shantytown" protests that Soule found in her NEXIS database over this six-year period.

The "shantytown" was first employed at an early protest at Columbia University's Hamilton Hall. To establish a presence there, the Columbia protesters dragged armchairs and sofas to the front of the building from a nearby dormitory. When night fell, they rigged up tarps and brought in blankets to keep warm. When Reverend Jesse Jackson came to speak in support of the protest, participation grew to over 5,000. Jackson's presence, the large number of African American demonstrators on campus, and the fact that Columbia had been the scene of the start of the 1967–1968 protest wave gained the protest national media attention and helped to trigger diffusion of a movement in favor of college divestment in South Africa (Soule 1997: 857).

"Naming" the Shantytown

There was no name for Columbia's collection of tarps, blankets, and odd bits of furniture when it was first assembled. But the practice was soon copied in divestment protests at campuses around the country. At Princeton and Santa Cruz, the tactic was called a "camp-out"; at Harvard a "sleep-in"; at Iowa, the students renamed the administration building "Biko Hall" after the murdered South African student leader. A number of other student groups sitting outside their colleges' administration buildings held what they called "sit-outs." In all, Soule identified forty-six shantytown protests between 1985, when the campaign against investment in South African firms had begun, and 1990, when it petered out. All these events used roughly the same performance – the erection by student activists of a makeshift structure to oppose their universities' investments in firms with ties to South Africa. While some made broader claims, all professed clear statements about the necessity of divestment.

The "naming" of the form that came to be known as "the shantytown" came only in the late spring of 1985, when students at Cornell University constructed a shack out of scraps of wood, tar paper, and plastic in front of the university's administration building. That shack, observed Soule, "was the first of what later became known as *shantytowns*, a performance and a name that eventually spread to similar structures around the country (Soule 1997: 858; Soule 1999).

Soule put most of her effort into constructing an event history of the shantytown protests and relating it to other variables. For example, she asked what kind of campuses tended to produce shantytown protests – large universities, mostly black or liberal arts colleges, or big state institutions? She also asked if there was a geographic pattern of proximate diffusion from Columbia to nearby campuses in the northeast, or whether the movement spread through the media, irrespective of location. And she examined the effects of the protests: were those campuses in which students built shantytowns more likely to divest than those that had no protests? (They were not.) But for linguistic purposes, what is important is that it was only after the Cornell students had invented the name *shantytown* that divestment protesters elsewhere adopted it. Then the term, as well as the practice, diffused across the country.

Viewed in its essence, the shantytown was simply a variation on the by-then familiar form of the sit-in, which had become modular in the course of the 1960s (Tilly and Tarrow 2007: 18–21). Its originality was to draw on the symbolism of impoverished South African black townships, so visible after the Sharpsville massacre and other protests in the 1980s, and to combine it with the material demand that universities divest themselves of South African securities. But because its symbolism was so closely associated with those townships and their protests against Apartheid, the shantytown form did not "travel" beyond the divestment campaign. Shanty building never became a part of the basic American repertoire of contention and it is mostly remembered, if at all, as "a failed innovation" (Soule 1999).[2]

---

[2] In a personal communication, Sarah Soule reports having found a few examples of the shantytown form during the 1990s. The shantytown protests against divestment failed in another way as well; when Soule carried out an analysis of the co-occurrence of shantytown protests with colleges' investment policies, she found that it was ineffective in forcing divestment. "Colleges and universities that had shantytowns," she concludes, "actually had slower rates of divestment than those that did not have them" (Soule 1999: 121).

The Rise and Decline of "Male Chauvinism"

In a landmark 2008 article, Jane Mansbridge and Katherine Flaster reported on a conversation that Mansbridge had in Chicago in 1992 with Sonia Rice, an African American woman on public assistance. Rice was describing a man of her acquaintance. "He's getting on my nerves," Rice said. "This one man is really touched, and I don't mean by God. He's gone. *He is a chauvinist pig. He is a chauvinist!*"

> MANSBRIDGE: What does he do?
> RICE: "He-he's a dipshit, is all ... and when I said he was a chauvinist pig, my girlfriend said, "You know it, you're right!" He really thinks he's the only rooster in the hen house. That's just what he's thinking, and he thinks when he clucks everybody's supposed to cringe. (Mansbridge and Flaster 648; italics added).

The terms *male chauvinist* and its extension, *male chauvinist pig,* arose in the 1960s and 1970s as part of the language of the new feminist movement. But it was actually an amalgam of two terms inherited from the past: *chauvinist* and *pig*. The first term derived from the French nineteenth-century term *chauviniste,* named after Nicolas Chauvin, an exaggerated patriot in Napoleon's army. It was then adopted by the American Left when Stalin, in 1928, called attention to minority issues. In response to Stalin's authoritative use of the term, it was adopted by the American Communist Party to designate a racist (Mansbridge and Flaster: 640–641).

The term *pig* had a separate derivation: it was at first used in the American New Left to designate the police and, by extension, other figures of authority. Putting the two terms together produced an evocative, if somewhat heterodox way of designating men who considered that men are naturally superior to women as "male chauvinist pig." But both terms begin to decline in movement usage fairly rapidly. Figure 10.2 uses Google Books and the NGram system to provide a rough idea of the appearance and decline of these two terms in American political discourse.

Clearly, the term *male chauvinist pig* must have had symbolic resonance for some American feminists. But it lacked strategic modularity, if only because it did not connect logically or politically to many of the issues that concerned most women: equal access to jobs and salaries; breaking the glass ceiling in business; access to sports and the professions. It also may have offended liberal feminists for whom denigrating men did not seem the best way to advance their cause. And it may have risked painting feminists as "man-haters," a caricature that would carry water to the mill of the cultural right. To put this failure of an evocative term to diffuse in the terms that David Strang and John Meyer developed to discuss *successful* diffusion, "male chauvinist pig" was not easy to "theorize" across the spectrum of issues and groups in the women's movement (1993).

Yet the term did not disappear when it fell out of favor with American feminists. Mansbridge and Flaster report from a Chicago-area survey in the early

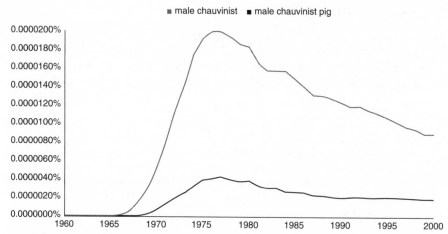

FIGURE 10.2. "Male Chauvinist" and "Male Chauvinist Pig" in American Culture, 1960–2000.
Source: N-gram analysis from Google Books.

1990s that 60-odd percent of women and over 40 percent of the men interviewed reported having used the term at some point (2008). This was the case regardless of level of education or political orientation. No more than the sexual behavior of powerful men like Dominique Stauss-Kahn, the former head of the IMF, who was arrested for rape in early 2011, the term "male chauvinist pig refuses to go away.[3]

The Diffusion of the Boycott

Social movement scholars have been impressed with the power of the media – and most recently that of the Internet – in diffusing forms of contentious politics. Often dramatic images – like the pictures of well-dressed young black college students brutalized by white thugs in the American South that appeared on American TV in the 1960s – are at least partially responsible for the rapid diffusion of new innovations. However, long before the advent of television, contentious episodes diffused through the media, even when the terms themselves had little symbolic resonance, because these terms were strategically modular. Such a term is the *boycott*, by which we usually mean the practice of shunning a person or refusing to purchase a product to punish its producer.

---

[3] The closest equivalent to male chauvinist that I could find in France before the Strauss-Kahn story broke in 2011 was the word *phallocrat*, a wonderful combination of the Greek term for a penis and the French term for an aristocrat – i.e., someone who thinks the possession of a male sex organ gave him a title of nobility.

The Prehistory of the Boycott

Americans and others had been practicing something resembling the boycott since the late eighteenth century. For example, the now doubly famous term *Tea Party* was only the most clamorous episode in a long series of attempts to limit the commercial control of the British colonial government by refusing to buy British items – from luxury goods to funeral apparel, to tea. In the nonimportation agreement signed in 1774, colonial representatives opposed the Stamp Act of 1765, the Townshend Acts of 1767 and the Coercive Acts of 1774 (Wood 1991). The Boston Tea Party was actually the action of a minority attempting to radicalize the situation when a voluntary nonimportation agreement appeared not to be working.

Probably the first organized use of the boycott – the English boycott of slave-produced sugar in the 1780s – depended on the social appropriation of preexisting networks of Protestant dissenters and on the use of the provincial press to announce the boycott and urge supporters to sign mass petitions to Parliament (Tarrow 2011a: ch. 5). The same strategy was adopted in the United States in the 1830s, when the National Negro Convention encouraged a boycott of slave-produced goods. Boycotts existed well before the term existed. It took another half century for Americans and others who wanted to punish wrongdoers or ban their products by shunning them to have a term of art to mobilize behind – the boycott.

Shunning Colonel Boycott

We owe the term *boycott* to a conflict between Irish peasants and a notorious Colonel Boycott, who was the land agent for Lord Erne during the Irish land wars of the 1870s and 1880s. When the 1880 harvest failed, Erne's peasants asked for a 20 percent reduction in their rents, which Boycott refused to grant. The Irish nationalist Charles Stewart Parnell had suggested that greedy landlords be ostracized rather than treated to violence. This was the tactic that was applied to Boycott. When his workers refused to work in the fields as well as in his house, and when the local mailman refused to deliver his mail and local shopkeepers stopped trading with him, Boycott was completely isolated (Marlow 1973). The term immediately spread to England when the *London Times* editorialized, on November 20th 1880, that "The people of New Pallas have resolved to 'boycott' them [i.e., the landlords] and refused to supply them with food or drink."

It is hardly surprising that a tactic used against an English lord with landholdings in Ireland should have been reported in the London press; what is more surprising is how rapidly the term spread across the Atlantic and how quickly American journalists grasped its strategic advantages. On November 16, 1880, the *Chicago Daily Tribune* wrote

> Boycotting is a new term added to the popular vocabulary of Ireland, after the manner of "bulldozing" and other similar additions to the American terms now passing into general use. Boycotting, though a peaceful means of coercion,

TABLE 10.2. *Diffusion of the Term* Boycott *to Different Countries from Ireland*

England	*Boycott*
United States	*Boycott*
France	*Boycotter*
Spain	*Boicoteo*
Italian	*Boicottagio*
Portuguese	*Boicotagem*

is perhaps a more efficient mode of intimidating than actual violence. It is a means within the letter of the law, and, involving no violence or breach of the peace, cannot be put down by force nor punished as a legal offense. (4)

The term then spread to France, Spain, Italy, Portugal, and elsewhere. What is most interesting is that it was adopted in a similar linguistic form in each of these countries, as Table 10.2 shows.

Why did a term that was derived from an obscure man's name spread so rapidly and so far? Despite the lack of symbolic resonance, boycotts enjoyed strategic modularity: the tactic of boycotting could be applied to a variety of targets by a variety of actors and organizations. In Poland in the 1930s it was used by the government to boycott Jewish-owned businesses; in California in the 1950s it was employed by farm worker sympathizers against grape growers (Ganz 2009); after the creation of the state of Israel it was used by Arab governments to boycott Israeli-made goods and those of countries that traded with Israel.[4] Strategic modularity more than made up for the symbolic poverty of the term *boycott*.

The Diffusion and Normalization of the Strike

Some contentious terms that arise in particular critical junctures do combine symbolic resonance with strategic modularity and these are the most durable and diffuse most widely. Such a term is *the strike,* a term that, strictly speaking, refers to the withdrawal of labor, but has come to mean a variety of types of collective action – think of rent strikes. The strike offers a good example of how forms of contention that began historically as disruptive confrontations become modular and ultimately conventional.

The first use of the term *strike* in English seems to date from the actions of the eighteenth-century English sailors who "struck" the sails of their ships as a sign of their unwillingness to work (Linebaugh and Rediker 1990: 240). Though mainly associated with industry, the strike predated industrialization.

[4] But there are objective limits: when a California environmental group proposed to boycott of goods produced by *maquiladora* factories following the example of the earlier grape boycott, their Mexican counterparts could not see people in a poor country like Mexico complying (Williams 2003).

As it became generally known that strikes could succeed by stopping production, striking spread from skilled to unskilled workers, from the large factory to smaller firms, from the withholding of labor to the withholding of produce, from industry to agriculture, and from there to the public services. By now, the strike has become a virtual part of the institutions of collective bargaining, with its own jurisprudence, rituals, and expectations among both challengers and opponents.

Strikes developed as a means for workers to put pressure on management, but in the course of the nineteenth century, they also became a source for building class solidarity. This was reflected in the increasing offering of mutual support across occupational and geographic lines and in the ritualization of the strike, which was designed to enhance solidarity. Strikers would parade within the precincts of the factory, carrying banners and tooting horns, chanting slogans, and singing songs of solidarity to induce their workmates to join them. Solidarity was also sometimes imposed, by "sending to Coventry" a worker who refused to down his or her tools.

Strikes can be employed in combination with other forms of contention: occupations, marches, industrial sabotage, petitions, and legal actions. Assemblies prepare the workers and elected strike committees; organizers in an especially militant sector try to bring out other workers; pickets block the gates of the plant to keep raw materials out. Strikers who want to gain community solidarity march from the factory through working-class neighborhoods in "turnouts" which – at their most successful – induce merchants to close their shutters and housewives to join their marches. From a spontaneous withdrawal of labor, the strike became the major means through which workers built and expressed solidarity, demonstrated their challenges, sought external support, and negotiated their differences with opponents from a position of enhanced, if temporary power.

But not without resistance to both the term and the practice of striking. Although strikes became common during the Industrial Revolution they were illegal in most Western countries until the weight of organized labor made it more rational to recognize and regulate strikes than to suppress them (Rokkan 1970). Even the term for striking was resisted: French authorities continued to refer to strikers as *coalitions* until late in the nineteenth century when the popular term *grève* was reluctantly recognized (Tournier 1992). In Germany, the term *streik*, which was adopted from the English word, was avoided until the end of the 1880s, and was not legally adopted until after 1945.[5] Industrialization, transnational communication, and common practice diffused the French and English terms for the withdrawal of labor at roughly the same time across European frontiers.

[5] There is evidence that the term *strikende Wasserarbeiter* (e.g., "striking sailors") had a similar meaning in sixteenth-century Germany to its original meaning in England, but the modern German usage for the strike derived from English in 1810. I am grateful to Bonnie Buettner for this information.

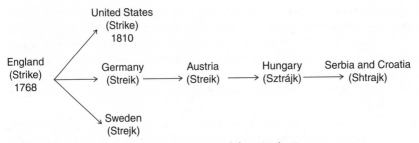

FIGURE 10.3. Diffusion of the English Word for "Strike."

We can tell a story about how this must have happened: German and Swedish industrialists imitated British manufacturing techniques, assembling large groups of workers in the same factories, where they came to understand their power to stop production, and thereby to squeeze profits, by withdrawing their labor power.[6] The German language would then have been the vehicle for the term's diffusion to Austria, and the lines of communication within the Habsburg Empire would have been responsible for the term's spread elsewhere in Central Europe and the Balkans, as Figure 10.3 suggests.

But industrialization, common language, and imperial connections cannot fully explain the diffusion of the language of the strike. For just as the English term was diffusing across central and northern Europe, the French term *grève* was spreading around Europe's southern tier. At its origins, *grève* did not have the evocative sense of the term *strike!* For centuries it had referred to the sand or gravel at the shore of the Seine in Paris, where boats would pull up to off-load their cargos. The first *grevistes* were not strikers at all, but unemployed men who would assemble at the *Place de Grève* seeking a day's work unloading barges. Gradually, from signifying *those without work*, the term came to mean those who *would not work* (Tournier 1992). Then, as Figure 10.4 shows, from France to Portugal, to Romania, and even to Turkey, workers, and those who wanted to organize them, adopted the French word for going on strike.

The Turkish story is perhaps the most interesting, because it demonstrates that political factors may be more important than either common language or industrialization in the diffusion of new terminology for contention. There had been a perfectly acceptable Arabic term for the withdrawal of labor in the Ottoman Empire; but when the Kemalists came to power after World War I and reformed the Turkish language, they wanted a term that would evoke modernity – and what could be more modern than a word that came from France, where many of them had studied? Symbolic resonance joined strategic modularity in the diffusion of the language of industrial conflict.[7]

---

[6] But note that it was not unskilled factory workers, but more-literate Leipzig printers who, in 1865, gave the term its currency in Germany.

[7] I am grateful to Berk Esen for the fieldwork that produced this information.

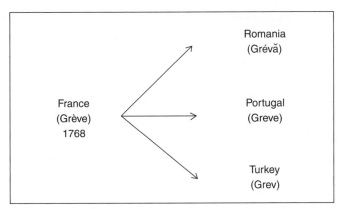

FIGURE 10.4. Diffusion of the French Word for "Strike."

Diffusion and the Political Process

Scholars who study the political contexts of contention have sometimes been insensitive to the meanings of mobilization, as Verta Taylor (2009) points out. That need not be the case, as the materials in this chapter suggest. After all, the term *male chauvinist* did not disappear as a movement term because it lacked symbolic resonance but because of the politically salient fact that it lent an uncomfortable antimale animus to those who employed it. Conversely, the shantytown was too resonant with the rather distant experience of poor South African blacks to diffuse to movements other than solidarity with the anti-Apartheid movement. Both in terms of resonance and adaptability, politics is far from detached from the language of contention.

A particularly clear linkage between the political process and language arises from research on the diffusion of the concept of sexual harassment from the United States to Western Europe. In this final section I will argue that symbolic resonance and strategic modularity came together to produce similar, but different, trajectories of this concept in the United States and Western Europe.

Sexual Harassment, the Courts, and Civil Rights in America

The term *sexual harassment* first appeared in the United States in the mid-1970s but was widely diffused after the publication of Catharine MacKinnon's book, *Sexual Harassment of Working Women,* published in 1979. Figure 10.5, from an N-Gram analysis of Google Books, tracks the appearance of this term in American books, alongside the narrower term, "violence against women."

In American jurisprudence, the term *sexual harassment* came to condemn a variety of behaviors, ranging from actual physical violence, to threats of retribution for denied sexual favors, to the creation of a hostile environment in the work place (Mink 2000: 23). Congress never explicitly defined sexual harassment but left it to the judiciary to say what the term actually meant. The key

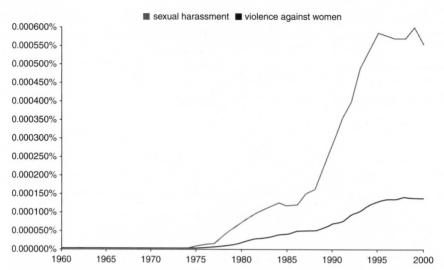

FIGURE 10.5. "Sexual Harassment" and "Violence Against Women" in American Culture, 1960–2000.

Source: N-gram analysis from Google Books.

Supreme Court case of *Meridor v. Vinson* (477 U.S. 57) established a broad reading of sexual harassment, leading government offices, private firms and educational institutions to develop elaborate procedures and substantive regulations for individual behavior.[8]

Sexual harassment was a new name for an old practice when it appeared in the United States in the 1970s (Zippel 2006: 11–12).[9] Only in 1981 did a court rule that sexual harassment could result in eligibility for employment benefits (Mink 2000: 4). Even managers who believed such complaints were valid did not take them seriously and the term *political correctness* soon came to be applied in the media to women who complained about sexual innuendoes or advances. But by 1980, well before any other advanced industrial democracy, the Equal Employment Opportunity Commission (EEOC) had established guidelines banning unwelcome sexual advances, the creation of a

[8] Particularly thorny was how to give a consistent meaning to "creating a hostile environment," which could go well beyond the relations between an individual claimant and an individual defendant (Mink 2000: 30). One of the first American claims of sexual harassment was filed by Lois Jenson in 1975 based on vulgar and obscene behavior by male coworkers. Jenson was joined by seventeen women coworkers in a class-action suit alleging a hostile environment. See *Jenson v. Eveleth Taconite Co.*, 824 Supp. 847 (D. Minn. 1993), decided amost twenty-five years later. See Zippel 2006: 45 for this and related cases.

[9] Until the 1980s, women who experienced unwanted sexual advances "had few words with which to name their experience" (Zippel 2006: 45). "Women who left their jobs could not file for unemployment, because state agencies did not recognize sexual harassment as cause for quitting," writes Zippel (46).

hostile environment, and quid pro quo sexual demands. In contrast, it was only in 1994 that Germany passed a Federal Employee Protection Law with a similar mandate and in 2002 that the European Union passed a Directive on Equal Treatment that went as far as the EEOC regulations (Zippel: 19).

Why was the United States a pioneer in recognizing and sanctioning sexual harassment? One reason surely was the stronger tradition of sexual reserve in relations between men and women in the United States, compared to Europe's more liberal sexual environment, which European opponents often used as a reason why they shouldn't follow in America's footsteps (Zippel 2006: 94). Another was the modular extension on the part of the courts and the Equal Employment Opportunity Commission of the concept of discrimination from race to gender (Mink 2000: 55–66; Zippel 2006: 50–53). Europeans, instead, drew on the continent's stronger tradition of worker's rights and on the international UN discourse of human rights (Friedman and Whitman 2003).

A third reason for American primacy in this field was the strength of the legal system in encouraging claimants to go to court. In contrast, European claimants had to take a longer, more circuitous parliamentary route for the recognition that sexual harassment was an offense (Zippel 2006: 26–28). And a fourth was the more dynamic Women's Rights Movement in the United States, which was evident as early as the mid-1970s, when groups like Working Women United arose out of a sexual discrimination case in Ithaca, New York (Ibid.: 53–57).

Trans-Atlantic Diffusion

Nevertheless, once sexual harassment was named, there was a cascade of diffusion of both the term and efforts to regulate the practice from North America to Western Europe. The early risers were the Anglo-American democracies of Canada, Australia, and the United Kingdom in the late 1970s; Spain in 1989; Sweden in 1991; Austria, Belgium, and France in 1992; Germany in 1994 and Finland in 1995 (Zippel 2006: 17–28). Moreover, with some national variations, the terms that were adopted closely mirrored American usage:

- In the Netherlands, "Initially Dutch feminists decided to translate the issue as 'unwanted intimacies' (*ongewenste intimiteiten*), putting the emphasis on the right of women to define what behavior they perceived as unwanted." The concept was, however, often ridiculed in the press and on the workfloor ("what intimacies do you want?"), and was therefore later replaced by the term for "sexual intimidation" (Roggeband 2010: 26).
- In France, "feminists … defined sexual harassment as a specific form of sexual violence in the workplace and labeled it as '*violences faites aux femmes au travail*,' But perhaps because (male) unionists' objected to the idea that women might be assaulted by fellow workers, the French Canadian translation '*harcèlement sexuele*' was eventually adopted" (Ibid.).
- "In Germany feminists chose the translation of '*sexuelle Belästigung*,' which refers to bullying, "but can also be used for physical attacks and intimidation by superiors" (Ibid.).

- The Spanish translation *"acoso sexual"* remained closely tied to the U.S. concept (Ibid.).
- In Italy, the term *molestie sessuale* was selected, which sounds violent to the English-speaking ear but can actually be used for all forms of annoyances in Italian.
- The same was true in Portugal, which, along with Greece, was one of Europe's latecomers, where the term chosen was *"asédio sexual."*

There were, of course, differences between the European and the American construction of the term. Of these, Kathrin Zippel notes three in particular:

First, in place of the U.S. discourse of discrimination that owed much to the precedent of the Civil Rights Movement, European advocates advanced a discourse of "dignity," which they claimed was more "European"; second, the impetus for reform came largely from "state feminists" in gender equality offices at both the national and European levels, compared to the stronger civil-society based movement in the United States; and third, given the stronger role of trade unions in Europe, the reforms relied on the implementation of work-place regulations through collective agreements between unions and employers. While this was an advantage in some ways, in others it slowed progress, because unions were often reluctant to admit that their members could be guilty of sexual harassment.

Mechanisms of Diffusion

How did the movement to sanction and regulate sexual harassment diffuse from the United States to Western Europe? Figure 10.6 lays out three processes of diffusion derived from my previous work on transnational activism (Tarrow 2005: ch. 6): *direct diffusion*, which depends on interpersonal ties between initiators and adopters of innovations; *indirect diffusion*, which relies on impersonal ties through the media or word-of-mouth; and *mediated diffusion*, which relies on the intermediation of third parties acting as translators or brokers among actors who might otherwise have no contact with one another or recognize their mutual interests.

All three processes of diffusion could be seen in the adoption of the discourse of sexual harassment in Western Europe:

- *Direct diffusion:* as in the diffusion of the New Left from the United States to Europe in the 1960s and 1970s (McAdam and Rucht 1993), there were both formal and informal personal ties between feminists in the United States and Western Europe. "Women labor unionists, activists involved in anti-violence movements, (pro-) feminist labor experts, and academic women diffused the concept in international conferences throughout the 1980s" (Zippel 2006: 87). Activists in Europe also borrowed strategies, such as consciousness raising, documenting harassment through surveys, and mobilizing protests around specific incidents (88);
- *Indirect diffusion:* Although women in Europe and America were reading the same books on violence against women (Zippel 2006: 88), in a period

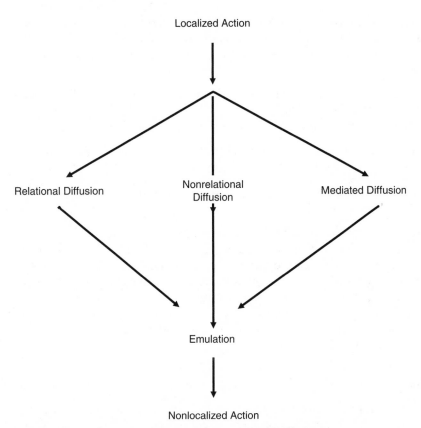

FIGURE 10.6. Alternative Routes to Transnational Diffusion.
Source: Adapted from Tarrow, *New National Transnational Activism*, ch. 1 © 2005 Sidney Tarrow. Reprinted with permission of Cambridge University Press.

in which the Internet had not yet come into its own, word of American reforms came mainly through the mainstream media. The problem was that these were either hostile or indifferent to sexual harassment. The Clarence Thomas case was emblematic: although it brought home the dangers of sexual harassment to many women in Europe it could also be used to show how "unreasonable" American women were on an issue that could be painted as "boys will be boys."

- *Mediated diffusion:* This pathway turns out to have been the most important. The lack of general receptivity to the discourse of sexual harassment in Europe left open a leading role for elite institutions – and particularly to the European Union. Alongside its general neoliberal stance on market issues, the EU – and, in particular, the European Commission – took a progressively liberal stance on rights, and, in particular, on gender equality (Alter and Vargas 2000; Caporaso and Jupille 2001; Cichowski

2001).[10] This involved a process of upward and then downward organizing as feminists first organized nationally, then transnationally, before the EU passed its 2002 directive and nudged its national members to adjust to it.

In her work on the diffusion of the sexual harassment frame, Conny Roggeband shows how two causal mechanisms – brokerage and scale shift – affected the reception and adaptation of sexual harassment in Europe. She writes;

> The example of the way sexual harassment became a central issue across Europe serves to demonstrate how diffusion is a political process in which actors at different levels adopt and adapt foreign examples to make national and transnational claims and change institutional legal settings, build alliances, and exert pressure. (2010: 22)

In particular, Roggeband points to a shift in the scale of feminist discourse to the European Union and to the "brokerage" role of the EU in spurring feminists in the various European countries to push for regulatory changes that recognized sexual harassment as an offense in their respective countries (29–31). The words *sexual harassment* carried emotional freight, but it was the intervention of a powerful and unifying force like the EU that spurred feminists in these countries to adopt and adapt a term that many had at first thought of as foreign through strategic modularity.

Conclusions

In this chapter, I have tried to extend the study of social movement outcomes to the invention and diffusion of new contentious language. I have also tried to merge the cultural approach to symbolic meanings with a perspective – strategic modularity – that comes from the political process tradition of social movement research. This combination of perspectives has helped to address a few specific questions:

- Why did *shantytown* fail to diffuse to other campaigns and movements? Because its symbolism was too closely tied to the anti-Apartheid movement and could not be adapted symbolically to more domestic issues.
- Why did the boycott spread from Ireland to England and America and beyond when the word *boycott* meant no more than a man's name? Because of its strategic modularity.
- And why did *male chauvinist* fall out of favor among feminists? Because it was better at capturing the boorish behavior of aggressive sexual partners than it was in mobilizing women politically.

---

[10] The commitment of members of the commission to sanctioning sexual harassment was no doubt through conviction but also because the commission "had been looking for issues that would consolidate its power and influence and help establish its profile as an active policy-maker" (Zippel 2006: 91).

- Why did *strike* spread so rapidly from England to other industrializing countries in Northern and Central Europe? Because of both its resonance and its strategic modularity.
- And why did *sexual harassment* diffuse so rapidly to the Anglo-American democracies and more slowly to Western Europe? Because activists in the first set of countries had a common law system they could use to make single claims directly and have them stick through precedent, while the latter had to depend on the slow-moving wheels of parliamentary politics and on downward scale shift from the European Union.

Several questions need to be tackled if we are to add the effect of contention on language to the study of movement outcomes: first, methodologically, is there a tension between the broad but thin cross-national approach I have used in this chapter and the thick but narrower ethnographic methods that would be necessary to understand the mechanisms that lead to the survival and diffusion of contentious language? Second, why are some terms that emerge from activist language eventually normalized into popular culture, while others are not? Third, *whose* language should we study? We may get different results depending on whether we look at the etymology of official terms for contention or at the language of popular culture. Finally, the biggest question is: "what role does language itself play in the survival and diffusion of a contentious practice? Wouldn't people have learned to strike, to boycott, to march and demonstrate, in the absence of these particular words for these forms of contentious action? Would some other term than *male chauvinist* have arisen for sexual aggression in the women's movement had that term not been available? And wouldn't the diffusion of the norm of gender equality have produced the practice of condemning sexually unwanted behavior even if the term *sexual harassment* had not been available?

These are questions that go to the heart of our understanding of the relationship between language and behavior. What I have tried to show in this chapter is that the repertoire of contention is both culturally and politically embedded; that the effects of contentious politics go well beyond their policy outcomes; and that language should matter more than it does in the study of contentious politics.

What's in a word? Plenty!

V

TRANSNATIONAL CONTENTION

Rooted Cosmopolitans and Transnational Activists

For many years, mainstream social movement scholars focused predominantly on contention within national boundaries. This was not an error: the social movement as a form developed in lock step with the development of the modern state (Tarrow 2011a: ch. 4; Tilly 1984). Even so, many of our predecessors saw political contention in global terms. When Marx and Engels called for workers of the world to unite, it was against what they saw as a global capitalist system; When Lenin wrote *Imperialism, the Highest Stage of Capitalism*, it was to point to the economic bases of colonial expansion (1977); and when Gramsci called for Italian communists to "do what they did in Russia," it was because he saw the peasants of the *Mezzogiorno* as part of the same world system as the Russian peasants who revolted in 1917 (Gramsci 1963).

The Marxists' successors in the world system school made the same transnational connection. They argued that the global reach of modern capitalism was producing exploitation, and thus resistance, in both the periphery and the semiperiphery of the globe (Arrighi ed. 1985). Like them, the Latin American *dependencia* school saw peripheral capitalism – and therefore the states of the global South – as servants of the interests of core capitalists and the states that served their interests. In contrast, mainstream social movement scholars – this author included – focused centrally on contention within the gates of national boundaries and gave little attention to contention that spilled over these boundaries.

But in the last decade or so, there has been a convergence between mainstream social movement scholarship and research influenced by global models (Smith 2004; 2007). In the areas of human rights, peace, the environment, development, and women's rights, both scholars and activists have been pushing against the territorial limitations of the "social movement school." Inspired by such writers as Margaret Keck and Kathryn Sikkink (1998) and by events like the Seattle WTO protest and the World Social Forum, these authors have

This chapter draws mainly on chapter 2 in my *New Transnational Activism*, Cambridge University Press, 2005.

concentrated on the role of "activists beyond borders" in forging links between North and South in the world system, and between social movements and international institutions and organizations.

When the new transnational activism first appeared in the 1990s there was enthusiasm among activists and scholars that it might be ushering in a new and expanded "global civil society." But increasingly, both groups began to appreciate the interactions between "the local" and the "global." But because of their structuralist cast, few of these studies paid attention to the individuals who transition between the local and the global – what I will call in this chapter, *rooted cosmopolitans* (but see Walgrave and Rucht eds. 2010). I will argue that these people do not permanently exit the gates of national politics. Many of them use the resources and opportunities of their national contexts on behalf of their transnational activities; others internalize international issues and conflicts into domestic politics; while still others are active at both the local and the global levels. It would reify what these individuals do to consider them all as part of "global social movements." Even as they navigate in transnational space, many of them are guided by domestic interests and values. The following example from the last century will introduce this broad group of people and tell my readers why I am so interested in the phenomenon of "rooted cosmopolitanism."

An Immigrant Activist

It is 1920 in the port of Hamburg, when a young man boards the steamer *Leviathan*, bound for New York City. Moishke Tarabeur has left his family's *shtetl* in what was then in Poland and is now part of Belarus, for life in the New World. Kletsk is one of thousands of mostly Jewish settlements between Warsaw and Moscow that has been caught in the war between Poland and the new Soviet state, only settled when the border was established just east of town. It has a flourishing cattle trade, but not yet the local shoe factory that would grow out of it under Soviet rule. Its 3,000-odd Jews worship in seven synagogues, alongside Catholic and Orthodox churches and a mosque for the Tatar minority. In the chaos and economic crisis that followed World War I, there were few sources of employment for young people and virtually no public services. Like thousands of others, Moishke has left home to escape poverty, disorder, and the antisemitism that invariably follows breakdowns of authority in this part of the world.

In 1928, by now naturalized with the "American" name of Morris, he travels home to see his family and seek a bride. He carries with him remittances for family members and money from his New York fraternal organization, the Kletzker Young Men's Benevolent Association (KYMBA), to provide the town with a health clinic. Greeted like a prince by his neighbors and friends, he stays on for nine months. By the time he leaves, the clinic is up and running and he returns to New York with a sheaf of photos to show his *landsmen* the medical marvels that their hard-earned cash has brought their home town.

Morris's activism on behalf of his *shtetl* doesn't end with transferring remittances from New York to Kletsk. In the 1930s, he becomes an officer of the

KYMBA. Soon after, working as a candy salesman, he becomes active in his labor union, the Teamsters, and then in organizations working to get Jews out of Europe before Hitler's hordes descend on them. At war's end he works with international aid agencies to locate Kletzker survivors in Europe's DP camps. By the late 1940s, he is collecting money to resettle displaced persons in Palestine and, by gradual extension, to fund the illegal arms purchases that will help to establish the state of Israel. Morris never thinks of himself as an activist, but as the global context changes from Jewish emigration to war and genocide to national renewal, my father imperceptibly transforms into what I call a "rooted cosmopolitan."

Rooted Cosmopolitanism

Rooted cosmopolitanism? What can this apparently contradictrory term mean? It is one that Ghanaian/British philosopher, Kwame Anthony Appiah, adopted about his own father, when he wrote that "The favorite slander of the narrow nationalist against us cosmopolitans is that we are rootless. What my father believed in, however, was a rooted cosmopolitanism, or, if you like, a cosmopolitan patriotism" (1996: 22). "In a final message my father left for me and my sisters," Appiah recalls, "he wrote, 'Remember you are citizens of the world.'" But as a leader of the independence movement in what was then the Gold Coast, he never saw a conflict between local partialities and a universality – between being part of the place you are from and a part of a broader human community (Appiah 2006: xviii).

Cosmopolitanism is not new, but its spread has been accelerated, in our era, by increasing connections across borders and by the enhanced capacities of citizens to mobilize both within and outside their own societies. In this chapter, I will argue – with Appiah – that true cosmopolitanism results, not from universal unity of views but from a *conversation* between people with different views (2006: xxi). I will then illustrate the phenomenon with findings from labor activists, global justice activists, and immigrants like my father, to both show how transnational activism has developed and explore its ambivalences and contradictions.

The Debate over Cosmopolitanism

> **Cosmopolitan,** *a.* 1. belonging to all parts of the world; not restricted to any one country or its inhabitants; 2. Having the characteristics which arise from, or are suited to, a range over many different countries; free from national limitations or attachments (*OED* 1999);
>
> **Rootless,** *a.* Without roots; destitute of roots (*OED* 1999);
>
> **Rootless cosmopolitan** ("bezrodny kosmopolit") was a Russian euphemism during Joseph Stalin's anti-Semitic campaign of 1948–1953, which culminated in the "exposure" of the "Doctors' plot."[1]

---

[1] From http://en.wikipedia.org/wik/Rootless_cosmopolitan.

Cosmopolitanism has had a bad press over the last century because it was used to justify purges of Jewish citizens by Stalin. But it was given a positive twist with philosopher Jeremy Waldron's 1992 article "Minority Cultures and the Cosmopolitan Alternative."[2] In this article, Waldron praised cosmopolitans as individuals who do not take their cultural identities to be defined by any bounded subset of the cultural resources available in the world (108). David Held vaunted the cosmopolitan in the same spirit as Waldron in his *Democracy and the Global Order* (1995). Yasemin Soysal followed in a similar vein in her book on "postnational citizenship" where she argued that universal rules are emerging to govern the status of immigrants" (1994). Martha Nussbaum brought the discussion to the United States with her essay "Patriotism and Cosmopolitanism" in 1996. Soon after, Stuart Hall saw cosmopolitanism as "the ability to stand outside of having one's life written and scripted by any one community" (2002: 26), while Craig Calhoun saw it as part of the advance of global democracy (2002: 90). On both sides of the Atlantic, scholars tended to define the term "cosmopolitan" cognitively, arguing, for the most part, that world citizenship should become the focus of civic education (1996: 11).

From Cognitive to Relational Cosmopolitans

It is not surprising that philosophers would adopt a cognitive definition of cosmopolitanism. Even Appiah defines it as "the idea that we have obligations to others, obligations that stretch beyond those to whom we are related by the ties of kith and kind, or even the more formal ties of a shared citizenship." He adds to it the complementary idea "we take seriously the value not just of human life but of particular human lives (2006: xv). But anthropologist Ulf Hannerz also defines cosmopolitanism cognitively when he writes that "interspersed among the most committed nationals, in patterns not always equally transparent, are a growing number of people of more varying experiences and connections. Some of them may wish to redefine the nation ... others again are in the nation but not part of it" (1996: 90).

After the turn of the century, as Europeans became concerned with plugging the holes in their borders and Americans were consumed with the threat of terrorism, the cosmopolitan debate subsided. Among mass publics and elites, empirical studies began to show a hardening of patriotic sentiments and a growing suspicion of immigrants. We see this in extreme form in the xenophobic movements and parties that gained ground in Western Europe (Rydgren 2004) and in the growing tide of anti-immigrant legislation in the American states. We also see it in the stubborn resistance of citizens of the EU to regard themselves as members of broader collectivities (Jung 2009). And we see it in the anti-Muslim mentality that has taken hold of people whose ideas of Muslims were shaped by the image of the falling towers of the World Trade Center and the London bombings of 2005.

---

[2] A good introduction will be found in Vertovec and Cohen, eds., 2002, and especially in Hollinger's chapter in that book.

But there may be a second reason for the decline in the debate about cosmopolitanism: in its focus on cosmopolitan *attitudes*, the debate failed to place cosmopolitans in their social and political contexts.[3] It is not that cosmopolitanism has no cognitive elements, but that cosmopolitan identities, like other identities, are the product of social *relations*. As James G. March and Johan P. Olson write:

> The emergence, development, and spread of understandings, identities, interests, and institutions *are shaped by interaction and involvement in political activities*. Interdependence, interaction, and communication lead to *shared experiences* and hence to shared meaning, to a convergence of expectations and policies, and to the *development of common institutions*. (1999: 319, emphasis added)

Appiah too moved toward a more relational concept of cosmopolitanism when he wrote, in his 2006 book, that "the model I'll be returning to is that of conversation – and, in particular, conversation between people from different ways of life (2006: xxi).

These views approached the relational view put forward by Robert Merton decades earlier. In his classical essay on types of influentials, Merton had written that the difference in basic orientation (i.e., cognition) between locals and cosmopolitans is bound up with the *structures of social relations* in which each type is implicated (1957: 394–395, emphasis added). It is through peoples' relations to significant others that cosmopolitan attitudes are shaped, and this takes us to the concept of "rooted" cosmopolitanism.

It was Mitchell Cohen, writing in *Dissent* in 1992, who first used the term *rooted cosmopolitanism* in a positive sense. Reacting against both marxism's "abstract proletarian internationalism" and the parochialism of advocates of "difference," Cohen called for "the fashioning of a dialectical concept of *rooted* cosmopolitanism, which accepts a multiplicity of roots and branches and that rests on the legitimacy of plural loyalties, of standing in many circles, but with common ground" (480, 483). What is "rooted" in this concept is that, as individuals move outside their spatial origins, they continue to be linked to place, to the social networks that inhabit that space, and to the resources, experiences and opportunities that place provides them. In the business world, in international organizations and institutions, in the "epistemic communities" that link professionals across borders, and in transgovernmental networks, we are finding more and more individuals whose primary ties are domestic but who are part of a complex international society. Some are normatively invested in

---

[3] For example, from a story in the *International Herald Tribune*, Hannerz tells of market women from Nigeria who board London-bound planes wearing loose-fitting gowns under which they hang dried fish to sell to their countrymen in Britain. "On the return trip," he points out, "they carry similarly concealed bundles of frozen fish sticks, dried milk, and baby clothes, all of which are in great demand in Lagos." "Is this cosmopolitanism?" asks Hannerz, and answers his question in the negative, because these market women continue to *think of themselves* as locals (1990: 238; 1996: 102–103, italics added).

international regimes and practices; others take advantage of them for primarily self-interested motives; but most rely on domestic resources and opportunities to launch their transnational activities and return home afterward. This is the pattern we will find among transnational activists.

Transnational Activists

Transnational activists I define as *individuals and groups who mobilize domestic and international resources and opportunities to advance claims on behalf of external actors, against external opponents, or in favor of goals they hold in common with transnational allies.* The unusual character of the contemporary period is not that it has detached individuals from their societies and set them loose elsewhere – think of Karl Marx; think of Mikhael Bakunin – but that it has produced a stratum of people who, in their lives and their activities, combine the resources and opportunities of their societies with membership in transnational networks and engage in activism beyond borders. These include such groups as:

- immigrants involved regularly in transnational political activities, but not all immigrants (Portes 2000: 265);
- labor activists from the South who forge ties with foreign unionists and NGOs, but not all workers (Anner et al. 2004; Waterman 2001);
- ecologists who gravitate around international institutions and organizations, but not all ecologists (Rohrschneider and Dalton 2002);
- religious activists who do missionary or service work in other countries, but not all religious activists;
- and members of transnational advocacy networks who link domestic activists to international institutions, but not all activists (Keck and Sikkink 1998).
- Transnational links have also produced "a dark side": clandestine cells of militants who attack citizens and institutions in the name of religion, and who trade in human beings across borders (Mendelson 2005).

Transnational activists, for the most part, are better educated than most of their compatriots, better connected, speak more languages, and travel more often (Appiah 2006: 79). They do not usually begin their careers at the international level but emerge from domestic political or social activities; only a small percentage ever become full-time international advocates or activists. Most return to their domestic activities, perhaps transformed by their experiences, but perhaps not. What makes them different than their domestic counterparts is their ability to shift between different scales of activity and take advantage of the expanded nodes of opportunity in a complex international society. In fact, it is best to see rooted cosmopolitans not as a distinct class of activists but as a loosely coupled network lodged both in national and in transnational space (Hadden 2011; Keck and Sikkink 1998).

A Diffusing Phenomenon

Although the data on the numbers of transnational activists are hard to assemble, there appears to have been a tremendous growth in their numbers over the last few decades. Fragmentary and incomplete evidence suggests that their numbers mushroomed in the late 1990s and the early years of the new century and – at least in the United States – declined somewhat as attention turned to domestic politics (Hadden and Tarrow 2007; Heaney and Rojas 2011). In Europe, transnational activism may also have leveled off, at least judging from the decline in the number of large transnational countersummits after the turn of the century.

We do possess solid data on the number of transnationally organized advocacy groups listed in the Yearbook of International Associations (YIA). Within that broad population, Jackie Smith's studies identified a subset of groups that were founded to promote some form of social or political change. The population of these transnational social movement organizations (TSMOs) "expanded at a tremendous rate over recent decades from fewer than 100 organizations in the 1950s to more than 1,000 today" [at the turn of the new century] (Smith, Wiest, and Eterovi 2004), as Table 11.1 shows.

Smith and Wiest found that through the turn of the new century, participation in TSMOs varied dramatically between the industrial countries of the North and the less-developed countries of the South. Western Europeans were active in more than 80 percent of these groups, and citizens of the United States and Canada participated in nearly 70 percent of them. On the other hand, although participation from the global South grew during the 1980s and 1990s, the countries of the South are still less present than northerners in the transnational social movement sector, according to Smith, Wiest, and Eterovi's findings (2004: 3). Despite the concentration of many TNGOs on the problems of the global South, there is still a net advantage for the richer, more well-connected citizens of the North, where resources are more plentiful and the core of international institutions are found.

The different sectors of transnational advocacy have almost all expanded over the last half-century, but at an uneven rate. Smith and Wiest's findings

TABLE 11.1. *Size and Geographic Dispersion of Transnational Social Movement Organizations*

Year	Number of TSMOs		Number of Countries in Memberships	
	# Orgs.	% Change	Mean (std. dev.)	Median
1973	183	–	33.89 (23.17)	28
1983	348	90%	31.02 (26.03)	23
1993	711	104%	33.13 (29.55)	23
2000 (observed)	959	35%	34.39 (32.46)	23
2003 (estimate)	1011	42%		

Sources: Smith, Wiest, and Eterovi 2004.

provide a good partial summary.[4] Human rights TSMOs listed in the Yearbook of International Associations increased in number from 41 in the 1973 YIA to 247 in 2000; environmental groups grew from 17 to 126 in the same period; peace groups from 21 to 98; while groups dedicated to self-determination and ethnic unity grew much more slowly (Smith 2004:16). The biggest percentage increases were found in what they call "development/empowerment" groups, which increased from 4 percent to 10 percent of the total over the three decades, and in multiissue groups, which increased from 7 percent to 15 percent over the same year period. A related trend was the rapid growth of groups organizing around a broad "global justice/peace/environmental" agenda, which grew from 4 percent of the total in 1973 to 11 percent in 2000 (Ibid.).

When scholars first began to take notice of transnational activism and advocacy in the 1990s, their major emphasis was on the "principled belief groups" who worked together on sectors like the environment, peace and justice, feminism, and human rights (Keck and Sikkink 1998; Risse-Kappen ed. 1995; Risse, Ropp, and Sikkink 1999). But if I am correct, and if global integration is as great as most observers think, the phenomenon of transnational activism is much broader than the boundaries of those who work on behalf of universal liberal norms. Two examples will help us to get a better picture of the wide range of transnational activism and advocacy in the world today.

Working Transnationals

When transnational activism first became an object of study in the 1990s, organized labor had "not been seen as a promising candidate for becoming a transnational social movement" (Evans 2005: 660). In contrast with this pessimistic view, Peter Evans finds three important ways in which unionists participate in transnational politics: by seeking basic rights, social contracts, and democratic governance (661–663). Some of these labor activists have become permanently active internationally, but others continue to operate on native ground on behalf of workers from elsewhere and in the name of global worker solidarity.

Working transnationalism shows how quite ordinary people can move back and forth between the local and the translocal among a variety of (not-necessarily compatible) identities. Nathan Lillie found such a group when he studied the "Flag of Convenience" campaign of the International Transport Workers' Federation (ITF). FOCs are flags flown on ships that sail under the registries of countries like Liberia that turn a blind eye to the labor conditions of their

---

[4] I say "partial" because we could not expect all transnational social change organizations to be registered in the Yearbook of International Associations. For an example from the human rights sector, see Evelyn Bush's careful analysis of human rights records in her "Measuring Religion in Global Civil Society," *Social Forces* 2007. Even so, we can assume that if there are unsampled organizations in the YIA data, we have no reason to expect the level of sampling error to have changed over time, so Smith and Wiest's figures on the rates of change in TNGOs are probably reliable.

seamen. FOC practices are the most effective way of causing a "race to the bottom" in employment conditions. But the ITF has stopped this race to the bottom, through the interaction between capital and organized labor and has improved conditions for a significant proportion of the seafaring workforce" (2006: 1).[5]

Also related to maritime commerce were the dockworkers who crossed the globe from Liverpool to California and from Sydney to Yokohama after they were bounced from their jobs in Liverpool by a port authority that wanted to bring in nonunion workers. Antonina Gentile has traced the peregrinations of these dockworkers and shown how they and their wives helped to mobilize their comrades around the globe against a ship that was refused unloading rights all over the globe (Gentile 2010). Gentile's work also shows how temporary "wildcat" groups intersect with more permanent labor NGOs, like the International Transport Federation, to defend labor's rights.

A third example of working transnationals are the Canadian, American, and Mexican unionists who – under the umbrella of the North American Free Trade Agreement (NAFTA) – have brought cases against management to special courts if the country of origin of the companies they work for, in cooperation with unions in that country. Through the treaty that binds the trade of the three countries, a North American Agreement on Labor Cooperation (NAALC) was signed.[6] In her research, Tamara Kay has shown that, while the policy success of NAALC has been modest, the process has brought together unionists of the three countries in cooperative relationships (Kay 2011). They remain "rooted" in their respective industrial relations systems but with transnational ties, understandings, and a greater confidence that they are not alone against the pressures of international capitalism.

Global Justice Activists

No grouping could be further in either spirit or tactics from these working transnationals than the new generation of global justice activists whose protests began to gather force after the "Battle of Seattle" in 1999. Yet here too, we find both transnational coordination and a deeply local rooting of transnational activism. Although Seattle was widely trumpeted as an incident in the struggle of the "South" against the "North," in fact most of the protesters who assembled there came from the American or Canadian Northwest and by far the largest proportion were unionists seeking protection for their jobs (Lichbach 2003). When Gillian Murphy and Margaret Levi traced the coalition that planned the Seattle protests, they found that the core of the participant

---

[5] The ITF uses a variety of strategies in its campaign, but the most interesting from the point of view of rooted cosmopolitanism is the use of a network of local union "inspectors" who have "transnationalized" the FOC campaign network tying rank-and-file port workers and local union officials directly into a global strategy to enforce a uniform global minimum wage scale on FOC vessels (Lillie 2006: ch. 4).

[6] Go to http://www.worldtradelaw.net/nafta/naalc.pdf for the terms of the NAALC agreement.

cadre was drawn from among activists who had worked together in domestic protests in the northwestern United States (Levi and Murphy 2006).

Donatella della Porta and her collaborators also found a deep domestic rooting of the Italian activists they interviewed during two major transnational protest campaigns.[7] They found a widespread rooting of these participants in the traditional sectors of Italian activism: a trade union background was reported by between 19 and 26 percent of them; political party alignment was claimed by roughly one-third; religious activism by between 18 and 20 percent; volunteers by between 41 and 49 percent and student activism by between 52 and 56 percent. These "transnational" activists came largely from familiar sectors of domestic politics and associations (Rieter et al. 2007: 66).

Both working transnationals and global justice activists take part in transnational activities but are rooted in domestic forms of activism and usually return to these activities in between their transnational experiences. They may become participants in enduring transnational coalitions and movement organizations or they may not; their "global identities" may be costumes put on during occasional external forays or may become a permanent part of their identities (della Porta 2004). But we are witnessing to an increasing extent the formation of a broad spectrum of activists who face both inward and outward and combine domestic and transnational forms of activism and advocacy. This can be well illustrated by those whose participation in "movements" results from their personal movement from their countries of origin to new host communities – immigrant activists. They will also illustrate what I earlier called the "dark side" of rooted cosmopolitanism.

Transnational Immigrant Communities

How has our more densely internationalized world affected the most familiar form of transnational movement – immigrants? Like my father in the 1940s, and like transnational activists in general, immigrant activists live in two worlds – in their case, the world of their adopted countries and that of their homelands. This has always been the case and, in describing them, we can draw on a century of evidence about a truly global phenomenon. But we also observe a dramatic expansion in immigrant transnationalism, from the traditional practice of sending remittances to home countries – remember the money my father carried back to Kletsk at the beginning of this chapter? – to participation in electoral politics to diasporic nationalism. And in the relationship of the latter to the more traditional forms of immigrant politics we will see the ambivalences and contradictions in transnational activism, for while most immigrant activists become "nesting pigeons" who increasingly integrate into their host countries, others are "birds of passage" who use them to provide cover for more lethal activities.

---

[7] These were the 2001 Genoa W-7 protest and the 2002 European Social Forum.

Back to History

In 1906, in language that was strikingly similar to what we hear today from advocates of postnational citizenship, Gino Speranza, an Italian official charged with the protection of this country's immigrants abroad, wrote the following: "The old barriers are everywhere breaking down. We may even bring ourselves to the point of recognizing foreign 'colonies' in our midst, on our own soil, as entitled to partake in the parliamentary life of their mother country" ([1906] 1974: 310).[8]

Speranza's hope for the recognition of foreign "colonies" in America was dashed by the First World War and by the restrictive immigration legislation that followed it, but it reminds us that immigrant transnationalism is not new. Like representatives of Mexican immigrants in the United States today, Speranza wanted the Italo-American "colony" in America to be represented in their home country's legislature; between Italian ports and New York and Buenos Aires there was constant back-and-forth traffic – as there is today between North American cities and the Caribbean; and immigrant remittances were responsible for supporting many southern Italian families and communities, as they do today in villages in Mexico. Immigrant transnationalism is nothing new.

But a host of factors make the connections among immigrants and their home countries more frequent and more integrated today than when Speranza wrote at the beginning of the last century. First of all, there was an epochal change in the state system between the beginning of the First World War and the mid-1920s. Where the bulk of pre-World War One immigrants came from the subject states of the great European empires – Habsburg, Prussian, Romanov – after the Versailles treaty that followed, nearly everyone had at least an imagined nation-state and, as a result, immigrant activism took on a radically new color. The League of Nations was a politically impoverished institution, but its title reflected this new reality quite accurately. Henceforth, immigrants would think of themselves in their new homes in connection to states that reflected their national origins, and not in terms of the empires to which they had been subjected.[9]

The post–World War II world added a host of new nation-states to those that were created after 1918 and did away with whatever vestiges of the imperial world had survived the war. Technological change, cheap air fares, and simplified electronic communication have been trumpeted as evidence of a new global village, but these are but the surface manifestations of new forms of economic and political integration. These include segmented production networks,

---

[8] I am grateful to Nancy Foner for calling this quotation to my attention and for her sensitive reflections on the old and the new immigrant transnationalism in her "Transnationalism Then and Now" (2001). Note that Speranza used the term *colony* in the sense of immigrant communities, not that of colonized societies by foreign states.

[9] I am grateful to Benedict Anderson for reminding me of this difference – obvious to me only after he had pointed it out.

diasporic investment in home country enterprises, and, of course, mass migration. If the number of migrants does not match the migrations from southern and eastern Europe of the late nineteenth and early twentieth centuries, the ties between home country and country of adoption are more likely to remain close; in many countries this includes dual nationality and home-country voting by immigrant communities (Foner 2001; Graham 2001). Where Speranza's Italian immigrants rarely returned to Naples or Catania – and when they did they most often stayed there – their successors from Santo Domingo or Mumbai can hop on a plane to see to their business interests at home or monitor their childrens' upbringing (Foner 2001: 42–43).

David Kyle (1999) describes the effects of these structural changes on a traditional clothing production area in highland Equador. Since its occupation by Spain, the region of Otavalo has specialized in the production and marketing of clothing. Now increased international trade and cheaper and easier international mobility have transformed it. As Alejandro Portes summarizes Kyle's thesis,

> During the last quarter of a century or so, Otavalans have taken to traveling abroad to market their colorful wares in major cities of Europe and North America. By so doing, they have also brought home a wealth of novelties from the advanced countries, including newcomers to their town. (Portes 2000: 260)

These transnational travelers are what we can call "nesting pigeons" because, though staying in one place, they combine the resources and opportunities they find at either end of migration chains. But others are what I call "birds of passage" whose residence in the diaspora serves as cover or ammunition for foreign forays. Both are "rooted" cosmopolitans, in the sense that their activism depends on links to both their home countries and their diaspora enclaves; but while "nesting pigeons" direct their efforts at the improvement of their home communities, "birds of passage" use the resources of receiving societies to subvert their home governments or aim their challenges at abstractions like "Western secularism" or concrete targets like the World Trade Center.

Nesting Pigeons

Transnational systems of exchange offer nesting pigeons incentives and resources to become politically active with their home countries as their targets. For example, in Los Angeles, Portes and his collaborators interviewed a Mr. Gonzalez, president of a civic committee of a small town in El Salvador. When asked why he intended to stay in Los Angeles in the face of discrimination and nativism, Gonzalez replied:

> I really live in El Salvador, not in LA. When we have the regular *fiestas* to collect funds for La Esperanza, I am the leader and I am treated with respect. When I go back home to inspect the works paid with our contributions I am as important as the mayor. (Portes 1999: 466)

How widespread is this pattern of transnational activism within immigrant communities, and what are its political implications? Because much of the evidence we have is ethnographic, it is difficult to generalize from it. But one source of systematic information does exist: a comparative study of the causes and consequences of the emergence of transnational communities among Colombian, Dominican, and Salvadoran immigrants in the United States in the 1990s.[10] Looking at "both electoral and nonelectoral activities aimed at influencing conditions in the home country ... on a regular basis," Luis Guarnizo and his collaborators report from this study that less than one-sixth of the three immigrant groups they studied are "core" transnational activists, while another one-sixth engage in such activities on an occasional basis (2003: 1225).

Are these proportions significant or trivial? Seen as a percentage of the enormous immigrant populations of New York, Los Angeles, Toronto, or London, they may seem derisory. But in the light of the shrinking proportion of civic involvement in these societies, they are impressive. Particularly in the United States, where participation in national elections has been steadily shrinking and citizens increasingly avoid involvement in politics, that one-sixth of struggling Columbians, Dominicans, and Salvadorans would engage regularly in homeland-directed political activities, and an additional sixth do so from time to time, seems highly significant for their home countries.

Who are these activists? The authors' findings help us to both recognize the stability of immigrant transnationalism and delimit its boundaries:

- First, home country context correlates closely with immigrant transnational activism in predictable ways. Reflecting their unstable and violent country, Colombian immigrants are least likely to take part in home country politics, while Salvadorans and Dominicans, coming from more stable political backgrounds, are more likely to do so (Ibid.: 1232).
- Second, the size of individuals' networks and their expectation that they will one day return to their homelands is significantly associated with political transnationalism (Ibid.).
- Third, "core transnationals are overwhelmingly married males, with high school or college education, and more, rather than less length of U.S. residence" (1238).

If we can generalize from these findings, it is not the least educated, the more marginal, or the most recent arrivals who are prone to become "nesting pigeons"; on the contrary, it is those who are most solidly rooted in their receiving societies. If this is the case, then not only the political context of

---

[10] The three-country study was directed by Alejandro Portes and Luis Eduardo Guarnizo. Between 1996 and 2000, they and their collaborators carried out three phases of data collection in Colombia, the Dominican Republic, and El Salvador. For each of the three target populations, data collection was carried out in two North American settlement cities and in the country of origin, using the same set of survey instruments and sampling designs in both cases. For the products of the project to date, see the website of the Center for Migration and Development at Princeton at http://cmd.princeton.edu/papers.html.

their countries of origin, but the opportunities and incentives of their places of arrival, condition the nature and possibilities of transnational activism (Waldinger and Fitzgerald 2004). For example, New York's fragmented and ethnically organized local politics offers far more opportunities and fewer constraints to Dominican immigrants in that city than, say, Los Angeles' more concentrated system does for Mexicans.[11]

The forms of exchange that immigrants engage in with their homelands are mainly traditional: sending remittances for public works projects. But immigrants increasingly support candidates for local office at home, lobby Mexican state governments to allocate resources to their communities, and engage in more collective forms of politics in their countries of origin. For example, there is evidence that Mexican community organizations in the United States are beginning to unite at the [Mexican] state level (R. Smith 2003). This is producing powerful regional pressure groups, based on immigrants' resources from north of the border, capable of negotiating with state governments on behalf of their home towns.

Transnational activists engage in more contentious forms of politics as well. When Mixtec leaders were arrested in Oaxaca, *Radio Bilingue* in Fresno, California, put pressure on the Mexican government. "If something happens in Oaxaca," declared a local organizer; "we can put protesters in front of the consulates in Fresno, Los Angeles, Madera" (Portes 1999: 474). Since the passage of NAFTA (the North American Free Trade Agreement), solidarity groups in Texas and California work to help workers in Mexican factories to fight exploitation, improve health conditions, and organize workers in the *maquiladora* factories (Williams 2003: 532–536). And in Western Europe there is growing evidence that immigrant groups are organizing to use their local resources to intervene in the politics of their home countries.[12]

But there is a gap between "core transnationals" – the one-third who are regularly involved in political contacts with their home countries – and the rest of the immigrant population, who are only occasionally involved in these practices. Core transnationals tend to engage in routine or contained immigrant politics, much of it oriented to improving the lives of their conationals who remained at home; peripheral transnationals are less routinely involved.

What explains the gap? Guarnizo and his collaborators speculate that the differences are due to sensitivity to contextual conditions. "While core transnationals stay involved in their home country politics via electoral or nonelectoral means, others become active only at special junctures such as highly contested elections or national disasters" (2003: 1238). Other conditions trigger diasporic nationalism among groups as diverse as Islamist radicals, Croatian

---

[11] I am grateful to Roger Waldinger for reminding me of this point in a personal communication.
[12] I make no effort here to survey the enormous literature on immigrant politics and communities in Europe. Perhaps the best-studied case is that of the Kurds. For good introductions to migrant transnationalism outside the United States, see Ostergaard-Nielsen 2001 and the papers collected in Al-Ali and Koser 2002.

nationalists, and supporters of Tamil independence. This takes us to the fundamental ambiguity in immigrant transnationalism: between the ameliorative activities of "nested pigeons" and the destructive potential of what we can call "birds of passage."

Birds of Passage

In the late 1990s, Benedict Anderson wrote worriedly of "long-distance nationalists" (1998). By this term, Anderson was referring to immigrant nationalists who mobilize resources from the diaspora to undermine their home governments. He observed that such activists – for example, Croatians in Canada, Irish in Boston, Kurds in Germany – could cheaply, easily, and without major risk to themselves incite and support violence in their countries of origin. Anderson could not have predicted the horrors that would be inflicted upon the world by the birds of passage who turned two airliners into flying bombs on September 11, 2001; but the phenomenon of long-distance religious militancy is a form of long-distance nationalism.

Systematic evidence lends support to Anderson's fears. When Paul Collier and Anke Hoeffler collected quantitative data on potential sources of the civil wars that have torn up communities across the world in the last few decades, they found no correlation with the proportion of the population living abroad – measured partially from the size of their immigrant communities in the United States. But they *did* find a robust correlation between diaspora size in the United States and "repeat conflicts" in the immigrants' home countries (2003: 2). Of course, the lethal character of diaspora nationalism does not depend on its geographic spread or on the number of immigrants living abroad. Like terrorism, with which it is often confused, diasporic nationalism is the exasperated recourse of small minorities for whom peaceful protest or mass organization are either impossible or have failed.

One source of long-distance nationalism is the odd dyslexia among diaspora nationalists between the contemporary reality of the countries they have left and their vision of the "true" homelands they cherish. Zlatko Skrbis's work on Croatian communities in Australia, for example, shows that the view of their homeland among Antipodian Croatians is at least fifty years out of date (Skrbis 1999). The same time warp, remarks Anderson, "is just as true of many American Irish, Armenians, Chinese, etc. To an amazing extent, they block out the real Ireland, Armenia, and China of the present."[13] And, we might add, the "Caliphate" of which many Islamist militants dream was nothing like the corrupt, authoritarian regimes in which they grew up.

Historical memories can distort identification with the homeland in a progressive, as well as a reactionary direction: liberal American Jews continue to support an Israel that no longer exists, both because they fear its increasingly unlikely destruction but also because they mistake the militaristic capitalist giant of today for the kibbutz society of fifty years ago. The source of much of

---

[13] In a personal communication to the author.

diaspora nationalism is identification with societies that no longer exist – or never did.[14]

Cosmopolitan Contradictions

In their radical goals and actions, the religious zealots and diaspora nationalists who have been responsible for many of the transnationally organized horrors of the new century are a world away from the benign world of the "nesting pigeons" – like my father, who send remittances to their families, invest in local enterprises, and attempt to influence elections in their home towns. But they are connected to their home countries by many of the same mechanisms. As Anderson writes:

> The Moroccan construction worker in Amsterdam can every night listen to Rabat's broadcasting services and has no difficulty in buying pirated cassettes of his country's favourite singers. The illegal alien, *Yakuza*-sponsored, Thai bartender in a Tokyo suburb shows his Thai comrades Karaoke videotapes just made in Bangkok. The Filipina maid in Hong Kong phones her sister in Manila, and sends money in the twinkling of an electronic eye to her mother in Cebu. The successful Indian student in Vancouver can keep in daily e-mail touch with her former Delhi classmates. (1998: 68)

Needless to say, it is mistaken to assume either that all immigrant transnationals are potential long-distance nationalists or that all forms of long-distance nationalism are violent. But it is striking that just as immigrant "nesting pigeons" use their ties to their home communities to foster development and keep family ties alive, "birds of passage" can cheaply, safely, and, in a self-satisfying way, "play national hero on the other side of the world" (Anderson 1998: 74).

The more aggressive forms of immigrant activism have impacts on both sending and receiving countries. On the one hand, the presence of long-distance activists in France or Italy feeds the xenophobic nationalism of a Le Pen or a Bossi. Resentful *Français de souche* (people who are French in origin: that is, white) who see young Arab women wearing the veil do not recognize it as a statement of female independence but as an unwillingness to give up the link to an unknown "other," across the Mediterranean. When middle class *Milanesi* living in an imagined *Padania* see Albanians or Moroccans sweeping the streets or washing dishes in the neighborhood pizzeria, they may be reminded of their own unregretted past in the poverty of Caltanisetta or Matera. And when well-established second-generation American immigrant groups, whose parents adapted eagerly to their receiving societies, observe the self-conscious multiculturalism of recent immigrants, it can seem a threat to their own assimilation.

---

[14] Even at the beginning of the state of Israel in 1948, less than 5 percent of the Jewish population lived on the land, and, of these, less than half lived on the *kibbutzim* with which most liberal American Jews identified. The American identification of the Jewish state with kibbutz communitarianism seems to have been in part the result of self-delusion on the part of American Jews and, in part, the result of a broad campaign of self-promotion by the Zionist cultural elite.

These mechanisms are interactive. Nativist xenophobia and diaspora extremism feed on one another; immigrant activists who sense their rejection by the indigenous population draw back from the hope of assimilation, thus fulfilling the prophecy of their antagonists that they do not wish to fit in. In turn, rejection feeds the divide within the immigrant community between those who feel themselves assimilated and those who retreat into a long-distance identity. We are witnessing this phenomenon all over Europe, as a younger generation of Islamic immigrants embraces a more radical form of Islam than their parents'.

It is in the weak and unauthoritative states of the South that we see the less visible effects of diasporic extremism. Some of the plans behind the dismantling of the Babri mosque in Ayodhya, which triggered the greatest South Indian bloodshed since partition, came from Indians living overseas; the most fanatical adherents of an independent Khalistan live in Melbourne and Chicago; "Tamilnet" links Tamil communities in Toronto, London and elsewhere to the violent struggles of the Tigers of Sri Lanka; and Croats living in Germany, Australia, and North America played "a malign role" in financing and arming Franjo Tudjman's breakaway state and pushing Germany and Austria to recognize it (Anderson 1998: 73–74).

Between nesting pigeons and birds of passage there are great differences, but there are also similarities and connections. The 9/11 killers dwelt unobserved in the Muslim community of Hamburg in the guise of nesting pigeons while awaiting the moment to zoom in on the World Trade Center and the Pentagon. In the liberal societies of the West, financial support for Croatian nationalism, Hindu xenophobia, and Islamist fundamentalism is nearly impossible to distinguish from well-meaning support for home-country charitable and educational works. The Tamil Tigers were enabled to engage in protracted insurgency against the Sri Lankan government in part through the support of the Tamil diaspora. In the complex international environment of the early twenty-first century, the activities of birds of passage are easily disguised within the routines of the nesting pigeons among whom they roost.

This does not mean that the hysterical witch hunt that was launched against the Muslim communities of the United States after September 11, 2001 is justified. Or that the veil of the Muslim schoolgirl in France is as dangerous to Republican secularism as the weapon of the suicide bomber. But it does suggest that transnational immigrant activism is multifaceted; that it often involves people with little self-conscious political intent as unconscious supporters; and that the complex internationalism of the world today no longer makes it possible to distinguish sharply between locals and cosmopolitans – at least where transnational activism is concerned. Birds of passage exist, as it were, within the gates of large, heterogeneous, and largely unknown immigrant communities.

Insiders and Outsiders

As the last section testifies, the growing population of advocacy groups and the activists who empower them is not homogeneous; some activists are "norms entrepreneurs" who attempt to diffuse deeply held beliefs to countries around the world (Keck and Sikkink 1998); others work at the international level on behalf of the "instrumental" goals of workers, women, indigenous peoples, or peasants. While some aim their activities at international institutions, others engage in service activities, and still others mediate between these levels. Cross-cutting these forms and trajectories of activism are two main types: some activists are classical "insiders," advocating before international institutions and taking part in highly-institutionalized service activities; while others are social movement "outsiders" who challenge these institutions and organizations (Hadden 2011).

In some sectors, NGO advocates and movement activists operate autonomously and may have little or no contact with one another. For example, advocates for conservation and radical ecologists know of one another's existence but operate at different levels of the polity, in relation to different opposite numbers, and using different forms of practice. In other sectors, NGOs and social movements cooperate, as they did during debates over the creation of a free trade zone of the Americas (Korzeneiwicz and Smith 2001) and, briefly, in the mobilization around the Copenhagen climate change summit in 2009 (Hadden 2011).

But in other sectors, there is fierce competition between NGO advocates and movement activists, and there are clear differences in their modes of action, forms of organization and their degree of opposition to those they challenge. We saw this most dramatically in the two groups of immigrant activists I called nesting pigeons and birds of passage; but in other groups of cosmopolitans there is as much competition and conflict as cohesion and cooperation. NGO advocates and movement activists constitute quite distinct networks that come together rarely if ever. Two such groups are the major climate change coalitions that Jennifer Hadden studied in Europe before and after the Copenhagen summit. By carrying out a detailed network analysis, Hadden showed that the Climate Action Network (CAN) and Climate Justice Now (CJN) were linked to one another by only a few threads and were divided by different modes of action, forms of organization and relations to their opposite numbers in the states and international organizations working on climate change (Hadden 2011).

Conclusions

As Hadden's work shows, there is no uniform meaning of cosmopolitanism or, more narrowly, of transnational activism. Rooted cosmopolitans are a broad stratum of individuals and groups found among many types of social actors today. Supported by technological change, by economic integration, and by cultural connections, the phenomenon of rooted cosmopolitanism expresses itself most dramatically in the ease with which young people participate in demonstrations outside their own borders, and transnational advocates navigate between London and Geneva and the vast reaches of the Global South. But when the demonstrations die down and when NGO advocates return home, more significant, but less easy to assess, are the lessons they bring to their own societies and the continued ties they have developed across borders.

While we still lack good evidence of transnational activism's magnitude or its rate of growth, we can see its importance in the expansion of the population of international NGOs; in the large number of European activists who traveled to Chiapas, to Porto Alegre and to Mumbai to militate in solidarity with peoples of the South since the turn of the new century; and in the spread of a capillary network of social actors throughout the world (Katz and Anheier 2005/2006). These grew up in the void created when the traditional Lefts declined at the start of the 1990s; but like the churches built by the early Christians on the ruins of destroyed temples, they may be the bases for new forms of cosmopolitan activism.

Some may wonder whether the revival of great power hegemony in the years since September 11, 2001 is destroying the foundations for this new transnational activism. It has certainly eroded the disposition of many to believe in a benevolent internationalist future (Tarrow 2005: ch. 11). But if, as I have argued, cosmopolitanism is relational – rather than simply cognitive – then the "conversations" that have been started across boundaries will produce more and more rooted cosmopolitans. When repression bites and public opinion turns against them – as many did in the United States after 9/11 – they will still retain the capacity to rebuild their relations across borders.

How do the activists we have encountered in this chapter navigate between "the local" and "the global" and between their home countries, other venues, and international institutions? I have said enough in this chapter to cast doubt on the narrative that a new global civil society will take the place of the society of states that we have inherited from the past. Because I don't think that state power is eroding, at least in the short run, rather than posit a "global civil society" on the march, we will do better to examine the specific processes that link the local and the global in the current period. This I will attempt to do in the final chapter, where I both criticize the dominant "strong globalization" model and examine the local/global links in the international human rights movement.

Transnational Contention and Human Rights

Behind the headlines on the war in the former Yugoslavia in the summer of 1994, a conflict roiled the waters of the Bay of Biscay. It pitted Spanish fishermen against their French and British competitors over fishing rights, with environmental issues and questions of national sovereignty in the background. As *The European* described it:

> Spanish tuna fishermen sailed home ... after a two-day battle with their French counterparts some 700 km. off Spain's northwestern coast of Galicia. The Spanish brought back a captured boat [the *Gabrielle*] they claim will support allegations that the French violate fishing quotas and methods.

Although it took an extreme form, this kind of conflict was becoming familiar in these days of depleted stocks of Atlantic fish, when massive mechanized trawlers roamed the seas, outfishing the small traditional fishing ships used by Spanish tuna men. These fishermen accused the French of using nets bigger than those permitted by European Union regulations, while the French insisted that their nets were legal and environmentalists wrung their hands at the growing threat to the world's oceans. In Paris, the government demanded the immediate restitution of the Gabrielle and sent its navy to capture a Spanish ship and tow it to a French port.[1]

As the ships of the two nations maneuvered on troubled waters, a war of words heated up between their capitals. In Madrid, the government complained at its uncontrollable fishermen and protested the state piracy carried out by the French. In Galicia, the tuna men who had made off with the *Gabrielle* were

---

[1] The sources for this account are "Spanish Fishermen Seize French Boat in Tuna War," *The European*, July 22–28, 1994, and "La armada francesa captura un barco de España en repesalia por el conflicto pesquero," *El País*, July 25, 1994.

The first part of this chapter is based on my chapter, "Fishnets, Internets, Catnets" in *Challenging Authority: The Historical Study of Contentious Politics*. edited by Michael Hanagan, Leslie Page Moch, and Wayne te Brake. Minneapolis: University of Minnesota Press, 1998, pp. 228–244. The second part is based on my "Insiders Outside and Outsiders Inside: Linking Transnational and Domestic Public Action for Human Rights." in *Human Rights Review* 11: 171–182.

convinced by their authorities to return her, while in Brussels, Spain's agriculture and fisheries minister met with his French counterpart, who agreed that EU inspectors would henceforth be allowed to initiate checks of French nets. By the end of the month, the French had agreed to limit the length of their nets to the 2.5 km. set down in the European Commission's regulations. The tuna war seemed to be over.

But a new storm soon blew up over the Bay of Biscay. Not trusting their government's willingness to defend their interests, an armada of Spanish tuna ships blockaded the ferries of the Cantabrian coast and – just for good measure – blocked the French port of Hendaye too. In early August, they were back on the high seas – this time hacking off the nets of two British boats and an Irish one, which they accused of using nets that were longer than the EU's statutory limit of 2.5 km. With typical British phlegm, Whitehall claimed that their nets were environmentally friendly: though longer than the 2.5 km. limit set by the EU, they made up for it with huge holes designed to let the dolphin through, while the apparently less intelligent tuna were caught.[2]

The conflict did not remain limited to the fishermen of the three nations. Soon the transnational environmental organization Greenpeace jumped into the fray, sending a ship to inspect the British and French nets. The French – who have a long and violent relationship with this organization – attacked its vessel with water cannon and a stun grenade, accusing Greenpeace of attempting to cut the nets of French trawlers. The activists denied it, claiming that they were only trying to record whether the French ships were taking endangered species, like dolphins.

Six months later, Spanish fishermen were back in the news, fishing for halibut outside Canada's self-declared 200-mile limit. Under pressure from the Newfoundland fishing fleet, the Canadians had declared a ban on fishing off the Grand Banks to allow badly depleted fish stocks to be renewed, but the Spanish paid them no heed. Finding a Spanish vessel just inside the 200-mile limit, the Canadian navy seized it and towed it into the harbor of St. John's, to the cheers and rotten tomatoes of the assembled fisherfolk. The Spanish responded with threatened trade sanctions if the Canadians did not desist.[3]

Given extensive coverage in all four national media, the story of the tuna wars was redolent with folkloric images: sputtering French officials, archaic Spanish ships, tight-lipped British sailors, and jeering "Fundy" fishermen. But beneath the folkloric surface of the tuna war, serious issues were at stake: the preservation of dwindling sea stocks; the protection of a Spanish industry that directly or indirectly employed 800,000 people; the power of a supranational

---

[2] "Atun contra Europa," *El País*, August 1, 1994, p. 8; and "Des chalutiers espagnols bloquent le port d'Hendaye," *Le Monde*, July 27, 1994; "Navy moves in to stop tuna war 'wolf packs,'" *London Times*, August 5, 1994, and "Los boniteros españoles rompen redes ilegales a barcos britànicos e irlandeses," *El País*, August 8, 1994.

[3] See "Canada Fishing Dispute Grows," *Manchester Guardian Weekly*, March 19, 1995; "Canadians Cut the Nets of Spain Ship," *New York Times*, March 28, 1995, and "When They Talk About Fish, the Mellow Canadians Bellow," *New York Times*, March 31, 1995.

institution – the European Commission – to interfere in people's lives; and the apparent helplessness of national governments to protect them. In the end it was the commission that produced a compromise solution. Three levels of conflict came together: transnational, international, and supranational.

Transnational Collective Action

For students of collective action and social movements, episodes like the one described previously raise important questions. On the one hand, in its repertoires, in the role of preexisting social networks and in the targeting of institutions, the tale was reminiscent of the great tradition of social movements in the West. On the other, there were new and disconcerting questions. Was this an idiosyncratic event involving marginal populations on the high seas or was it typical of the new phenomenon that social scientists were beginning to call "transnational collective action" (della Porta et al. 1999[2009]; Guidry et al. 2000; Keck and Sikkink 1998; Smith et al. 1997; Tarrow 2001, 2005)?

Already in the mid-1990s, there were episodes that suggested the need to expand the vision of social movement scholars beyond borders: in England, striking dockworkers encouraged their peers in other ports to boycott unloading a ship from Liverpool (Gentile 2010). In Mexico, a peasant rebellion gained support from sympathizers around the world and brought foreign activists to Chiapas chanting "Ya basta!" (Olesen 2005); soon "global justice" protesters from many countries would converge on Seattle and Genoa to protest the World Trade Association and the G-8 Summit; and in 2003 millions of people demonstrated against the imending invasion of Iraq (Walgrave and Rucht 2010). Was a new world of "global social movements" on the horizon?

As I pointed out in the last chapter, in the areas of human rights, peace, the environment, development, and women's rights, both scholars and activists have been pushing against the territorial limitations of the "social movement school." They have done so with the major narrative of "globalization" as a background variable. This, I will argue, says both too much and too little: too much, because globalization has contradictory effects on transnational contention; and too little, because many of the most lively episodes of transnational contention cannot be reasonably traced to globalization.

In this chapter, I examine an important sector of transnational collective action that is not traceable to globalization – human rights. Based on the intersection of two main variables – *the sites of action* and *the degree of local/ transnational interaction* – I deduce and describe four processes of transnational activism that have emerged over the past two decades. I will argue that we will make more progress by disaggregating what some have called "global social movements" into their component processes than by deducing the coming of a "global civil society" from what I will call the "strong globalization thesis."

The Strong Globalization Thesis

The reasoning behind the "strong thesis" of globalization goes something like this: Sometime around the end of World War II, assisted by the liberalization of international trade and the appearance of a new economic hegemon, the United States, a global capitalist economy began to emerge. Its most basic aspect, writes Kevin Robins, was a shift to a world "in which all aspects of the economy – raw materials, labour information and transportation, finance, distribution, marketing – are integrated or interdependent on a global scale" (1995: 345). Moreover, "they are so on an almost instantaneous basis.... The forces of globalization thereby tend to erode the integrity and autonomy of national economies" (Ibid.).

Robins' insistence on the "instantaneous" expression of integration and interdependence takes us to the second element of the thesis: the appearance of global communications structures that weave core and periphery of the world system together. Decentralized and private communications technologies accelerate this growth, providing individuals and groups with independent means of communication (Bennett 2003; Frederick 1995; Ganley 1992). The result of this growth in worldwide economics and global communications is that citizens of the North and West and those of the East and South have been brought closer together, making the former more cosmopolitan and the latter more aware of their inequality (see Chapter 11). This has made it possible for northern advocates and activists to speak the same language and work around the same goals as their counterparts in the South, and has contributed to the beginning of the formation of a "global civil society."

Scholars of social movements have become increasingly aware of the transnational processes that carry contention beyond borders. First, a number of them have derived a broad concept of *"global social movements"* from the strong globalization thesis. For these scholars, resistance to globalization created an entirely new field of contention (Evans 2005, McMichael 2005; Smith and Johnston eds. 2002). Second, struck by the role of international institutions in triggering episodes of transnational contention, many scholars have seen these institutions as *opportunity structures* to which transnational actors gravitate (Joachim and Locher eds. 2009; Kay 2010; O'Brien et al. 2000; Tarrow 2001). This is particularly true in Europe, the region of the world in which international institutions are most fully developed.[5]

Third, especially after the dramatic Seattle protest against the WTO in 1999, many scholars were intrigued by the advent of *transnational countersummits*, which were organized to protest international summits like the meetings of the WTO, the World Bank/International Monetary Fund, the G-8, and the European Union (Pianta et al. 2003; Wood 2003, 2007).

---

[5] For representative work that centers on Europe, see della Porta, Kriesi and Rucht eds. 1999 [2009]; della Porta, Andretta, Mosca, and Rieter 2006; della Porta ed. 2009; Imig and Tarrow eds. 2001; and Joachim and Locher eds. 2009.

Global social movements, international opportunities, summits and countersummits: these features of the post-1990s world have blown a refreshing breath of fresh air to a field that had become almost entirely nation-centered. But as in all new research programs, there are puzzles and ambiguities in this paradigm, and they relate to each of the aspects of the study of the new transnational politics sketched above: first, the globalization thesis may be too strong; second, many actors who appear in transnational conflicts are predominantly domestic; and third, not all transnational activism can be traced to social movement organizations.

The Weaknesses of the Strong Thesis
Even before the current age of economic integration, social movements in similar forms and with similar goals were diffusing across boundaries through word of mouth, immigration, proselytism and transnational movement organizations. Antislavery – perhaps the first successful modern transnational movement – spread in the early nineteenth century through the combination of movement missionaries, colonial administrators, and the British navy (Drescher 1987; Sikkink 1995).

Most important, many of the most robust transnational movements in the world today are *not* responses to globalization – at least not in a direct sense. Think of the human rights movement: although we might think that it has diffused through globalization, its targets are authoritarian and less-than-authoritarian states that abuse their citizens' rights. The most dramatic transnational protest in the first decade of the new century was the global opposition to the advent of the Iraq War on February 15, 2003, in which the target was not globalization but a renascent American imperialism (Walgrave and Rucht eds. 2010). And as for Islamist militantism, it diffused through religious networks and reactions against western secularism, not against globalization (Sageman 2004).

The "Domesticity" of "Transnational Actors
Exciting as it is for scholars to focus on the activists who come together across borders to protest against neoliberal capitalism and/or hegemonic states, this does not make these activists "transnational": rather, as I argued in the last chapter, they are rooted cosmopolitans, who join transnational protest movements as a side product of their domestic activities. Think of the "global justice" activists who gathered at the international counter-summit in Seattle in 1999. Although the "Battle of Seattle" was widely trumpeted as an incident in the struggle of the "global South" against the "global North," the largest proportion of activists were actually American trade unionists seeking protection for their jobs (Levi and Murphy 2006; Lichbach and DeVries 2007).

Even in Western Europe, Donatella della Porta and Manuela Caiani found that among the participants in European social forums 32 percent were or had been members of trade unions, 35 percent in political parties, 58 percent in student groups, 32 percent in youth squats, and 43 percent in environmental associations (della Porta and Caiani 2009: 143). When Doug Imig and I studied European protest events targeting the European Union, we found that the vast majority were mounted on domestic ground, and often against the activists' own governments (Imig and Tarrow 2001).

Social Movements, NGOs, and Others

Although the concept of "social movement" is often used as an umbrella label for all transnational actors, most transnational actors – like the fisherman we met in the "Tuna War" – do not fit the definition of social movements. Consider the examples we met in the last chapter: the port workers who took their fight against international maritime companies from Liverpool to Oakland, Yokohama and Sydney (Gentile 2010); the immigrant workers in Southern California who intervene in local political campaigns in their native villages in Mexico (Portes 2000); the lawyers who use United States law in campaigns of legal mobilization to indict human rights violators in Mexico and Libya (Davis 2008): these are not social movements, as the term has developed over the past 200 years.

Most important among these nonsocial movement actors are the transnational advocacy groups (TNGOs) that have sprung up around the world in the areas of development, the environment, feminism, human rights, and peace (Siméant 2011; Smith et al. 1997; Smith and Wiest 2012).[6] In their organizations, their sources of funding, their use of the techniques of advocacy rather than disruptive forms of action, NGOs are quite different from social movements (Tarrow 2011: ch. 12). Lumping these organizations together with movements may be inspiring to supporters and exciting to students, but it lends them a character that is not justified by their forms of action. Most important, it obscures what is particular about them: they operate routinely within the gates of both national and international institutions.

These variations and weaknesses should not disguise the fact that there has been a broad growth in transnational forms of organization, an expanding repertoire of transnational contention, and a growing stratum of transnational activists. Not every instance of transnational action is the result of globalization; not every activist who participates in a countersummit is a transnational activist; and not all transnational groups are part of a "global social

---

[6] It is significant that the very term advocacy was first popularized by institutional actors in the 1980s to designate something that was not quite as contained as lobbying but was far more conventional – and manageable – than protesting (Siméant 2011). Both the English term advocacy and its French equivalent *plaidoyer* (i.e., "to plead") were originally legal terms with which officials of the World Bank, the United Nations, and the European Union were far more comfortable than with the term protest. Siméant adds that the term advocacy "appears as a new category of international aid that emerges at the end of the 1980s. A working paper of the World Bank in 1989 describes "policy advocacy groups" as "indigenous or international, often focused on human rights or environment issues; involvement in project work includes contributions to planning, monitoring and stimulating corrections." I am grateful to Professor Siméant for allowing me to cite her unpublished work.

movement." I think we will do better to examine the various mechanisms and processes that bridge domestic and international politics in a sustained way. In the rest of this book I will illustrate this approach by specifying four key processes of local/transnational interaction from recent research in the area of human rights.

Transnational Processes of Human Rights

Two main assumptions will guide the rest of this chapter:

- *First,* many of the actors who take part in transnational action are domestic, and many transnational processes are experienced domestically, while others take activists outside their own boundaries;
- *Second,* some of these processes are unidirectional – based on structural or indirect effects – while others are reciprocal and depend on networking.

From these two sets of assumptions, the four processes of international/ domestic interaction potrayed in Table 12.1 are derived: the first process is what I call *internalization:* local or national collective action constructed around international issues – most visibly in response to actions taken by international institutions or foreign actors. I will illustrate internalization in the campaigns for human rights by Koreans in Japan, drawing on the work of Kiyoteru Tsutsui and Hwa Ji Shin (2008).

The second process is what I call *externalization:* the employment of political opportunities provided by international institutions, regimes, or treaties for external political action. Drawing on work by feminist and IR scholars, I will show how nonstate actors in Belgium and Britain used the European Court of Justice to make claims on their own governments or on other governments.

The third process is the *formation of insider/outsider coalitions,* a term that Kathryn Sikkink derived from her work on human rights campaigns in Argentina (2005: 165). I will illustrate it from Sally Merry's work on

TABLE 12.1. *Transnational Processes in Human Rights Campaigns*

	Type of Process	
	Unidirectional	Reciprocal
Domestic	Internalization (Koreans in Japan)	Insider/Outsider Coalition (International Women's Rights)
Site of Interaction *International*	Externalization (Gender equality in the EU)	Transnationalization (European unemployed Movement)

Source: Sidney Tarrow, "Insiders Outside and Outsiders Inside: Linking Transnational and Domestic Public Action for Human Rights," *Human Rights Review 11:171–182.*

transnational coalitions to combat violence against women in Asia (Merry 2006).

The final process I will examine is the *transnationalization of collective action:* by this I mean the sustained cooperation of domestic actors when they work together across national boundaries. Drawing on Richard Balme and Didier Chabanet's work (Balme and Chabanet 2008; Chabanet 2002), I will use the example of the European marches of the unemployed to illustrate this process, which comes closest to the form of transnational social movements that activists hope to create.

The Internalization of Human Rights Norms in Japan

Thirty-five years of Japanese occupation of Korea left a large number of Korean immigrants in Japan at war's end, and 600,000 of them stayed there, despite the fact that they were denied Japanese citizenship (Tsutsui and Shin 2008: 396). This left them with major economic, social, legal, and political disabilities in a country that prides itself on its ethnic unity. To make things worse, the war on the Korean peninsula split Koreans in Japan into northern- and southern-oriented factions.

But as the cold war waned and Japan began to move cautiously into the international community, many Koreans began to mobilize against discrimination. They framed their campaign in four main ways: against the practice of mandatory fingerprinting (civil rights); for alien suffrage (political rights); for participation in the national pension system (social/economic rights); and for ethnic education and Korean language training (cultural rights) (397). These claims were slow to receive recognition by the Japanese government. But as Japan became more integrated into what the authors call "world society," there was a greater chance for pressures on the government to work (392).

A key turning point was the ratification of two key international covenants on human rights in the UN system and their impact on Japan. As Tsutsui and Shin put it; "Global human rights discourses ... enabled resident Koreans to see their problems as universal rights issues that affected all of them" (397). In all four rights areas, but more effectively in some than in others, Tsutsui and Shin show how "global norms, combined with resident Koreans' activism, have produced specific policies" (399). This was internalization.

The modest successes of Koreans in Japan in gaining civil, economic, and cultural rights lend support to the idea that international norms are being inserted in domestic politics – what I call "internalization." But we would also be right to ask: how much of the heavy lifting was done by the appropriation of global vocabularies by activists and how much by other factors: first, the adoption of international human rights norms by a Japanese government anxious to rejoin the community of nations; second, by the support of influential allies – the South Korean government and international human rights groups; third, by the growing unity of north and south Koreans in Japan as the Cold War ebbed and memories of the Korean war receded into the past; and, fourth by the external support of international activists? This takes us to the second process I want to discuss: externalization, the movement of insider activists outside of their national communities into international institutions.

Externalization of Gender Equality in Europe

If Koreans in Japan framed their claims domestically in global terms, British and other European women's groups have been going outside their political communities to claim their rights in European institutions. The European Court of Justice (ECJ) and the European Court of Human Rights (ECHR) are two of the most interesting channels for nonstate public actors to engage in external activism. They show how international tribunals can serve as a kind of "coral reef" to attract social actors whose weakness at home leads them to look for a venue in which their rights may be recognized. Let's look at the European Court of Justice and the role of nonstate actors in changing European policies toward gender equality.[6]

The ECJ was originally conceived as an agent to prevent member-states from defecting from agreed-upon policies. But over the years, and with the help of the European Commission, the court transformed the European legal order in a supranational direction, and this has allowed weak social actors – like women – to significantly improve their positions in the labor market. From 1970 to the late 1990s, 177 cases involving gender equality laws came before the court (Cichowski 2001: 122).

The process began with the activation of the EU legal system by a Belgian stewardess and her lawyer in 1976. Having reached the age of forty, Gabrielle Defrenne, a Belgian national working as a stewardess for Sabena airlines, was told to take another job or lose her position with the airline. After working through the national judicial system unsuccessfully, Ms. Defrenne brought her case to the European Court of Justice. The ECJ ruled in her favor on the grounds of equal protection, because a male steward in her position was not required to change jobs (Caporaso and Jupille 2001).

The implications of the Defrenne decision became the foundation for a long line of equal pay decisions by the ECJ, many of which came from the UK and a majority of which adjusted women's pay scales upward. In this effort the British Equal Opportunity Commission combined with the trade unions, with an external assist from the European Commission, and pushed to develop the cases that led the court to hold that British practices undermined the European Treaties (Alter and Vargas 2000: 458–459). The European Commission even organized joint seminars with the British unions to advise claimants on how to use European law to best advantage (Ibid.: 459).

---

[6] For the role of NGOs and social movements in the European Court of Human Rights, see Dolidze, Anna, "The European Court of Human Rights' Evolving Approach to Non-Governmental Organizations," in Laurence Boulle (ed.) *Globalisation and Governance* (SiberInk Publishers, Cape Town) 2011.

The key decision came in 1982 when the court found the United Kingdom to be in violation of the Equal Pay Directive. To this decision, the UK government offered stiff resistance but the ultimate results were dramatic, both in terms of the government's compliance with the court's decisions (Chicowski 2001: 130), and in compromising the long-held principle of the sovereignty of the UK Parliament (Caporaso and Jupille 2001: 40–41). Through resistance to a government that was not responsive to their demands, British women's groups used a process of international access to put forward their claims.

But externalizing internal demands abroad is difficult and we see far fewer examples of it than of our first process – internalization. For in "going outside," actors lose access to the domestic resources and opportunities they know and know how to use. This is why international institutions are important magnets for externalization – institutions like the ECJ, the European and inter-American courts of human rights and perhaps, in the future, the International Criminal Court.

Insider-Outsider Women's Rights Coalitions

Following a line of research that began with her important collaborative work with Margaret Keck in the 1990s (Keck and Sikkink 1998), Kathryn Sikkink has identified what she calls "the insider-outside coalition," which can result when domestic and international opportunities are both relatively open and "domestic activists ... privilege domestic political opportunities but will keep international activism as a complementary and compensatory option." Domestic political change is closer to home and more directly addresses the problems activists face, so they will concentrate their attention there. However, she writes, "activists who have learned how to use international institutions ... will keep this avenue open in case of need" (2005: 164–165). Sikkink goes on to show how Argentinian human rights groups, which had developed international connections during the dictatorship, kept these connections in reserve when domestic opportunities opened up and formed new transnational coalitions to further new goals at home (166).

Although she does not use the term "insider-outsider coalition," Sally Merry's findings about campaigns targeting violence against women produce good examples of the process that Sikkink has described. The substantial progress that has been made in the UN system in combating violence against women cannot be seen as the result of externalization. Although the UN – the major site of treaty progress on human rights – affords many NGOs consultative status, NGO representatives' work is largely limited to the lobbies and balconies of UN meetings and they are frequently even denied the right to speak at these meetings. Moreover, domestic activists from the South must overcome enormous resource deficiencies to even participate in UN events – not only because of the expense and distance involved but because large and usually Northern-based NGOs have preferred status.

The struggle against violence against women in the global South would have made little progress against male-dominated ruling groups and their employment of "cultural" interpretations (Merry 2006: 92–98) if they had not formed insider-outsider coalitions. Merry argues that the Convention against All Forms of Discrimination Against Women (CEDAW) – much like domestic law – works through "the cultural production of norms" (89). Adopted by the General Assembly in 1979, CEDAW has give rise to a complex and slow-moving set of procedures involving country reports, commission hearings in Geneva, and attempts to escape surveillance on the part of recalcitrant states.[7]

Yet NGOs have indirect effects at these global conferences. As Merry learned from her interviews, "most observers of the process agree that it is the NGOs that raise new issues, do the research to develop them, generate public support, and reach the media" (69). The role of women's NGOs also seems to have been growing over the past few decades. At the Beijing Plus 5 meeting in 2000, for example, they "prepared at least 112 alternative reports assessing their countries' compliance with the Platform for Action…. organized two all-day sessions and … provided guidance about the UN system and advice on lobbying. Despite government discomfort, the human rights system depends on NGO activities" (70–71).

But the most significant role for these actors still occurs at the domestic level. Although governments can escape surveillance through the CEDAW system, "they face internal pressure from national NGOs, which may be supported by international donors and therefore active even if the country does not have enough wealth to support them…. It was primarily domestic NGOs that used the hearings to exert pressure on their governments to comply" (88). These are examples of insider-outsider coalitions.

Transnationalization of the Unemployed in Europe

What of transnational social movements? This is even more difficult process than forming insider/outsider coalitions. Doug Imig and I learned how difficult it is by assembling a data set of contentious European political events covering the fourteen years from January 1, 1984 through December 31, 1997 from *Reuters* press releases. Within this record, we found accounts of some 9,872 discrete contentious political events, launched by a broad range of social actors. But most of them were purely domestic – almost 95 percent of the total). States are still the predominant targets of nonstate actors (Imig and Tarrow 2001).

But what of the remaining 5 percent? Were they truly transnational coalitions? When we looked at these events in detail, we found that 490 contentious events fit our definition of European protests, but only a minute percentage

---

[7] Merry reports that by 2000, there were 242 overdue reports to CEDAW from 165 state parties to the treaty. Overall, 78 percent of state parties had overdue reports, many file superficial reports, and some do not even send representatives to meetings. See Merry 87–88 for these findings.

of them were actually *transnational*: e.g., coalitions of actors from different European countries with common aims and engaged in coordinated collective action across borders. Almost 83 percent of the EU-directed protests we found were examples of internalization or externalization of single actors, while 17 percent were transnational.[8]

What were these transnational events about? Here are some examples: in April 1993, workers from across the European community launched strikes and took to the streets in protest of the failure of their own governments to halt and reverse the steep rise in unemployment. From 1996 on, anti-GM campaigners coordinated their efforts against the approval of genetically modified foods. And in 1998 a major campaign of farmers' protests was mounted against changes in the CAP by farmers' groups coordinated by their national organizations. And as the Amsterdam summit approached, women's groups coordinated campaigns to lobby their national governments to support a gender equality plank in the treaty (Helfferisch and Kolb 2001).

The Amsterdam Treaty was the occasion for one of the most dramatic transnational protest events in EU history – the European Marches against Unemployment, Job Insecurity, and Social Exclusion (Chabanet 2002). For not only did 50,000 people turn out against the holding of that EU Summit; "What made the event even more remarkable," wrote Richard Balme and Didier Chabanet, " was the presence of demonstrators from many countries" and the fact that "small teams of marchers had crisscrossed Europe before converging on the Netherlands and calling people onto the street" (Balme and Chabanet 2008: 133–134). This was a true transnational movement coalition.

But apart from a brief revival, the "marches" of the unemployed were eventually reduced to the fate of many transnational movements – an internet communications network, albeit an active one.[9] The reasons are not hard to discern. The unemployed are historically the hardest social group to coordinate – especially when they live far from one another and speak different languages; the unemployment policies of the different EU member-states are widely divergent and have shown little sign of convergence, despite EU urging (Balme and Chabanet 2008: 128–133). As for the EU itself, the treaties give it little discretion over unemployment, apart from periodic attempts to identify best practices and put forward frameworks for fighting it (Ibid.: 134). Even in the EU – where a robust opportunity structure exists for social movements to organize around and where neoliberalism is highly organized – transnational collective action is hard to organize, faces shifting targets, and is difficult to sustain.

---

[8] In some sectors, like the environment, "Europrotests" have continued to increase (Poloni-Staudinger 2008). On the other hand, the total number of protests targeting the EU has remained fairly steady since the 1990s, with a brief uptick around the turn of the new century. For these findings see Uba and Uggla 2011.

[9] Http://www.euromarches.org.

Coda

In this chapter, I argued first that there have been dramatic increases in transnational contention across a number of dimensions. I argued that although globalization is a powerful and heterogeneous process, many of these actions have little or nothing to do with globalization. Moreover, many of the actors we met in the chapters were primarily domestic and many would be hard to classify as social movements without giving that term a very loose meaning.

From the two defining variables I used – the level at which collective action is organized and the degree of interaction among the participants – I derived four main processes. None of these processes has radically shifted the global balance from domestic to international politics or created anything resembling a "global social movement" and all of them worked within international institutions and domestic power structures. All of them are, in terms of the title of this volume, "at the gates" of institutional politics, both domestic and international. But taken together they reveal a number of avenues for activists and for advocates of human rights:

- First, they can translate international norms and practices into domestic politics, where elements of the public can be educated to go beyond parochial concerns;
- Second, they can give domestic actors the experience of working with external allies, experiences which they can take home with them to dignify and broaden interest-based actions;
- And, third, in the case of both insider-outsider coalitions and transnationalization of collective action, they can produce at least temporary cross-border coalitions, the closest the we have come to seeing the creation of global social movements.

This is a much more mixed picture of the prospects for a "global civil society" than we find in much of the literature on transnational contention. Think back to the "Tuna War" with which I began this chapter: it was a contingent conjuncture involving mainly domestic actors, one transnational NGO – Greenpeace – four governments, and an international institution, the European Commission. But this is my major point about how transnational contention has developed: not through something as threatening as "globalization" or as promising as the formation of "global social movements," but a network of relations in which rooted cosmopolitans link the domestic and the international in loosely coupled campaigns of collective action.

To those who hope for a process of "globalization from below" this may sound a pessimistic note. But by bringing actors from the domestic level into contact with international institutions and transnational actors, these processes are effecting the creation of a class of people who can broker links between the domestic and the international arenas. They are familiarizing domestic actors with the international arena and legitimating the involvement of international actors in the domestic realm. That translation is unlikely to be either dramatic or complete. Consider what Merry writes about human rights ideas about violence against women: they percolate into local communities in a limited and fragmentary way, "primarily through the mediation of activists who translate the global language into locally relevant terms" (Merry 2006: 218). To activists impatient for change, this may not sound like much. But to anyone who has encountered the resistance of national parochialism, the molasses effects of international bureaucracies, and the obstruction of antagonistic actors, such a translation could be a significant step toward the construction of a more humane and more equal world.

That struggle is taking new forms, engaging new actors, and traversing borders in ways that could not have been imagined, even in the recent past. But it takes place mainly within the gates of the polity; it involves mechanisms – like diffusion and scale shift – like the ones that have been examined in this book; and it is only the latest in a long sequence of conflicts over power and rights, as the final episode in this book will suggest.

Back to the Future
In a dismal winter chill, a rebellion has broken out in a minor country over issues that might not have been noticed in more tranquil times. When the elite responds with an uncertain mixture of repression and paralysis, the rebellion mushrooms, spreading to a neighboring regional power which has problems of its own. But in this second country, dissidents are already organized, and they join "the street" in what turns into a major revolutionary insurrection. The military and the police are divided; moderate elements of the elite defect to the insurgents; foreign allies are nowhere to be seen; and the government, which has ruled through a combination of autocracy and liberal reform, falls.

Word of the collapse of this powerful state spreads like wildfire across the region. Soon neighboring countries are caught up in what has become a spring time of freedom in an area of the world that has been under the thumb of autocracy for decades. But the nature of the conflagration varies from place to place: in some countries, civil war breaks out; in others, governmental forces savagely repress the protesters; in still others, rebellion is avoided through a combination of military threats and economic payoffs. What seemed like a spring time of freedom soon erodes into a summer of discontent.

Within the turbulent states, the liberal consensus of the early days of the rebellion soon passes, as workers, state officials, and competing social groups seize the opportunity to mount claims of their own. Preexisting ethnic conflicts divide once-solidary coalitions; here and there, minority ethnic groups are attacked; traditional rural groups do not follow the lead of their more sophisticated urban compatriots. As the spark of rebellion spreads, concern for their stability leads powerful international actors to intervene. Some counsel reform, others close their borders to the "contagion" they fear will infect their own people, and still others intervene militarily. What began as a springtime of freedom ends partly in reform, partly in repression, and almost everywhere in disillusionment.

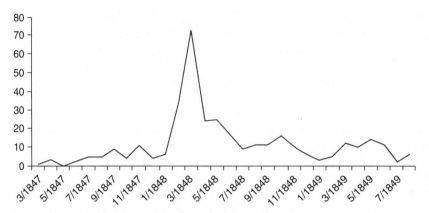

FIGURE 12.1. "1848" Events: France, Germany, Italy, and the Habsburg Empire.
Source: Sarah Soule and Sidney Tarrow, "The 1848 Revolutions." Unpublished paper,
presented to the Social Science History Association Annual Meeting, New Orleans,
1991.

If you guessed that this thumbnail sketch described "The Arab Spring" of
2011, when rebellion broke out in Tunisia and spread to Egypt and from there
to a ring of more repressive states in North Africa and the Middle East, you
would not have been wrong. But you would also be correct if you guessed that
it described what took place in Europe in the spring and summer of 1848.
The "small state" where rebellion first broke out was actually not Tunisia, but
Italy, where timid reforms by a new Pope triggered outbreaks of violence; the
"Egypt" of 1848 was France – the most important state in Western Europe,
where the fall of King Louis Philippe in February "unleashed a torrent of
regime contention" across the continent (Weyland 2009: 393); and the more
repressive states to which the revolution then spread were not the Bahrain, the
Libya, the Syria and Lebanon of 2011, but the Germany, Austria, Hungary, and
the smaller states of the Habsburg Empire. Figure 12.1, drawn from an over-
view of the 1848 events from the work of French historian Jacques Godechot
(1971), gives us a sense of how rapidly the revolution spread through France,
Italy, Germany, and the Habsburg Empire in the spring of 1848.[10]

Of course, big events – revolutions, civil wars, genocides – almost always
look similar when viewed holistically – and this is as good a reason as any
to disaggregate them into their component episodes and processes. As Jack
Goldstone argues in a recent article,[11] the regimes attacked in North Africa

[10] I am grateful to Sarah Soule for the analysis she carried out of these "1848" events with me two
    decades ago, and for her help in excavating them from her data files.
[11] Jack Goldstone, "Not 1848. Not 1989. The 2011 Arab revolts in historical perspective,"
    presented to the annual meeting of the Social Science History Association, Boston. Also see
    his "Understanding the Revolutions of 2011: Weakness and Resilience in Middle Eastern
    Autocracies." *Foreign Affairs* 90 (May/June): 8–16.

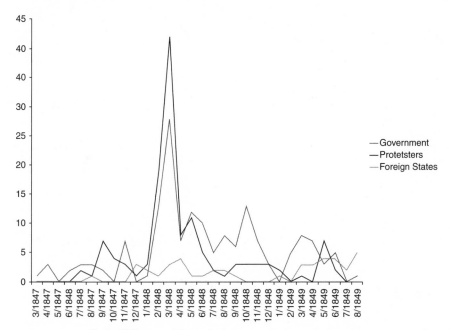

FIGURE 12.2. "1848" Events: Major Actors.
Source: Sarah Soule and Sidney Tarrow, "The 1848 Revolutions." Unpublished paper, presented to the Social Science History Association Annual Meeting, New Orleans, 1991.

and the Middle East in 2011 were nothing like the constitutionalizing monarchy of Orléanist France, the petty duchies of the German states, or the autocratic Prussian and Habsburg Empires of 1848. They were mainly military dictatorships with a patina of fraudulent representative institutions with powerful security apparatuses that would have been impossible for rulers in the middle of the nineteenth century to construct. They were also part of transnational networks of communication fed by print, radio, and TV and the internet to a degree that could not have been imagined a century and a half ago.

Yet in a number of ways these two revolutions reinforce themes that have been canvassed in the previous chapters:

First, contentious politics involves not only protesters but their governments, third parties, and even foreign states. From the spring of 1848 to the summer of 1849 Godechot's account shows that governments and foreign states were increasingly involved in the resolution or suppression of the movements in many of these countries. Figure 12.2, also drawn from Godechot's accounts, shows how, toward the end of the cycle of contention, foreign intervention rose. That foreign intervention in the Libya of 2011 was carried out in the name of "protecting civilians" does not make the intervention of the United States, Britain, and France and the Arab League any less portentous.

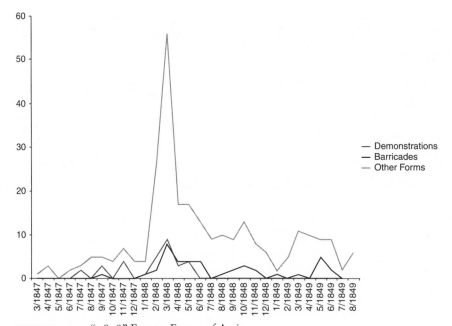

FIGURE 12.3. "1848" Events: Forms of Action.
Source: Sarah Soule and Sidney Tarrow, "The 1848 Revolutions." Unpublished paper, presented to the Social Science History Association Annual Meeting, New Orleans, 1991.

Second, in 1848, as in 2011, there was much violence but there were also many conventional and disruptive forms that did not rise to the level of violence: marches, public meetings, and celebrations in the streets as rulers gave way with amazing alacrity and ordinary citizens joined the protesters in expressions of joy. Figure 12.3 catalogues the demonstrations, the barricades, and other forms of actions coded from Godechot's calendar of 1848–1849 events and shows that while barricades were common at the high point of contention, demonstrations were just as common and "other events" outstripped both of these forms. News reports in the spring of 2011 emphasized the violence, repressive actions, and joyous demonstrations of the crowds in Tahir Square and elsewhere; but under the surface, as this book goes to press, it is already clear that a wide range of forms of action – conventional, contentious, and violent – marked the Middle Eastern and North African Revolutions.[12]

---

[12] As I conclude this chapter, a number of scholars are already hard at work cataloguing and analyzing the repertoire of contention that has emerged from the Middle Eastern and North African revolts of the Spring of 2011. For a unique journalistic perspective, see "Arab spring: an interactive timeline of Middle East protests" by the *Guardian* newspaper at www.guardian.co.uk/world/interactive/2011/mar/22/middle-east-protest-interactive-timeline.

Finally, even in the absence of radio, television, or the Internet, the 1848 events spread rapidly across Europe in ways so rapid and so complex that the patterns of diffusion cannot easily be described. Take the barricade: as he walked from his home to Parliament amid the tumult of Paris in revolution in February 1848, Alexis de Tocqueville saw men systematically cutting down trees and putting up barricades. "These barricades," he observed

> were skillfully constructed by a small number of men who worked industri-ously – not like criminals fearful of being caught *in flagrante delicto*, but like good workmen who wanted to do their job expeditiously and well. Nowhere did I see the seething unrest I had witnessed in 1830, when the whole city reminded me of one vast, boiling cauldron. (Tocqueville 1992: 39)

As insurrection spread across Europe, the barricade emerged at the quintessen-tial form of revolutionary activity, virtually synonymous with revolution, much as the occupation of central city squares has become the magnetizing action of insurgents in the Middle East today.

It is too soon to say whether the revolutions of 2011 will provide historians with similar evidence of how cycles of contention produce new forms of col-lective action. But surely, the occupation of public space in Egypt and Yemen and the thwarted attempts to do the same in Bahrain and Syria will have a similar place in the hagiography of these revolutions that the barricade did in 1848. And although I am not ready to categorize these new eruptions as "the Facebook/Twitter revolution" as some have done, the power of personal media to diffuse contention was demonstrated in these events as never before.

I do not close this book with the parallels between 1848 and 2011 in order to argue that nothing ever changes under the sun. That would be contrary to the historical spirit of the volume. I do so to call, as I have done elsewhere in this book, for a determined search for the mechanisms that connect social actors to their governments, their institutions, and to third parties who may not share their aspirations, but who interact with them in episodes of conten-tious politics. Only by identifying and examining such mechanisms, and seeing how they travel from one social actor to another, from reformist to revolution-ary cycles, and from one epoch of history to the next, will we understand the role of strangers at the gates in social and political change.

Bibliography

Abbott, Andrew. 1988a. "Transcending General Linear Reality." *Sociological Theory* 6:169–186.

1988b. "From Causes to Events." *Sociological Methods and Research* 20:428–455.

Abrams, Philip. 1982. *Historical Sociology.* Ithaca, NY and London: Cornell University Press.

Accornero, Aris. 1967. *I comunisti in fabbrica: Documenti delle lotte operaie.* Florence: Centro G. Francovich.

Accornero, Aris, Renato Mannheimer, and Chiara Saraceno (Eds.). 1983. *L'identitá comunista: I militanti, le strutture, la cultura del PCI.* Rome: Riuniti.

Ackerman, Bruce. 1994. "Rooted Cosmopolitanism." *Ethics* 104:516–535.

Al-Ali, Najde, and Khalid Koser (Eds.). 2002. New Approaches to Migration? Transnational Communities and the Transformation of Home. New York: Routledge.

Alberoni, Francesco. 1968. *Statu nascenti.* Bologna: Il Mulino.

1979. "Movimenti e instituzioni nell'Italia tra il 1960 e il 1970." Pp. 233–269 in *La crisi italiana,* edited by Luigi Graziano and Sidney Tarrow. Turin: Einaudi.

Allison, Paul. 1982. "Discrete-time Methods for the Analysis of Event Histories." Pp. 61–98 in *Sociological Methodology,* edited by Samuel Leinhardt. San Fancisco: Jessey Basis.

Almond, Gabriel A. 1988. "The Return to the State." *American Political Science Review* 82:853–874.

Alter, Karen, and Jeannette Vargas. 2000. "Explaining Variation in the Use of European Litigation Strategies: EC Law and UK Gender Equality Policy." *Comparative Political Studies* 33:452–482.

Altschuler, Glenn C., and Stuart M. Blumin. 2000. *Rude Republic: Americans and their Politics in the Nineteenth Century.* Princeton, NJ: Princeton University Press.

Amenta, Edwin. 2005. "Political Contexts, Challenger Strategies, and Mobilization: Explaining the Impact of the Townsend Plan." Ch. 1 in *Routing the Opposition: Social Movements, Public Policy and Democracy,* edited by David Meyer, Valerie Jenness, and Helen Ingram. Minneapolis: University of Minnesota Press.

2006. *When Movements Matter: The Townsend Plan and the Rise of Social Security.* Princeton, NJ: Princeton University Press.

Amenta, Erwin, and Neal Caren. 2004. "The Legislative, Organizational, and Beneficiary Consequences of State-Oriented Challengers." Pp. 461–488 in *The Blackwell Companion to Social Movements*, edited by David A. Snow, Sarah Soule, and Hanspeter Kriesi. Oxford: Blackwell.

Amenta, Edwin, Drew Halfmann, and Michael P. Young. 1999. "The Strategies and Contexts of Social Protest: Political Mediation and the Impact of the Townsend Movement in California." *Mobilization* 4:1–24.

Amenta, Edwin, and Yvonne Zylan. 1991. "It Happened Here: Political Opportunity, the New Institutionalism, and the Townsend Movement." *American Sociological Review* 56:250–265.

Aminzade, Ronald. 1983. *Ballots and Barricades: Class Formation and Republican Politics in France, 1830–1871*. Princeton, NJ: Princeton University Press.

1992. "Historical Sociology and Time." *Sociological Methods and Research* 20:456–480.

Aminzade, Ronald R., and Doug McAdam. 2001. "Emotions and Contentious Politics." Ch. 2 in *Silence and Voice in the Study of Contentious Politics*, edited by Ronald R. Aminzade, Jack Goldstone, Doug McAdam, Elizabeth Perry, William H. Sewell, Jr., Sidney Tarrow, and Charles Tilly. Cambridge: Cambridge University Press.

Anderson, Benedict. 1991. *Imagined Communities. Reflections on the Origin and Spread of Nationalism*. London: Verso.

1998. *The Spectre of Comparisons: Nationalism, Southeast Asia and the World*. New York: Verso.

Anderson, Perry. 1962. "Report on the Debate of the Central Committee of the PCI on the Twenty-Second Party Congress of the CPSU." *New Left Review* 13–14:152–160.

1976. *Considerations on Western Marxism*. London: New Left Books.

Andress, David. 2005. *The Terror*. New York: Farrar, Straus, and Giroux.

Anner, Mark, Ian Greer, Marco Hauptmeier, Nathan Lillie, and Nik Winchester. 2004. "The Industrial Determinants of Transnational Solidarity: Global Interunion Politics in Three Sectors." *European Journal of International Relations* 12:7–27.

Appelby, Joyce, Lynn Hunt, and Margaret Jacobs. 1994. *Telling the Truth About History*. New York and London: Norton.

Appiah, Kwame Anthony. 1996. "Cosmopolitan Patriots." Pp. 21–29 in *For Love of Country*, edited by Joshua Cohen. Boston: Beacon Press.

2006. *Cosmopolitanism: Ethics in a World of Strangers*. New York and London: Norton.

Apter, David E. 1965. *The Politics of Modernization*. Chicago: University of Chicago Press.

Arrighi, Giovanni (Ed.). 1985. *Semiperipheral Development: The Politics of Southern Europe in the Twentieth Century*. Beverly Hills, CA: Sage Publications.

1990. "Marxist Century, American Century: The Making and Remaking of the World Labour Movement." *New Left Review* 179:29–63.

1994. *The Long Twentieth Century: Money, Power, and the Origins of Our Times*. London: Verso.

Arrighi, Giovanni, Terence Hopkins, and Immanuel Wallerstein. 1986. "Dilemmas of Antisystemic Movements." *Social Research* 53:185–206.

Arrighi, Giovanni, Terence K. Hopkins, and Immanuel Wallerstein (Eds.). 1989. *Antisystemic Movements*. London: Verso.

Ashenfelter, Orley, and John Pencavel. 1969. "American Trade Union Growth, 1900–1960." *Quarterly Journal of Economics* 83:434–448.

Baker, Keith M. 1990. *Inventing the French Revolution. Essays on French Political Culture in the 18th Century.* Cambridge: Cambridge University Press.

Baker, Keith M., and Steven L Kaplan. 1991. "Introduction." in Roger Chartier, *The Cultural Origins of the French Revolution.* Durham, NC: Duke University Press.

Balme, Richard, and Didier Chabanet. 2008. *European Governance and Democracy: Protest and Power in the EU.* Lanham, MD: Rowman and Littlefield.

Banfield, Edward, and Laura Fasano Banfield. 1958. *The Moral Basis of a Backward Society.* Glencoe, IL: The Free Press.

Baran, Paul A. 1957. *The Political Economy of Growth.* New York: Monthly Review.

Barbagli, Marzio, and Piergiorgio Corbetta. 1978. "Partito e movimento: Aspetti del rinnovamento del PCI." *Inchiesta* 8:3–46.

Beccalli, Bianca. 1971. "Scioperi e organizazzione sindacale: Milano 1950–1970." *Rassegna Italiana di sociologia* 12:83–120.

Becchelloni, Giovanni (Ed.). 1973. *Cultura e ideologia della nuova sinistra: Materiali per un inventorio della cultura politica della riviste del dissenso marxista.* Milan: Comunita.

Beissinger, Mark R. 2002. *Nationalist Mobilization and the Collapse of the Soviet Union.* Cambridge: Cambridge University Press.

2009. "An Interrelated Wave." *Journal of Democracy* 20:74–77.

Benda, Harry. 1966. "Reflections on Asian Communism." *Yale Review* 56:1–16.

Ben-Eliezer, Uri. 1997. "Rethinking the Civil-Military Relations Paradigm: The Inverse Relation Between Militarism and Praetorianism through the Example of Israel." *Comparative Political Studies* 30:356–374.

Bennett, W. Lance. 2003. "Communicating Global Activism." *Information, Communication & Society* 6:142–168.

Bensel, Richard F. 1991. *Yankee Leviathan. The Origins of Central Authority in America, 1859–1877.* New York and Cambridge: Cambridge University Press.

Billington, Ray Allen. 1938. *The Protestant Crusade, 1800–1860. A Study of the Origins of American Nativism.* New York: Macmillan.

Binder, Amy J. 2002. *Contentious Curricula. Afrocentrism and Creationism in American Public Schools.* Princeton, NJ: Princeton University Press.

Blackmer, Donald L. M., and Sidney Tarrow (Eds.). 1975. *Communism in Italy and France.* Princeton, NJ: Princeton University Press.

Blanning, T. C. W. 1986. *The Origins of the French Revolutionary Wars.* London and New York: Longman.

Blocker, Jack S., Jr. 1989. *American Temperance Movements: Cycles of Reform.* Boston: Twayne Publishers.

Boix, Carles, and Susan Stokes (Eds.). 2007. *Oxford Handbook of Comparative Politics.* Oxford and New York: Oxford University Press.

Boli, John, and George Thomas. 1997. "World Culture in the World Polity." *American Sociological Review* 62:171–190.

Bond, Doug and Joe Bond. 1995. "Protocol for the Assessment of Nonviolent Direct Action (PANDA) Codebook for the P2 Data Set." Cambridge, MA: Harvard University, Center for International Affairs.

Bosi, Lorenzo, and Katrin Uba. 2009. "Special Focus Issue on Social Movement Outcomes." *Mobilization* 14:409–504.

Bourricaud, François. 1982. "France: The Prelude to the *loi d'orientation* of 1968." Pp. 63–102 in *Universities, Politicians and Bureaucrats*, edited by Hans Daalder and Edward Shils. Cambridge: Cambridge University Press.

Brady, Henry E., and David Collier (Eds.). 2004. *Rethinking Social Inquiry: Diverse Tolls, Shared Standards.* Lanham, MD: Rowman & Littlefield.

Braudel, Fernand. 1972. *The Mediterranean and the Mediterranean World in the Age of Philip II.* New York: Harper and Row.

Bridges, Amy. 1986. "Becoming American: The Working Classes in the United States before the Civil War." Ch. 5 in *Working Class Formation: Nineteenth Century Patterns in Western Europe and the United States,* edited by Ira Katznelson and Aristide R. Zolberg. Princeton, NJ: Princeton University Press.

Bright, Charles, and Susan Harding. 1984. *Statemaking and Social Movements: Essays in History and Theory.* Ann Arbor: University of Michigan Press.

Bright, Charles C. 1984. "The State in the United States during the Nineteenth Century." Pp. 121–122 in *Statemaking and Social Movements: Essays in History and Theory,* edited by Charles Bright and Susan Harding. Ann Arbor: University of Michigan Press.

Brockett, Charles D. 1995. "A Protest-Cycle Resolution of the Repression/Popular Protest Paradox." Pp. 117–44 in *Repertoires and Cycles of Collective Action,* edited by Mark Traugott. Durham, NC: Duke University Press.

Browning, Rufus P., Dale Rogers Marshall, and David H. Tabb. 1984. *Protest is Not Enough. The Struggle of Blacks and Hispanics for Equality in Urban Politics.* Berkeley and Los Angeles: University of California Press.

Bunce, Valerie. 1981. *Do New Leaders Make a Difference? Executive Succession and Public Policy under Capitalism and Socialism.* Princeton, NJ: Princeton University Press.

Bunce, Valerie, and Sharon Wolchik. 2006. "Favorable Conditions and Electoral Revolutions." *Journal of Democracy* 17:5–18.

2006. "International Diffusion and Postcommunist Electoral Revolutions." *Communist and Postcommunist Studies* 39:283–304.

2011. *Defeating Authoritarian Leaders in Mixed Regimes: Electoral Struggles, U.S. Democracy Assistance, and International Diffusion in Post-Communist Europe and Eurasia.* New York and Cambridge: Cambridge University Press.

Burrows, Donald. 1976. *Music and Revolution: Verdi.* Milton Keynes: Open University Press.

Burstein, Paul. 1985. *Discrimination, Jobs, and Politics: The Struggle for Equal Opportunity in the United States.* Chicago: University of Chicago Press.

Burstein, Paul, and William Freundenberg. 1978. "Changing Public Policy: The Impact of Public Opinion, Anti-War Demonstrations, and War Costs on Senate Voting on Vietnam War Motions." *American Journal of Sociology* 84:99–122.

Burstein, Paul, and April Linton. 2002. "The Impact of Political Parties, Interest Groups and Social Movements on Public Policy: Some Recent Evidence and Theoretical Concerns." *Social Forces* 81:380–408.

Bush, Evelyn L. 2007. "Measuring Religion in Global Civil Society." *Social Forces* 85:1645–1665.

Caizzi, Bruno (Ed.). 1955. *Antologia della questione meridionale.* Milan: Communitá.

Calhoun, Craig. 1995. "New Social Movements of the Early Nineteenth Century." Pp. 173–216 in *Repertoires and Cycles of Collective Action,* edited by Mark Traugott. Durham, NC and London: Duke University Press.

2002. "The Class Consciousness of Frequent Travelers: Towards a Critique of Actually Existing Cosmopolitanism." Pp. 86–109 in *Conceiving Cosmopolitanism: Theory,*

Context, and Practice, edited by Steven Vertovec and Robin Cohen. Oxford: Oxford University Press.

Capdevielle, Jacques, and Rene Mouriaux. 1988. *Mai 68: L'entre-deux de la modernité. Histoire de trente ans.* Paris: Presses de la Fondation Nationale des Sciences Politiques.

Caporaso, James A., and Joseph Jupille. 2001. "The Europeanization of Gender Equality Policy and Domestic Structural Change." Pp. 21–43 in *Transforming Europe: Europeanization and Domestic Change*, edited by Maria Green Cowles, James A. Caporaso, and Thomas Risse. Ithaca, NY: Cornell University Press.

Cardoso, Ferndando Henrique and Enzo Faletto. 1979. *Dependency and Development in Latin America.* Berkeley and Los Angeles: University of California Press.

Carwadine, Richard. 1993. *Evangelicals and Politics in Antebellum America.* New Haven, CT: Yale University Press.

Cattaneo Institute. 1968. *La presenza sociale del PCI e della DC.* Bologna: Mulino.

Cazzaniga, Gian Mario. 1967. "Cronache e documenti del movimento studentesco." *Nuovo Impegno* 8:19–37.

Cederman, Lars-Erik, and Luc Giradin. 2007. "Beyond Fractionation: Mapping Ethnicity onto Nationalist Insurgencies." *American Political Science Review* 101:1–13.

Chabanet, Didier. 2002. "Les marches européennes contre le chômage, la précarité et les exclusions." Ch. 12 in *L'action collective en Europe*, edited by Richard Balme, Didier Chabanet, and Vincent Wright. Paris: Presses de Sciences Po.

Chalendar, Jacques de. 1970. *Une loi pour l'université.* Paris: de Brouwer.

Chapman, Brian. 1955. *The Prefects in Provincial France.* London: Allen and Unwin.

Charlot, Jean. 1989. "The Aftermath of May '68 for Gaullism, the Right and the Center." Pp. 62–81 in *May '68: Coming of Age*, edited by D. L. Hanley and A. P. Kerr. London: Macmillan.

Chartier, Roger. 1991. *The Cultural Origins of the French Revolution.* Durham, NC: Duke University Press.

Cichowski, Rachel A. 2001. "Judicial Rulemaking and the Institutionalization of the European Union Sex Policy." Ch. 6 in *The Institutionalization of Europe*, edited by Alec Stone Sweet, Neil Fligstein, and Wayne Sandholtz. Oxford: Oxford University Press.

   2007. *The European Court and Civil Society.* New York and Cambridge: Cambridge University Press.

Cobb, Richard. 1987. *The People's Armies: Instrument of the Terror in the Departments. April 1793 to Floréal Year II.* New Haven, CT and London: Yale University Press.

Cohen, David William. 1994. *The Combing of History.* Chicago: University of Chicago Press.

Cohen, Mitchell. 1992. "Rooted Cosmopolitanism." *Dissent* 390:478–483.

Collier, David, and Ruth Collier. 1991. *Shaping the Political Arena: Critical Junctures, the Labor Movement, and Regime Dynamics in Latin America.* Princeton, NJ: Princeton University Press.

Collier, Paul, and Anke Hoeffler. 2003. "Greed and Grievance in Civil War." *Oxford Economic Papers* 56:563–595.

Comitato centrale. 1951a. *Documenti.* Roma: Partito comunista italiano.

   1951b. *Risoluzione della Direzione.* Roma: Partito comunista italiano.

Costain, Anne, and Andrew McFarland (Eds.). 1998. *Social Movements and American Political Institutions*. Lanham, MD: Rowman and Littlefield.

Cross, Whitney. 1950. *The Burned-Over District: The Social and Intellectual History of Enthusiastic Religion in Western New York, 1800–1850*. Ithaca, NY and London: Cornell University Press.

Dalton, Russell J. 2006. *Citizen Politics: Public Opinion and Political Parties in Advanced Industrial Democracies*. Washington, DC: CQ Press.

Daniele, Piergiorgio. 1978. "L'organizazzione dell'utenza casa a Milano: Rapporto tra sviluppo dei sindacati inquilini e territorio urbano." State University of Milan, Unpublished report.

d'Anieri, Paul, Claire Ernest, and Elizabeth Kier. 1990. "New Social Movements in Historical Perspective." *Comparative Politics* 22:445–458.

Darnton, Robert. 1984. *The Great Cat Massacre and Other Episodes in French Cultural History*. New York: Basic Books.

Davis, Jeffrey. 2008. *Justice Across Borders: The Struggle for Human Rights in U.S. Courts*. New York and Cambridge: Cambridge University Press.

de Pasquale, Piero. 1956. "Dalla politica di Salerno alla crisi del frontismo meridionale." *Rinascita* 13:542–545.

della Porta, Donatella. 1995. *Social Movements, Political Violence and the State: A Comparative Analysis of Italy and Germany*. New York: Cambridge University Press.

   2004. "Multiple Belongings, Flexible Identities, and the Construction of 'Another Politics': Between the European Social Forum and Local Social Fora." Pp. 175–202 in *Transnational Protest and Global Activism*, edited by Donatella della Porta and Sidney Tarrow. Lanham, MD: Rowman and Littlefield.

   (Ed.). 2007. *The Global Justice Movement: Cross-National and Transnational Perspectives*. Boulder, CO: Paradigm Publishers.

   (Ed.). 2009. *Another Europe*. London: Routledge.

Della Porta, Donatella, Massimo Andretta, Lorenzo Mosca, and Herbert Reiter. 2006. *Globalization from Below: Transnational Activists and Protest Networks*. Minneapolis: Unniversity of Minnesota Press.

della Porta, Donatella, and Manuela Caiani. 2009. *Social Movements and Europeanization*. Oxford and New York: Oxford University Press.

della Porta, Donatella, and Mario Diani. 1999. *Social Movements: An Introduction*. Oxford: Blackwell Publishers.

della Porta, Donatella, Hanspeter Kriesi, and Dieter Rucht (Eds.). 1999 [2009]. *Social Movements in a Globalizing World*. Houndsmills, England: Macmillan Press.

della Porta, Donatella, and Sidney Tarrow. 1986. "Unwanted Children: Political Violence and the Cycle of Protest in Italy." *European Journal of Political Research* 14:607–632.

   2012. "Double Diffusion: The Co-Evolution of Police and Protests in Transnational Contention." *Comparative Political Studies* 45: in press.

Diani, Mario. 1995. *Green Networks: A Structural Analysis of the Italian Environmental Movement*. Edinburgh: Edinburgh University Press.

Diani, Mario, and Giovanni Lodi. 1988. "Three in One: Currents in the Milan Ecology Movement." Pp. 103–124 in *From Structure to Action: Comparing Social Movement Research across Cultures. International Social Movement Research*, edited by Bert Klandermans, Hanspeter Kriesi, and Sidney Tarrow. Greenwich, CT: JAI Press.

Dolidze, Anna. 2011. "The European Court of Human Rights' Evolving Approach to Non-Governmental Organizations." Pp. 207–231 in *Globalization and Governance*, edited by Laurence Boulle. Cape Town, South Africa: Siber Ink Publishers.

Downs, Anthony. 1957. *An Economic Theory of Democracy*. New York: Harper.

Drescher, Seymour. 1987. *Capitalism and Antislavery: British Mobilization in Comparative Perspective*. New York: Oxford University Press.

——— 1991. "British Way, French Way: Opinion Building and Revolution in the Second French Slave Emancipation." *American Historical Review* 96:709–734.

Dryzek, John. 1996. *Democracy in Capitalist Times: Ideals, Limits, and Struggles*. New York: Oxford University Press.

Dubois, Pierre. 1978. "New Forms of Industrial Conflict, 1960–74." Vol. II, Ch. 1 in *The Resurgence of Class Conflict in Europe since 1968*, edited by Colin Crouch and Alessandro Pizzorno. London: Macmillan.

Dumoulin, Olivier. 1986. "Evenementielle (Histoire)." Pp. 271–272 in *Dictionnaire des sciences historiques*, edited by Andre Burguiére. Paris: Presses Universitaires de France.

Durkheim, Emile. 1964. *Suicide: A Study in Sociological Interpretation*. Glencoe, IL: Free Press.

Earl, Jennifer. 2004. "The Cultural Consequences of Social Movements." Pp. 508–550 in *The Blackwell Companion to Social Movements*, edited by David Snow, Sarah Soule, and Hanspeter Kriesi. Oxford: Blackwell.

Eisinger, Peter K. 1973. "The Conditions of Protest Behavior in American Cities." *American Political Science Review* 67:11–28.

Ergas, Yasmine. 1982. "1968–79: Feminism and the Italian Party System." *Comparative Politics* 14:253–280.

Evans, Peter. 2005. "Counter-Hegemonic Globalization: Transnational Social Movements in the Contemporary Global Political Economy." Ch. 32 in *Handbook of Political Sociology*, edited by Thomas Janoski, Alexander Hicks, and Mildred Schwartz. New York: Cambridge University Press.

Evans, Peter, Deitrich Rueschemeyer, and Theda Skocpol, Eds. 1985. *Bringing the State Back In*. New York and Cambridge: Cambridge University Press.

Favre, Pierre. 1990. *La Manifestation*. Paris: Presses de la Fondation Nationale des Sciences Politiques.

Fearon, James D., and David Laitin. 2003. "Ethnicity, Insurgency, and Civil War." *American Political Science Review* 97:75–90.

FEN (Federation de l'Education Nationale). 1969. "Les Etats généraux de l'université nouvelle." *Enseignement public* 5:1–44.

Ferri, Franco. 1952. "Questione meridionale e unità nazionale in Gramsci." *Rinascita* 9:6–10.

Fillieule, Olivier. 1994. "Contribution à une théorie comprehensive de la manifestation: Les formes et les determinants de l'action manifestante dans la France des années quatre-vingts." Paris: Institut d'Etudes Politiques.

——— 1995. "Methodological Issues in the Collection of Data on Protest Events: Police Records and National Press France." Unpublished paper.

Fiori, Giuseppe. 1971. *Antonio Gramsci: Life of a Revolutionary*. New York: Dutton.

Floud, Roderick. 2006. *Height, Health, and History: Nutritional Status in the United Kingdom, 1750–1980*. Cambridge and New York: Cambridge University Press.

Fomerand, Jacques. 1974. "Policy-Formulation and Change in Gaullist France: The 1968 Orientation Act of Higher Education." PhD Dissertation: City University of New York.

——— 1975. "Policy Formulation and Change in Gaullist France. The 1968 Orientation Act of Higher Education." *Comparative Politics* 8:59–89.

Foner, Nancy. 2001. "Transnationalization Then and Now: New York Immigrants Today and at the Turn of the Twentieth Century." Pp. 35–57 in *Migration, Transnationalization and Race in a Changing New York*, edited by Hector R. Cordero-Guzmán, Robert C. Smith, and Ramón Grosfoguel. Philadelphia: Temple University Press.

Fortunato, Giustino. 1911. *Il Mezzogiorno e lo Stato Italiano*. Bari: Laterza.

Franklin, James. 2009. "Contentious Challenges and Governmental Responses." *Political Research Quarterly* 62:700–714.

Franzosi, Roberto. 1987. "The Press as a Source of Socio-Historical Data: Issues in the Methodology of Data Collection from Newspapers." *Historical Methods* 20:5–16.

Franzosi, Roberto. 1995. *The Puzzle of Strikes: Class and State Strategies in Postwar Italy*. Cambridge: Cambridge University Press.

Frederick, Howard H. 1995. "North American NGO Computer Networking: Computer Communications in Cross-Border Coalition-Building: The Case of Mexico." in *Program for Research on Immigration Policy*. Santa Monica, CA: Rand Corporation; Ford Foundation.

Friedman, Gabrielle, and James Q. Whitman. 2003. "The European Transformation of Harassment Law." *Columbia Journal of European Law* 9:241–264.

Fromm, Erich. 1969. *Escape from Freedom*. New York: Avon.

Furet, François. 1978. *Penser la révolution française*. Paris: Gallimard.

——— 1981. *Interpreting the French Revolution*. London: Cambridge University Press.

——— 1992. "Terreur." Pp. 293–315 in *Dictionnaire critique de la Révolution française. Evenements*, edited by François Furet and Mona Ozouf. Paris: Flammarion.

Furet, François, and Mona Ozouf (Eds.). 1992. *Dictionnaire critique de la Révolution française*. Paris: Flammarion.

Furtado, Celso. 1964. *Development and Underdevelopment*. Berkeley and Los Angeles: University of California Press.

Galli, Georgio, and Alfonso Prandi. 1970. *Patterns of Political Participation in Italy*. New Haven, CT: Yale University Press.

Gamson, William A. 1975. *The Strategy of Social Protest*. Homewood, IL: Dorsey Press.

——— 1990. *The Strategy of Social Protest*. Belmont, CA: Wadsworth. 2nd enlarged edition.

Ganley, Gladys D. 1992. *The Exploding Political Power of Personal Media*. Norwood, NJ: Ablex Publishers.

Ganz, Marshall. 2009. *Why David Sometimes Wins: Leadership, Organization, and Strategy in the California Farm Worker Movement*. Oxford and New York: Oxford University Press.

Geertz, Clifford. 1973. *The Interpretation of Cultures: Selected Essays*. New York: Basic Books.

Gentile, Antonina. 2010. "Historical Varieties of Labor Contention and Hegemony in Transnational Docker Campaigns." Unpublished PhD Thesis: Johns Hopkins University.

George, Alexander L., and Andrew Bennett. 2005. *Case Studies and Theory Development in the Social Sciences*. Cambridge and London: MIT Press.

Gitlin, Todd. 1987. *The Sixties: Years of Hope, Days of Rage*. New York: Bantam.

Giugni, Marco. 1998. "Was it Worth the Effort? The Outcomes and Consequences of Social Movements." *Annual Review of Sociology* 98:371–393.

　1999. "Introduction: How Social Movements Matter: Past Research, Present Problems, Future Developments." Pp. xiii–xxxiii in *How Social Movements Matter*, edited by Marco Giugni, Doug McAdam, and Charles Tilly. Minneapolis and St. Paul: University of Minnesota Press.

　2001. "L'impact des mouvements ecologistes, antinucléaires et pacifistes sur les politiques publiques: Le cas des Etats-Unis, de l'Italie et de la Suisse, 1974–1995." *Revue Française de Sociologie* 42:641–668.

　2008. "Welfare States, Political Opportunities, and the Mobilization of the Unemployed: A Cross National Analysis." *Mobilization* 13:297–310.

Giugni, Marco, and Sakura Yamasaki. 2009. "The Policy Impact of Social Movements: A Replication Through Qualitative Comparative Analysis." *Mobilization* 14:467–484.

Givan, Rebecca K, Kenneth Roberts, and Sarah A Soule (Eds.). 2010. *The Diffusion of Social Movements: Actors, Mechanism, and Political Effects*. New York and Cambridge: Cambridge University Press.

Godechot, Jaques 1971. *Les révolutions de 1848*. Paris: Albin Michel.

Golden, Miriam. 1988. *Labor Divided: Austerity and Working-Class Politics in Contemporary Italy*. Ithaca, NY: Cornell University Press.

Goldfield, Michael. 1982. "The Decline of Organized Labor: NLRB Union Certification Election Results." *Politics and Society* 11:167–210.

Goldstone, Jack A. 1991. *Revolution and Rebellion in the Early Modern World*. Berkeley and Los Angeles: University of California Press.

　1998. "Social Movements or Revolutions? On the Evolution and Outcomes of Collective Action." Ch. 6 in *From Contention to Democracy*, edited by Marco Giugni, Doug McAdam, and Charles Tilly. Lanham, MD: Rowman and Littlefield.

　2011. "Understanding the Revolutions of 2011: Weakness and Resilience in Middle Eastern Autocracies." *Foreign Affairs* 90:8–16.

Goldstone, Jack A., and Charles Tilly. 2001. "Threat (and Opportunity): Popular Action and State Response in the Dynamics of Contentious Action." Ch. 7 in *Silence and Voice in the Study of Contentious Politics*, edited by Ronald R. Aminzade et al. New York: Cambridge University Press.

Goodin, Robert E., and Hans-Dieter Klingeman (Eds.). 1996. *A New Handbook of Political Science*. Oxford: Oxford University Press.

Goodwin, Jeff. 1994. "Toward a New Sociology of Revolutions." *Theory and Society* 23:731–766.

　2001. *No Other Way Out : States and Revolutionary Movements, 1945–1991*. Cambridge and New York: Cambridge University Press.

Goodwin, Jeff, and James M. Jasper. 1999. "Caught in a Winding, Snarling Vine: The Structural Bias of Political Process Theory." *Sociological Forum* 14:27–54.

　(Eds.). 2004. *Rethinking Social Movements: Structure, Meaning, and Emotion*. Lanham, MD: Rowman and Littlefield.

Goodwin, Jeff, James M. Jasper, and Francesca Polletta (Eds.). 2001. *Passionate Politics: Emotions and Social Movements*. Chicago: University of Chicago Press.

Gough, Hugh. 1998. *The Terror in the French Revolution*. New York: St. Martin's.

Gould, Roger. 1995. *Insurgent Identities: Class, Community, and Protest in Paris from 1848 to the Commune.* Chicago: University of Chicago Press.

1998. "Political Networks and the Local/National Boundary in the Whiskey Rebellion." Ch. 3 in *Challenging Authority: The Historical Study of Contentious Politics,* edited by Michael P. Hanagan, Leslie Page Moch, and Wayne te Brake. Minneapolis and St. Paul: University of Minnesota Press.

Gourevitch, Peter Alexis. 1978. "Reforming the Napoleonic State." Pp. 28–63 in *Territorial Politics in Industrial Nations,* edited by Luigi Graziano, Peter J. Katzenstein, and Sidney Tarrow. New York: Praeger.

1980. *Paris and the Provinces: The Politics of Local Government Reform in France.* Berkeley: University of California Press.

Graham, Pamela M. 2001. "Political Incorporation and Re-Incorporation: Simultaneity in the Dominican Migrant Experience." Pp. 87–108 in *Migration, Transnationalization and Race in a Changing New York,* edited by Hector R. Cordero-Guzmán, Robert C. Smith, and Ramón Grosfoguel. Philadelphia: Temple University Press.

Gramsci, Antonio. 1955. *Note sul Machiavelli, sulla politica e sullo stato moderno.* Turin: Einaudi.

1963. "Alcuni temi della quistone meridionale." in *Antologia degli scritti.* Roma: Editori Riuniti.

1963. *Antonio Gramsci: Antologia degli scritti.* Roma: Editori Riuniti.

1971. *Selections from the Prison Notebooks of Antonio Gramsci.* New York: International Publishers.

Gramsci Institute. 1962. *Tendenze nel capitalismo italiano.* Rome: Riuniti.

Grazioli, Marco. 1979. "Il movimento studentesco in Italia nell'anno accademico 1967–68: Ricostruzione ed analisi." Unpublished PhD thesis, State University of Milan, Milan, Italy.

Grignon, Claude, and Jean-Claude Passeron. 1970. *Innovation in Higher Education: French Experience Before 1968.* Paris: OECD Case Studies in Higher Education.

Groux, Guy. 1988. "Les cadres et le mouvement de mai; un moment, une rupture." In René Mouriaux, ed. *Colloque sur Acteurs et terrains du mouvement social de 1968.* Paris: CRMSS, pp. 142–153.

Groux, Guy, and Jean-Marie Pernot. 2008. *La Grève.* Paris: Les Presses de Sciences Po.

Guarnizo, Luis Eduardo, Alejandro Portes, and William Haller. 2003. "From Assimilation to Transnationalism: Determinants of Transnational Political Action among Contemporary Migrants." *American Journal of Sociology* 108:1211–1248.

Guidry, John A., Michael D. Kennedy, and Mayer N. Zald (Eds.). 2000. *Globalizations and Social Movements: Culture, Power, and the Transnational Public Sphere.* Ann Arbor: University of Michigan Press.

Gurr, Ted Robert. 1970. *Why Men Rebel.* Princeton, NJ: Center for International Studies, Princeton University.

Gurr, Ted R. 1987. *The State and the City.* Chicago: University of Chicago Press.

Gurr, Ted Robert, Barbara Harff, Montey G. Marshall, and James R. Scarritt. 1993. *Minorities at Risk.* Washington, DC: U.S. Institute for Peace.

Hadden, Jennifer. 2011. "Contesting Climate Change: Civil Society Networks and Collective Action in the European Union." Unpublished PhD Dissertation, Ithaca, NY: Cornell University.

Hadden, Jennifer, and Sidney Tarrow. 2007. "Spillover or Spillout: The Global Justice Movement in the United States after 9/11." *Mobilization* 12:359–376.

Haines, Herbert H. 1984. "Black Radicalization and the Study of Civil Rights: 1957–1970." *Social Problems* 32:21–43.

Hall, Stuart. 2002. "Political Belonging in a World of Multiple Identities." Pp. 25–31 in *Conceiving Cosmopolitanism: Theory, Context, and Practice*, edited by Steven Vertovec and Robin Cohen. Oxford: Oxford University Press.

Han, Shin-Kap. 2008. "The Other Ride of Paul Revere." *Mobilization* 14:155.

Hanagan, Michael. 1980. *The Logic of Solidarity*. Urbana: University of Illinois Press.

Hanagan, Michael, and Chris Tilly (Eds.). 2011. *Contention and Trust in Cities and States*. New York: Springer.

Hannerz, Ulf. 1990. "Cosmopolitans and Locals in World Culture." *Theory, Culture and Society* 7:237–251.

1996. *Transnational Connections: Culture, People, Places*. London: Routledge.

Heaney, Michael T., and Fabio Rojas. 2011. "The Partisan Dynamics of Contention: Demobilization of the Antiwar Movement in the United States, 2007–2009." *Mobilization* 16:44–64.

Heclo, Hugh. 1974. *Modern Social Policies in Britain and Sweden: From Relief to Income Maintenance*. New Haven, CT: Yale University Press.

Hedström, Peter, and Richard Swedberg (Eds.). 1998. *Social Mechanisms: An Analytical Approach to Social Theory*. Cambridge: Cambridge University Press.

Held, David. 1995. *Democracy and the Global Order: From the Modern State to Cosmopolitan Governance*. Cambridge: Polity Press.

Helfferish, Barbara, and Felix Kolb. 2001. "Multilevel Action Coordination in European Contentious Politics: The European Women's Lobby." Ch. 7 in *Contentious Europeans: Protest and Politics in an Emerging Polity*, edited by Doug Imig and Sidney Tarrow. Lanham, MD: Rowman and Littlefield.

Hellman, Judith Adler. 1987. *Journeys among Women: Feminism in Five Italian Cities*. New York: Oxford University Press.

Hellman, Stephen. 1975. "The PCI's Alliance Strategy and the Case of the Middle Classes." Pp. 372–419 in *Communism in Italy and France*, edited by Donald L. M. Blackmer and Sidney Tarrow. Princeton, NJ: Princeton University Press.

1980. "Il PCI e la eredità ambigua dell-autunno caldo: Evidenza del caso Torinese." *Il Mulino* 29:246–295.

Hervieu-Leger, Daniele. 1988. "May 1968 et les Catholiques: Le cas de la Mission Etudiante." in *Colloque sur Acteurs et terrains du mouvement social de 1968*. Paris: CRSMSS.

Hirschman, Albert O. 1982. *Shifting Involvements, Private Interest and Public Action*. Princeton, NJ: Princeton University Press.

Hobsbawm, Eric J. 1959. *Social Bandits and Primitive Rebels*. Glencoe: The Free Press.

1974. "Peasant Land Occupations." *Past and Present* 62:120–152.

1978. "The Left and the Crisis of Organization." *New Society* 44:63–66.

Hoffer, Eric. 1951. *The True Believer*. New York: Harper and Row.

Hollinger, David. 2002. "Not Universalists, Not Pluralists: The New Cosmopolitans Find Their Own Way." Pp. 227–239 in *Conceiving Cosmopolitanism: Theory, Context, and Practice*, edited by Steven Vertovec and Robin Cohen. Oxford: Oxford University Press.

Hunt, Lynn. 1984. *Politics, Culture and Class in the French Revolution*. Berkeley: University of California Press.

Imig, Doug, and Sidney Tarrow (Eds.) 2001. *Contentious Europeans: Protest and Politics in an Emerging Polity*. Lanham, MD: Rowman and Littlefield.

Imig, Doug, and Sidney Tarrow. 2001. "Mapping the Europeanization of Contention: Evidence from a Quantitative Data Analysis." Ch. 2 in *Contentious Europeans: Protest and Politics in an Emerging Polity*, edited by Doug Imig and Sidney Tarrow. Lanham, MD: Rowman and Littlefield.

Isaac, Larry, and Larry Griffin. 1989. "Ahistoricism in Time-Series Analyses of Historical Process: Critique, Redirection, and Illustrations from U.S. Labor History." *American Sociological Review* 54:873–890.

Jasper, James. 1998. "The Emotions of Protest: Affective and Reactive Emotions in and around Social Movements." *Sociological Forum* 13:397–424.

Jenkins, J. Craig. 1985. *The Politics of Insurgency: The Farm Worker Movement in the 1960s*. New York: Columbia University Press.

Jenkins, J. Craig, and Craig Eckert. 1986. "Channeling Black Insurgency: Elite Patronage and the Development of the Civil Rights Movement." *American Sociological Review* 51:812–830.

Jenkins, J. Craig, and Charles Perrow. 1977. "Insurgency of the Powerless: Farm Worker Movements (1946–1972)." *American Sociological Review* 42:249–268.

Joachim, Jutta, and Birgit Locher (Eds.). 2009. *Transnational Activism in the UN and the EU*. London and New York: Routledge.

Johnson, Chalmers A. 1962. *Peasant Nationalism and Communist Power*. Stanford CA: Stanford University Press.

Johnson, Paul E. 1978. *A Shopkeeper's Millennium: Society and Revivals in Rochester, New York, 1815–1837*. New York: Hill and Wang.

Jung, Jai Kwan. 2009. "Growing Supranational Identities in a Globalizing World? A Multi-level Analysis of the World Vales Surveys." *European Journal of Political Research* 47:578–609.

Kalyvas, Stathis N. 1996. *The Rise of Christian Democracy in Europe*. Ithaca, NY: Cornell University Press.

2006. *The Logic of Violence in Civil War*. New York and Cambridge: Cambridge University Press.

Kaplan, Steven L. 1982. "The Famine Plot Persuasion." in *The American Philosophical Society*. Philadelphia.

1993. *Adieu 1789*. Paris: Fayard.

Katz, Hagal, and Helmut Anheier. 2006. "Global Connectedness: The Structure of Transnational NGO Networks." Ch. 7 in *Global Civil Society 2005/6*, edited by Marlies Glasius, Mary Kaldor, and Helmut Anheier. London: Sage Publications.

Katzenstein, Mary F. 1990. "Feminism within Institutions: Unobtrusive Mobilization." *Signs* 16:27–54.

1998. *Faithful and Fearless: Moving Feminist Protest inside the Church and Military*. Princeton, NJ: Princeton University Press.

Katznelson, Ira. 1981. *City Trenches: Urban Politics and the Patterning of Class in the United States*. New York: Pantheon Books.

2002. "Flexible Capacity: The Military and Early American Statebuilding." Ch. 4 in *Shaped by War and Trade. International Influences on American Political Development*, edited by Ira Katznelson and Martin Shefter. Princeton, NJ: Princeton University Press.

Kay, Tamara. 2010. *NAFTA and the Politics of Labor Transnationalism*. New York and Cambridge: Cambridge University Press.

Keck, Margaret, and Kathryn Sikkink. 1998. *Activists beyond Borders: Transnational Activist Networks in International Politics*. Ithaca, NY and London: Cornell University Press.

Keniston, Kenneth. 1968. *Young Radicals*. New York: Harcourt, Brace Jovanovich.

Kestnbaum, Meyer. 2000. "Citizenship and Compulsory Military Service: The Revolutionary Origins of Conscription in the United States." *Armed Forces and Society* 27:7–36.

——— 2002. "Citizen-Soldiers, National Service and the Mass Army: The Birth of Conscription in Revolutionary Europe and North America." *Armed Forces and Society* 20:117–144.

——— 2005. "Mars Revealed: The Entry of Ordinary People into War Among States." Pp. 249–285 in *Remaking Modernity: Politics, History and Sociology*. Durham, NC and London: Duke University Press.

Kirchheimer, Otto. 1966. "The Transformation of the European Party Systems." Ch. 6 in *Political Parties and Political Development*, edited by Joseph LaPalombara and Myron Weiner. Princeton, NJ: Princeton University Press.

Kitschelt, Herbert. 1986. "Political Opportunity Structures and Political Protest: Anti-Nuclear Movements in Four Democracies." *British Journal of Political Science* 16:57–85.

Klandermans, Bert. 1984. "Participation and Mobilization: Social-psychological Expansions of Resource Mobilization Theory." *American Sociological Review* 49:583–600.

——— 1990. "Linking the 'Old' and the 'New': Movement Networks in the Netherlands." Pp. 123–136 in *Challenging the Political Order*, edited by Russell Dalton and Manfred Kuechler. New York: Oxford University Press.

Klandermans, Bert, Hanspeter Kriesi, and Sidney Tarrow (Eds.). 1988. *From Structure to Action: Comparing Social Movement Participation Across Cultures*. Greenwich, CT: JAI Press.

Klandermans, Bert, Conny Roggeband, and Jacquelien van Stekelenberg (Eds.). 2011. *The Changing Dynamics of Contention*. Minneapolis and St. Paul: University of Minnesota Press.

Klandermans, Bert, and Suzanne Staggenborg (Eds.). 2002. *Methods of Social Movement Research*. Minneapolis and St. Paul: University of Minnesota Press.

Kolb, Felix. 2007. *Protest and Opportunities: The Political Outcomes of Social Movements*. Frankfurt and New York: Campus.

Koopmans, Ruud. 1993. "The Dynamics of Protest Waves: West Germany, 1965 to 1989." *American Sociological Review* 58:637–658.

——— 2004. "Protest in Time and Space: The Evolution of Waves of Contention." Ch. 2 in *The Blackwell Companion to Social Movements*, edited by David A. Snow, Sarah A. Soule, and Hanspeter Kriesi. Malden and Oxford: Blackwell.

Kornhauser, William. 1959. *The Politics of Mass Society*. New York: Free Press.

Korzeniewicz, Roberto P., and William S. Smith. 2001. "Protest and Collaboration: Transnational Civil Society Networks and the Politics of Summitry and Free Trade in the Americas." in *Programa de Estudios sobre Instituciones Económicas Internationales (PIEI) de FLASCO*. Buenos Aires, pp. 1–32.

Kramnick, Issac. 2007. "Introduction." in Alexis de Tocqueville. *Democracy in America. An Annotated Text, Backgrounds, Interpretations*. New York: W.W. Norton.

Kriesi, Hanspeter, et al. 1995. *The Politics of New Social Movements in Western Europe*. Minneapolis and St. Paul: University of Minnesota Press.

Kryder, Daniel. 2000. *Divided Arsenal: Race and the American State During World War Two*. New York and Cambridge: Cambridge University Press.

Kuran, Timur. 1991. "Now Out of Never: The Element of Surprise in the East European Revolution of 1989." Pp. 7–48 in *Liberalization and Democratization: Change in the Soviet Union and Eastern Europe* edited by Nancy Bermeo. Baltimore, MD: Johns Hopkins University Press.

Kyle, David. 1999. "The Otavalo Trade Diaspora: Social Capital and Transnational Entrepreneurship." *Ethnic and Racial Studies* 22:422–446.

Lange, Peter, Sidney Tarrow, and Cynthia Irvin. 1989. "Mobilization, Social Movements and Party Recruitment: The Italian Communist Party since the 1960s." *British Journal of Political Science* 20:15–42.

LaPalombara, Joseph. 1964. *Interest Groups in Italian Politics*. Princeton, NJ: Princeton University Press.

1987. *Democracy, Italian Style*. New Haven, CT: Yale University Press.

Le Bon, Gustave. 1977. *The Crowd: A Study of the Popular Mind*. New York: Penguin.

Lefebvre, Georges. 1947. *The Coming of the French Revolution* (trans. R. R. Palmer). Princeton, NJ: Princeton University Press.

Lefebvre, Henry. 1965. *La Proclamation de la Commune*. Paris: Gallimard.

Lenin, V. I. 1929. *What Is to be Done? Burning Questions of Our Movement*. New York: International Publishers.

1972. "The Agrarian Programme of Social-Democracy in the First Russian Revolution, 1905–1907." Pp. 217–429 in *Collected Works*. Moscow: Progress Publishers.

1977. *Imperialism, the Highest Stage of Capitalism*. New York: International Publishers.

Lepetit, Bernard. 1988. *Les villes dans la France moderne, 1740–1840*. Paris: Albin Michel.

Levi, Margaret, and Gillian Murphy. 2006. "Coalitions of Contention." *Political Studies* 54:651–667.

Lichbach, Mark. 2003. "Global Order and Local Resistance: The Neoliberal Institutional Trilemma and the Battle of Seattle." Unpublished Paper. College Park, MD: University of Maryland.

Lichbach, Mark, and Helma DeVries. 2007. "Mechanisms of Globalized Protest Movements." Pp. 461–496 in *The Oxford Handbook of Comparative Politics*, edited by Charles Boix and Susan C. Stokes. New York and Oxford: Oxford University Press.

Lillie, Nathan. 2006. *A Global Union for Global Workers: Collective Bargaining and Regulatory Politics in Maritime Shipping*. New York and London: Routledge.

Linebaugh, Peter, and Marcus Rediker. 1990. "The Many-Headed Hydra: Sailors, Slaves, and the Atlantic Working Class in the Eighteenth Century." *Journal of Historical Sociology* 3:225–252.

Lloyd, Christopher. 1993. *The Structures of History*. Oxford and Cambridge: Blackwell.

Lohmann, Susanne. 1993. "A Signaling Model of Informative and Manupulative Political Action." *American Political Science Review* 87:319–333.

Lotringer, Sylvere, and Christian Marazzi (Eds.). 2007. *Autonomia: Post-Political Politics*. Cambridge, MA: MIT Press.

Lowi, Theodore. 1971. *The Politics of Disorder*. New York: Basic Books.

Lumley, Robert. 1983. "Social Movements in Italy, 1968–78." Unpublished paper, Centre for Contemporary Cultural Studies: University of Birmingham.

  1990. *States of Emergency: Cultures of Revolt in Italy from 1968 to 1978.* London: Verso.

Lutz, Vera. 1962. *Italy: A Study in Economic Development.* Oxford: Oxford University Press.

Lynn, John A. 1983. *The Bayonets of the Republic: Motivation and Tactics in the Army of Revolutionary France, 1791–94.* Urbana and Chicago: University of Illinois Press.

Machiavelli, Niccolo. 1977. *The Prince.* New York: W.W. Norton & Company.

MacKinnon, Catharine. 1979. *Sexual Harassment of Working Women.* New Haven, CT and London: Yale University Press.

Magna, Nino. 1978. "Per una storia dell'operaismo in Italia: Il trentennio postbellico." Pp. 295–345 in *Operaismo e centralitá operaia,* edited by Fabrizio D'Agostini. Rome: Riuniti.

Maheu, Louis. 1995. *Social Movements and Social Classes: The Future of Collective Action.* London: Sage Publications.

Mahoney, James, Erin Kimball, and Kendra Koiva. 2009. "The Logic of Historical Explanation in the Social Sciences." *Comparative Political Studies* 42:114–146.

Maier, Pauline. 1972. *From Resistance to Revolution: Colonial Radicals and the Development of American Opposition to Britain, 1765–1776.* New York: Knopf.

Mansbridge, Jane, and Katherine Flaster. 2008. "The Cultural Politics of Everyday Discourse: The Case of 'Male Chauvinist.'" *Critical Sociology* 33:627–660.

March, James G., and Johan P. Olson. 1999. "The Institutional Dynamics of International Political Orders." Pp. 303–330 in *Exploration and Contestation in the Study of World Politics,* edited by Peter J. Katzenstein, Robert Keohane, and Stephen Krasner. Cambridge, MA: MIT Press.

Margadant, Ted W. 1979. *French Peasants in Revolt: The Insurrection of 1851.* Princeton, NJ: Princeton University Press.

Marlow, Joyce. 1973. *Captain Boycott and the Irish.* New York: Saturday Review Press.

Marshall, Thomas H. 1964. *Class, Citizenship and Social Development.* Garden City, NY: Doubleday.

Marx, Gary T., and James L. Wood. 1975. "Strands of Theory and Research in Collective Behavior." *Annual Review of Sociology* 1:363–428.

Marx, Karl. 1963. *The Poverty of Philosophy.* New York: International Publishers.

  1978. "The Eighteenth Brumaire of Louis Bonaparte " Pp. 594–617 in *The Marx-Engels Reader,* edited by Robert C. Tucker. New York and London: Norton.

Matynia, Elzbieta. 2009. *Performative Democracy.* Boulder, CO: Paradigm.

McAdam, Doug. 1983. "Tactical Innovation and the Pace of Insurgency." *American Sociological Review* 48:735–754.

  1995. "'Initiator' and 'Spin-Off' Movements: Diffusion Processes in Protest Cycles." Pp. 217–240 in *Repertoires and Cycles of Collective Action,* edited by Mark Traugott. Durham, NC: Duke University Press.

  1996. "Conceptual Origins, Current Problems, Future Directions." Pp. 23–40 in *Comparative Perspectives on Social Movements: Political Opportunities, Mobilizing Structures, and Cultural Framings,* edited by Doug McAdam, John McCarthy, and Mayer N. Zald. Cambridge: Cambridge University Press.

1999. "The Biographical Impact of Activism." Ch. 6 in *How Social Movements Matter*, edited by Marco Giuni, Doug McAdam, and Charles Tilly. Minneapolis and St. Paul: University of Minnesota.

1999 [1982]. *Political Process and the Development of Black Insurgency, 1930–1970*. Chicago: University of Chicago Press.

McAdam, Doug, Nella Van Dyke, Allison Munch, and Jim Shockey. 1998. "Social Movements and the Life-Course." Unpublished paper, Tucson, AZ: University of Arizona.

McAdam, Doug, and Dieter Rucht. 1993. "The Cross-National Diffusion of Movement Ideas." *The Annals of the American Academy of the Political and Social Sciences* 528:56–74.

McAdam, Doug, and Sidney Tarrow. 2012. "Social Movements and Elections: Toward a Broader Understanding of the Context of Contention." Ch. 6 in *The Changing Dynamics of Contention*, edited by Jacquelien van Stekelenburg, Conny Roggeband, and Bert Klandermans. Minneapolis and St. Paul: University of Minnesota Press.

McAdam, Doug, Sidney Tarrow, and Charles Tilly. 2001. *Dynamics of Contention*. New York and Cambridge: Cambridge University Press.

McAdam, Doug, Sidney Tarrow, and Charles Tilly. 2009. "Toward an Integrated Perspective on Social Movements and Revolution." Pp. 142–173 in *Comparative Politics: Rationality, Culture, and Structure*, edited by Mark Irving Lichbach and Alan S. Zuckerman. New York: Cambridge University Press, second edition.

McCarthy, John. 1987. "Pro-Life and Pro-Choice Mobilization: Infrastructure Deficits and New Technologies." Pp. 49–66 in *Social Movements in an Organizations Society*, edited by Mayer N. Zald and John McCarthy. New Brunswick, NJ: Transaction Books.

McCarthy, John, David Britt, and Mark Wolfson. 1991. "The Institutional Channeling of Social Movements in the Modern State." *Research in Social Movements, Conflict and Change* 13:45–76.

McCarthy, John, Clark McPhail, and Jackie Smith. 1996. "Images of Protest: Estimating Selection Bias in Media Coverage of Washington Demonstrations." *American Sociological Review* 61:478–499.

McCarthy, John, David Schweingruber, and Clark McPhail. 1999. "Policing Protest in the United States, 1960–1995." Ch. 2 in *Policing Protest*, edited by Donatella della Porta and Herbert Reiter. Minneapolis and St. Paul: University of Minnesota Press.

McCarthy, John, and Mayer N. Zald. 1973. *The Trend of Social Movements in America: Professionalization and Resource Mobilization*. Morristown, NJ: General Learning Press.

1977. "Resource Mobilization and Social Movements: A Partial Theory." *American Journal of Sociology* 82:1212–1241.

(Eds.). 1987. *Social Movements in an Organizational Society: Collected Essays*. New Brunswick, NJ: Transaction Publishers.

McMichael, Philip. 2005. "Globalization." Pp. 587–606 in *Handbook of Political Sociology*, edited by Thomas Janoski, Robert Alford, Alexander M. Hicks, and Mildred Schwartz. New York and Cambridge: Cambridge University Press.

McVey, Ruth. 1970. *The Social Roots of Indonesian Communism*. Brussels: Center d'Etude du Sud-Est Asiatique et de l'Extreme Orient.

Melucci, Alberto. 1980. "The New Social Movements: A Theoretical Approach." *Social Science Information* 19:199–226.

1985. "The Symbolic Challenge of Contemporary Movements." *Social Research* 52:789–815.

1988. "Getting Involved: Identity and Mobilization in Social Movements." Pp. 329–48 in *From Structure to Action: Comparing Social Movements Across Cultures*, edited by Bert Klandermans, Hanspeter Kriesi, and Sidney Tarrow. Greenwich, CT: JAI Press.

1989. *Nomads of the Present: Social Movements and Individual Needs in Contemporary Society*. Philadelphia: Temple University Press.

Mendelson, Sarah. 2005. *Barracks and Brothels: Peacekeepers and Human Trafficking in the Balkans*. Washington, DC: Center for Strategic and International Studies.

Merry, Sally Engle. 2006. *Human Rights and Gender Violence: Translating International Law into Local Justice*. Chicago: University of Chicago Press.

Merton, Robert K. 1957. *Social Theory and Social Structure*. Glencoe, IL: The Free Press.

Meyer, David S. 2005. "Introduction. Social Movements and Public Policy: Eggs, Chickens, and Theory." Pp. 1–26 in *Routing the Opposition: Social Movements, Public Policy and Democracy*, edited by H. Ingram, V. Jenness, and D. Meyer. Minneapolis and St. Paul: University of Minnesota Press.

Meyer, David S. and Josh Gamson. 1995. "The Challenge of Cultural Elites: Celebrities and Social Movements." *Sociological Inquiry* 65:181–206.

Meyer, David S., and Suzanne Staggenborg. 1994. "Movements, Countermovements, and the Structure of Political Opportunity." *American Journal of Sociology* 101:1628–1660.

1998. "Countermovement Dynamics in Federal Systems: A Comparison of Abortion Politics in Canada and the United States." *Research in Political Sociology* 8:209–240.

Meyer, David S., and Sidney Tarrow (Eds.). 1998. *The Social Movement Society: Contentious Politics for a New Century*. Lanham, MD: Rowman and Littlefield.

Meyer, John, John Boli, and George Thomas et al. 1998. "World Society and the Nation-State." *American Journal of Sociology* 103:144–181.

Meyer, John, John Boli, and David Frank. 1997. "The Structuring of a World Environmental Regime, 1870–1990." *International Organization* 51:623–651.

Michels, Robert. 1962. *Political Parties: A Sociological Study of the Oligarchical Tendencies of Modern Democracy*. New York: Collier Books.

Mink, Gwendolyn. 2000. *Hostile Environment: The Political Betrayal of Sexually Harassed Women*. Ithaca, NY and London: Cornell University Press.

Minkoff, Debra C. 1995. *Organizing for Equality: The Evolution of Women's and Racial-ethnic Organizations in America, 1955–1985*. New Brunswick, NJ: Rutgers University Press.

1996. "The Sequencing of Social Movements." Unpublished Paper. New Haven, CT: Yale University.

Mische, Ann. 2008. *Partisan Publics: Communication and Contention Across Brazilian Youth Activist Networks*. Princeton, NJ and Oxford: Princeton University Press.

Mitrany, David. 1961. *Marx against the Peasant: A Study in Social Dogmatism*. New York: Collier.

Mobilization. 2003. "Book Symposium: Focus on Dynamics of Contention." *Mobilization* 8:107–141.

2010. "Dynamics of Contention, Ten Years On." *Mobilization* 16:1–116.

Moen, Matthew C. 1996. "The Evolving Politics of the Christian Right." *PS: Political Science and Politics* 29:461–464.

Moore, Robert Lawrence. 1994. *Selling God: American Religion in the Marketplace of Culture*. New York: Oxford University Press.

Moore, Sally Falk. 1987. "Explaining the Present: Theoretical Dilemmas in Processual Ethnography." *American Ethnologist* 14:727–736.

Morin, Edgar, Claude Lefort, and Jean-Marc Coudray. 1968. *La Brêche: Premières reflexions sur les évenements*. Paris: Fayard.

Mornet, Daniel. 1989. *Les origines intellectuelles de la Révolution française, 1715–1787*. Lyon: La Manufacture.

Nitti, Francesco Saverio. 1958. *Scritti sulla questione meridionale*. Bari: Laterza.

Nora, Pierre. 1974. "Le retour de l'évenement " Pp. 210–230 in *Faire de l'Histoire*, edited by Jacques Le Goff and Pierre Nora. Paris: Gallimard.

Nossiter, John Thomas. 1982. *Communism in Kerala: A Study in Political Adaptation*. London: Royal Institute of International Affairs.

Nussbaum, Martha C. 1996. "Patriotism and Cosmopolitanism." Pp. 4–17 in *For Love of Country*, edited by Joshua Cohen. Boston: Beacon Press.

O'Brien, Robert, Anne Marie Goetz, Jan Aart Scholte, and Marc Williams. 2000. *Contesting Global Governance: Multilateral Economic Institutions and Global Social Movements*. Cambridge: Cambridge University Press.

Offe, Claus. 1985. "New Social Movements: Challenging the Boundaries of Institutional Politics." *Social Research* 52:817–868.

Olesen, Thomas. 2005. *International Zapatismo: The Construction of Solidarity in the Age of Globalization*. London: ZED Books.

Olzak, Susan. 1989. "Analysis of Events in the Study of Collective Action." *Annual Review of Sociology* 15:119–186.

——— 1992. *Dynamics of Ethnic Competition and Conflict*. Stanford, CA: Stanford University Press.

Ortoleva, Peppino. 1988. *Saggio sui movimenti del 1968 in Europa e in America*. Rome: Editori Riuniti.

Osa, Maryjane. 2003. *Solidarity and Contention: Networks of Polish Opposition*. Minneapolis: University of Minnesota Press.

Ostergaard-Nielsen, Eva. 2001. "Transnational Political Practices and the Receiving State: Turks and Kurds in Germany and the Netherlands." *Global Networks* 1:261–282.

Overstreet, Gene D., and Marshall Windmuller. 1959. *Communism in India*. Berkeley and Los Angeles: University of California Press.

Parisi, Arturo, and Gianfranco Pasquino. 1980. "Changes in Italian Electoral Behavior: The Relationships between Parties and Voters." Pp. 6–30 in *Italy in Transition: Conflict and Consensus*, edited by Peter Lange and Sidney Tarrow. London: Cass.

Partito comunista italiano. 1954. *Forza e attivitá del partito*. Roma: Partito comunista italiano; Sezione d'organizazzione.

——— 1961. *L'organizazzione del PCI*. Roma: Partito comunista italiano; Sezione d'organizazzione.

——— 1962. *L'organizazzione del partito*. Roma: Partito comunista italiano; Sezione d'organizazzione.

——— 1964. *Dati sull'organizzazione del PCI*. Roma: Partito comunista italiano; Sezione d'organizazzione.

Passeron, Jean-Claude. 1986. "1950–1980: L'université mise à la question: changement de decor ou changement de cap?" Pp. 367–420 in *Histoire des universités en France*, edited by Jacques Verger. Toulouse: Privat.

Perlmutter, Edward. 1987. "Modeling the Polity: Autoriduzione in Turin." Unpublished Paper.

———. 1988. "Intellectuals and Urban Protest: Extraparliamentary Politics in Turin, Italy, 1968–1976." Unpublished PhD Dissertation. Cambridge, MA: Harvard University.

Pero, Luciano. 1967. "La crisi del movimento studentesco: Indicazioni per una comprensione e una soluzione." *Questitalia* 114–115:53–69.

Perrot, Michelle. 1987. *Workers on Strike: France 1871–1890*. New Haven, CT and London: Yale University Press.

Persinos, John F. 1994. "Has the Christian Right Taken Over the Republican Party?" *Campaigns and Elections* 15:21–24.

Pianta, Mario, Federico Silva, and Duccio Zola. 2003. "Parallel Summits, Social Fora, Global Days of Action (Update)." Ch. 7 in *Global Civil Society 2003*, edited by Helmut Anheier, Marlies Glasius, and Mary Kaldor. London: Sage Publications.

Piven, Frances Fox, and Richard Cloward. 1972. *Regulating the Poor*. New York: Vintage Books.

———. 1977. *Poor People's Movements: Why They Succeed, How They Fail*. New York: Vintage.

Pizzorno, Alessandro. 1978. "Political Exchange and Collective Identity in Industrial Conflict." Vol. II, Pp. 277–298 in *The Resurgence of Class Conflict in Western Europe since 1968*, edited by Colin Crouch and Alessandro Pizzorno. London: Macmillan Press.

Pocock, John Greville Agard. 1975. *The Machiavellian Moment: Florentine Political Theory and The Atlantic Republican Tradition*. Princeton, NJ: Princeton University Press.

Poloni-Staudinger, Lori. 2008. "The Domestic Opportunity Structure and Supernational Activity: An Explanation of Environmental Group Activity at the European Union Level." *European Union Politics* 9:531–555.

Popkin, Samuel. 1977. *The Rational Peasant. The Political Economy of Rural Society in Vietnam*. Berkeley: University of California Press.

Portes, Alejandro. 1999. "Conclusion: Towards a New World—The Origins and Effects of Transnational Activities." *Ethnic and Racial Studies* 22:463–477.

———. 2000. "Globalization from Below: The Rise of Transnational Communities." Pp. 253–270 in *The Ends of Globalization: Bringing Society Back In*, edited by Don Kalb, Marco van der Land, Richard Staring, Bart van Steenbergen, and Nico Wilterdink. Lanham, MD: Rowman and Littlefield.

Prebisch, Raúl. 1950. *The Economic Development of Latin America and its Principal Problems*. New York: United Nations Press.

Regalia, Ida. 1985. *Eletti e abbandonati*. Bologna: Il Mulino.

Regalia, Ida, Mario Regini, and Emilio Reyneri. 1978. "Labour Conflicts and Industrial Relations in Italy." Vol. I, Ch. 4 in *The Resurgence of Class Conflict in Western Europe since 1968*, edited by Colin Crouch and Alessandro Pizzorno. New York: Holmes and Meier.

Rice, C. Duncan. 1982. "The Missionary Context of the British Anti-Slavery Movement." Pp. 150–163 in *Slavery and British Society, 1776–1846*, edited by James Walvin. Baton Rouge: Louisiana State University Press.

Rieter, Herbert, Massimiliano Andretta, Donatella Della Porta, and Lorenzo Mosca. 2007. "The Global Justice Movement in Italy." Pp. 52–78 in *The Global Justice Movement*, edited by Donatella Della Porta. Boulder, CO and London: Paradigm.

Riley, Denise. 1988. *Am I That Name? Gender and the Category of Women in History.* Minneapolis and Minnesota: University of Minnesota Press.

Risse, Thomas, Stephen C. Ropp, and Kathryn Sikkink. 1999. *The Power of Human Rights: International Norms and Domestic Change.* Cambridge and New York: Cambridge University Press.

Risse-Kappen, Thomas (Ed.). 1995. *Bringing Transnational Relations Back In: Non-state Actors, Domestic Structure and International Institutions.* New York: Cambridge University Press.

Robins, Kevin. 2005. "Globalization." Pp. 345–346 in *Social Science Encyclopedia,* edited by Adam Kuper and Jessica Kuper. London: Routledge.

Rochon, Thomas R. 1998. *Culture Moves: Ideas, Activism, and Changing Values.* Princeton, NJ: Princeton University Press.

Roggeband, Conny. 2010. "Transnational Networks and Institutions: How Diffusion Shaped the Politicization of Sexual Harassment in Europe." Ch. 2 in *The Diffusion of Social Movements: Actors, Mechanisms, and Political Effects,* edited by Rebecca Kolins Givan, Kenneth M. Roberts, and Sarah A. Soule. Ithaca, NY and London: Cornell University Press.

Rohrschneider, Robert, and Russell Dalton. 2002. "A Global Network? Transnational Cooperation among Environmental Groups." *The Journal of Politics* 64:510–533.

Rojas, Fabio. 2007. *From Black Power to Black Studies: How a Radical Social Movement Became an Academic Discipline.* Baltimore, MD and London: Johns Hopkins University Press.

Rokkan, Stein, with Angus Campbell, Per Torscvik, and Henry Valen. 1970. *Citizens, Elections, Parties.* New York: Vintage.

Root, Hilton. 1987. *Peasants and Kings in Burgundy. Agrarian Foundations of French Absolutism.* Berkeley and Los Angeles: University of California Press.

Rosenau, James. 1990. *Turbulence in World Politics: A Theory of Change and Continuity.* Princeton, NJ: Princeton University Press.

Rousseau, Jean-Jacques. 1972. *The Government of Poland.* Indianapolis, IN and New York: Bobbs-Merrill.

Rousseau, Jean Jacques. 1978. *On the Social Contract with the Geneva Manuscript and Political Economy.* New York: St. Martin's.

Roy, William G. 2010. *Reds, Whites, and Blues: Social Movements, Folk Music, and Race in the United States.* Princeton, NJ: Princeton University Press.

Rucht, Dieter. 1988. *Themes, Logics and Arenas of Social Movements: A Structural Approach.* Greenwich, CT: JAI Press.

——— 1989. "Environmental Movement Organizations in West Germany and France: Structure and Interorganizational Relations." Pp. 61–94 in *Organizing for Change: Social Movement Organizations across Cultures. International Social Movement Research,* edited by Bert Klandermans. Greenwich, CT: JAI Press.

——— 1990. "Campaigns, Skirmishes and Battles: Anti-Nuclear Movements in the USA, France and West Germany." *Industrial Crisis Quarterly* 4:193–222.

——— 1991. "Sociological Theory as a Theory of Social Movements? A Critique of Alain Touraine." Pp. 355–384 in *Research on Social Movements: The State of the Art in Western Europe and the USA,* edited by Dieter Rucht. Boulder, CO: Westview Press.

Rucht, Dieter, and Stefaan Walgrave (Eds.). 2008. *The World Says No to War.* Minneapolis and St. Paul: University of Minnesota Press.

Rupp, Leila J., and Verta Taylor. 1987. *Survival in the Doldrums: The American Women's Rights Movement, 1945 to the 1960s.* New York: Oxford University Press.

Ryan, Mary P. 1989. "The American Parade: Representations of the Nineteenth-Century Social Order." Pp. 131–153 in *The New Cultural History: Studies on the History of Society and Culture,* edited by Lynn Hunt. Berkeley CA: University of California Press.

Rydgren, Jens. 2004. "Right-Wing Populist Parties in Denmark." *West European Politics* 27:474–502.

Sabel, Charles. 1982. *Work and Politics.* Cambridge: Cambridge University Press.

Sageman, Mark. 2004. *Understanding Terror Networks.* Philadelphia: University of Pennsylvania Press.

Sahlins, Marshall. 1985. *Islands of History.* Chicago: University of Chicago Press.

　　1991. "The Return of the Event, Again: With Reflections on the Beginnings of the Great Fijan War of 1843 to 1855 between the Kingdoms of Bau and Rewa." Pp. 37–100 in *Clio in Oceania: Toward a Historical Anthropology,* edited by Aletta Biersack. Washington, DC: Smithsonian Institution Press.

Salmon, Pierre. 1982. "France: The *loi d'orientation* and its Aftermath." Pp. 103–124 in *Universities, Politicians and Bureaucrats,* edited by Hans Daalder and Edward Shils. Cambridge: Cambridge University Press.

Salvati, Michele. 1981. "May 1968 and the Hot Autumn of 1969: The Responses of Two Ruling Classes." Pp. 329–363 in *Organizing Interests in Western Europe,* edited by Suzanne Berger. Cambridge: Cambridge University Press.

Salvemini, Gaetano. 1955. *Scritti sulla questione meridionale.* Turin: Einaudi.

Sambanis, Nicholas, and Annalisa Zinn. 2003. "The Escalation of Self-Determination Movements: From Protest to Violence." Unpublished Paper. New Haven, CT: Yale University.

Sarat, Austin, and Stuart A. Scheingold (Eds.). 2006. *Cause Lawyering and Social Movements.* Stanford, CA: Stanford University Press.

Sartori, Giovanni. 1966. "European Political Parties: The Case of Polarized Pluralism." Ch. 5 in *Political Parties and Political Development,* edited by Joseph LaPalombara and Myron Weiner. Princeton, NJ: Princeton University Press.

Schama, Simon. 1989. *Citizens: A Chronicle of the French Revolution.* New York: Knopf.

Scheinman, Lawrence. 1965. *Atomic Energy Policy in France under the Fourth Republic.* Princeton, NJ: Princeton University Press.

Schnapp, Alain, and Pierre Vidal-Naquet. 1971. *The French Student Uprising: November 1967–June 1968: An Analytical Record.* Boston, MA: Beacon.

　　1988. *Journal de la commune étudiante: Textes et documents, novembre 1967-juin 1968.* Paris: Seuil.

Schram, Stuart. 1967. *Mao Tse-Tung.* Harmonsworth, England: Penguin.

Schumaker, Paul D. 1975. "Policy Responsiveness to Protest-Group Demands." *Journal of Politics* 37: 488–521.

Schwartz, Michael. 1976. *Radical Protest and Social Structure: The Southern Farmers' Alliance and Cotton Tenancy, 1880–1890.* Chicago: University of Chicago Press.

Sciubba, Roberto, and Rossana Sciubba Pace. 1976. *Le comunitá di base in Italia.* Rome: Coines.

Scoccimaro, Mauro. 1945. "Dottrina marxista e politica comunista." *Rinascita* 1:135–138.

Selbin, Eric. 1993. *Modern Latin American Revolutions*. Boulder, CO: Westview Press.

Selden, Mark. 1971. *The Yenan Way in Revolutionary China*. Cambridge, MA: Harvard University Press.

Sewell, William H., Jr. 1980. *Work and Revolution in France: The Language of Labor From the Old Regime to 1848*. New York and Cambridge: Cambridge University Press.

1986. "Artisans, Factory Workers, and the Formation of the French Working Class, 1789–1848." Pp. 45–70 in *Working Class Formation: Nineteenth Century Patterns in Western Europe and the United States*, edited by Ira Katznelson and Aristide R. Zolberg. Princeton, NJ: Princeton University Press.

1990. "Collective Violence and Collective Loyalties in France: Why the French Revolution made a Difference." *Politics and Society* 18:527–552.

1994a. A Rhetoric of Bourgeois Revolution: The Abbé Sieyes and "What is the Third Estate?" Durham, NC: Duke University Press.

1994b. "The Sans-Culotte Rhetoric of Subsistence." Pp. 249–269 in *The French Revolution and the Creation of Modern Political Culture*, edited by Keith M. Baker. Oxford and New York: Pergamon.

1996. "Historical Events as Transformations of Structures: Inventing Revolution at the Bastille." *Theory and Society* 25:841–881.

2005. *Logics of History. Social Theory and Social Transformation*. Chicago University of Chicago Press.

Shefter, Martin. 1986. "Trade Unions and Political Machines: The Organization and Disorganization of the American Working Class in the Late Nineteenth Century." Pp. 197–276 in *Working-class Formation: Nineteenth Century Patterns in Western Europe and the United States*, edited by Ira Katzelson and Aristide R. Zolberg. Princeton, NJ: Princeton University Press.

Shorter, Edward, and Charles Tilly. 1974. *Strikes in France, 1830–1968*. Cambridge: Cambridge University Press.

Sikkink, Kathryn. 1995. "Historical Precursors to Modern Transnational Issue Networks: Campaigns against Slavery, Footbinding, and Female Circumcision." Presented to the Annual Conference of the American Political Science Association, Chicago.

2005. "Patterns of Dynamic Multilevel Governance and the Insider—Outside Coalition." Pp. 151–173 in *Transnational Protest and Global Activism*, edited by Donatella Della Porta and Sidney Tarrow. Lanham, MD: Rowman and Littlefield.

Sil, Rudra and Peter J. Katzaenstein. 2010. "Analytical Eclecticism in World Politics: Reconfiguring Problems and Mechanisms across Research Traditions." *Perspectives on Politics* 8:411–431.

Silver, Beverly J. 2003. *Forces of Labor: Workers' Movements and Globalization since 1870*. Cambridge: Cambridge University Press.

Siméant, Johanna. 2011. "La deuxième vie de l'advocacy: Sur la diffusion internationale de l'advocacy comme pratique et imperative de conformation de la société civile." Paris: University of Paris I.

Skocpol, Theda. 1979. *States and Social Revolutions: A Comparative Analysis of France, Russia and China*. New York and Cambridge: Cambridge University Press.

1992. *Protecting Soldiers and Mothers: The Political Origins of Social Policy in the United States*. Cambridge, MA: Harvard University Press.

1994. *Social Revolutions in the Modern World.* New York and Cambridge: Cambridge University Press.

Skocpol, Theda, and Kenneth Finegold. 1982. "State Capacity and Economic Intervention in the New Deal." *Political Science Quarterly* 97:255–278.

Skowronek, Stephen. 1982. *Building a New American State: The Expansion of National Administrative Capacities, 1877–1920.* New York and Cambridge: Cambridge University Press.

Skrbis, Zlatko. 1999. *Long Distance Nationalism: Diasporas, Homelands and Identities.* Brookfield, England: Ashgate Publishing.

Smelser, Neil J. 1962. *The Theory of Collective Behavior.* New York: Free Press of Glencoe.

Smith, Jackie. 2004. "Exploring Connections between Global Integration and Political Mobilization." *Journal of World-Systems Research* 10:255–285.

2007. *Global Visions/Rival Networks: Social Movements for Global Democracy.* Baltimore, MD: Johns Hopkins University Press.

Smith, Jackie, Charles Chatfield, and Ron Pagnucco (Eds.). 1997. *Transnational Movements in Global Politics.* Syracuse, NY: Syracuse University Press.

Smith, Jackie, and Hank Johnston (Eds.). 2002. *Globalization and Resistance: Transnational Dimensions of Social Movements.* Boulder, CO, New York and Lanham, MD: Rowman and Littlefield.

Smith, Jackie, and Ellen Reese. 2009. "The World Social Forum Process." *Mobilization* 13:373–394.

Smith, Jackie, and Dawn R. Wiest. 2012. *Social Movements in the World System: The Politics of Crisis and Transformation.* New York: Russell Sage Foundation.

Smith, Jackie, Dawn Wiest, and Ivana Eterovi. 2004. "Uneven Globalization: Understanding Variable Participation in Transnational Social Movement Organizations." Department of Sociology, Unpublished Paper, Stony Brook, NY: SUNY Stony Brook.

Smith, Robert R. 2003. "Migrant Membership as an Instituted Process: Transnationalization, the State and the Extra-Territorial Conduct of Mexican Politics." *International Migration Review* 37:297–343.

Smithey, Lee A., and Michael P. Young. 2010. "Parading Protest: Orange Parades in Northern Ireland and Temperance Parades in Antebellum America." *Social Movement Studies* 9:393–410.

Snow, David A., and Robert D. Benford. 1988. "Ideology, Frame Resonance, and Participant Mobilization." Pp. 197–217 in *From Structure to Action: Social Movement Participation Across Cultures*, edited by Bert Klandermans, Hanspeter Kriesi, and Sidney Tarrow. Greenwich, CT: JAI Press.

1992. "Master Frames and Cycles of Protest." Pp. 133–155 in *Frontiers in Social Movement Theory*, edited by Aldon Morris and Carol McClurg Mueller. New Haven, CT: Yale University Press.

Snow, David A., E. Burke Rochford, Jr., Steven K. Worden, and Robert D. Benford. 1986. "Frame Alignment Processes, Micromobilization and Movement Participation." *American Sociological Review* 51:464–481.

Snow, David A., Sarah A. Soule, and Hanspeter Kriesi, eds. 2004. *The Blackwell Companion to Social Movements.* Malden, MA and Oxford: Blackwell.

Soboul, Albert. 1958. *Les sans-culottes parisiens en l'An II; mouvement populaire et gouvernement révolutionnaire, 2 juin 1793–9 thermidor An II.* Paris: Libraire Clavreuil.

Sofri, Ariano. 1985. "Intervento." Pp. 141–144 in *Democrazia Proletaria, 1968–76*. Milan: Mazzotta.

Somers, Margaret. 1992. "Narrativity, Narrative Identity, and Social Action: Rethinking English Working-Class Formation." *Social Science History* 16:591–630.

1993. "Where is Sociology After the Historic Turn? Knowledge Cultures, Narrativity and Historical Epistemologies." *Comparative Studies in Society and History* 21:204–213.

Soule, Sarah A. 1995. "The Student Anti-Apartheid Movement in the United States: Diffusion of Tactics and Policy Reform." Unpublished PhD Thesis, Ithaca, NY: Cornell University.

1997. "The Student Divestment Movement in the United States and Tactical Diffusion: The Shantytown Protest." *Social Forces* 75:855–882.

1999. "The Diffusion of an Unsuccessful Innovation: The Case of the Shantytown Protest Tactic." *The Annals of the American Academy of the Political and Social Sciences* 566:120–134.

2004. "Diffusion Processes within and across Movements." Ch. 13 in *The Blackwell Companion to Social Movements*, edited by David A. Snow, Sarah A. Soule, and Hanspeter Kriesi. Malden, MA and Oxford: Blackwell.

Soule, Sarah A. 2009. *Contention and Corporate Social Responsibility*. New York: Cambridge University Press.

Soule, Sarah A., and Sidney Tarrow. 1991. "The 1848 Revolutions." Social Science History Association Annual Meeting.

Soysal, Yasemin. 1994. *Limits of Citizenship: Migrants and Postnational Membership in Europe*. Chicago, IL: University of Chicago Press.

Speranza, Gino C. 1974 [1906]. "Political Representation of Italo-American Colonies in the Italian Parliament." Pp. 309–310 in *The Italians: Social Backgrounds of an American Group*, edited by Francesco Cordasco and Eugene Bucchioni. Clifton, NJ: Augustus M. Kelley.

Spriano, Paolo. 1964. *The Occupation of the Factories*. London: Pluto.

Steinberg, Marc W. 1995. "The Roar of the Crowd: Repertoires of Discourse and Collective Action Among the Spitalfields Silk Weavers in Nineteenth-Century London." Pp. 57–87 in *Repertoires and Cycles of Collective Action*, edited by Mark Traugott. Durham, NC and London: Duke University Press.

1999. *Fighting Words*. Ithaca, NY: Cornell University Press.

Stinchecombe, Arthur 1987. "Review of *The Contentious French* by Charles Tilly." *American Journal of Sociology* 93:1248.

Stone, Lawrence. 1979. "The Revival of Narrative: Reflections on a New Old History." *Past and Present* 85:3–24.

1982. *The Family, Sex and Marriage in England, 1500–1800*. New York: Harper Collins Publishers.

Stout, Harry S. 1991. *The Divine Dramatist: George Whitefield and the Rise of Modern Evangelicalism*. Grand Rapids, MI: Eerdmans.

Strang, David, and John Meyer. 1993. "Institutional Conditions for Diffusion." *Theory and Society* 22:487–511.

Strayer, Joseph R. 1970. *On the Medieval Origins of the Modern State*. Princeton, NJ: Princeton University Press.

Streeck, Wolfgang, and Kathleen Thelen. 2005. "Introduction: Institutional Change in Advanced Political Economies." Pp. 1–39 in *Beyond Continuity: Institutional*

Change in Advanced Political Economies, edited by Wolfgang Streeck and Kathleen Thelen. Oxford: Oxford University Press.

Sutherland, Donald. 1994. "The Vendée: Unique or Emblematic?" Pp. 99–114 in *The French Revolution and the Creation of Modern Political Culture*, edited by Keith Michael Baker. Oxford and New York: Pergamon.

SVIMEZ (Associazione per lo sviluppo del Mezzogiorno). 1961. *Un secolo di Statistiche Nord e Sud, 1861–1961*. Roma: SVIMEZ.

Sylos-Labini, Paolo. 1975. *The Successor Generation*. London: Butterworth.

Szymanski, Anne-Marie E. 2003. *Pathways to Prohibition: Radicals, Moderates, and Social Movement Outcomes*. Durham, NC: Duke University Press.

Tarde, Gabriel. 1989. *L' Opinion et la Foule*. Paris: Presses Universitaires de France.

Tarrow, Sidney. 1967a. *Peasant Communism in Southern Italy*. New Haven, CT: Yale University Press.

1967b. "Political Dualism and Italian Communism." *American Political Science Review* 61:39–53.

1974. *Partisanship and Political Exchange in Italian Local Politics*. Beverly Hills, CA: Sage Publications.

1983. "Struggling to Reform: Social Movements and Policy Change." Western Societies Paper: Ithaca, NY: Cornell University.

1988. "Old Movements in New Cycles of Protest: The Career of an Italian Religious Community." Pp. 281–303 in *From Structure to Action: Comparing Social Movement Participation across Cultures*, edited by Bert Klandermans et al. Greenwich, CT: JAI.

1989. *Democracy and Disorder: Protest and Politics in Italy, 1965–1974*. New York: Oxford University Press.

1990. "The Phantom at the Opera: Political Parties and Social Movements in Italy in the 1960s and 1970s." Pp. 251–273 in *Challenging the Political Order*, edited by Russell Dalton and Manfred Kuechler. New Haven, CT: Yale University Press.

1991. "Comparing Social Movement Participation in Western Europe and the United States: Problems, Uses, and a Proposal for Synthesis." Pp. 392–420 in *Research on Social Movements. The State of the Art in Western Europe and the USA*, edited by Dieter Rucht. Boulder, CO: Westview.

1993. "Social Protest and Policy Reform: May 1968 and the Loi d'Orientation." *Comparative Political Studies* 25:579–607.

1998a. "Fishnets, Internets and Catnets: Globalization and Transnational Collective Action." Pp. 228–244 in *Challenging Authority: The Historical Study of Contentious Politics* edited by Michael Hanagan, Leslie Page Moch, and Wayne te Brake. Minneapolis: University of Minnesota Press.

1998b. "Studying Contentious Politics: From Event-ful History to Cycles of Collective Action." Pp. 33–64 in *Acts of Dissent: New Developments in the Study of Protest*, edited by Dieter Rucht, Ruud Koopmans, and Friedhelm Neidhardt. Berlin: Sigma.

2001. "Transnational Politics: Contention and Institutions in International Politics." *Annual Review of Political Science* 4:1–20.

2005. *The New Transnational Activism*. Cambridge and New York: Cambridge University Press.

2006. "Confessions of a Recovering Structuralist." *European Political Science* 5:7–20.

2007. "Inside Insurgencies: Politics and Violence in an Age of Civil War." *Perspectives on Politics* 5:587–600.

2008. "Charles Tilly and the Practice of Contentious Politics." *Social Movement Studies* 7:225–246.

2009. "Outsiders Inside and Insiders Outside: Linking Transnational and Domestic Public Action for Human Rights." *Human Rights Review* 11:171–182.

2010. "Bridging the Quantitative-Qualitative Divide." Pp. 171–180 in *Rethinking Social Inquiry: Diverse Tolls, Shared Standards*, edited by Henry E. Brady and David Collier. Lanham, MD: Rowman and Littlefield.

2011a. *Power in Movement.* 3rd Edition. New York and Cambridge: Cambridge University Press.

2011b. ""Red of Tooth and Claw:" The French Revolution and the Political Process – Then and Now." *French Politics, Culture, and Society* 29:93–110

Tarrow, Sidney, and Doug McAdam. 2005. "Scale Shift in Transnational Contention." Ch. 6 in *Transnational Protest and Global Activism*, edited by Donatella della Porta and Sidney Tarrow. Lanham, MD: Rowman and Littlefield.

Tartakowsky, Danielle. 2004. *La manif en éclat.* Paris: Dispute.

Taylor, Michael. 1988. "Rationality and Revolutionary Collective Action." Pp. 63–97 in *Rationality and Revolution*, edited by Michael Taylor. Cambridge: Cambridge University Press.

Taylor, Verta. 2009. "Culture, Identity, and Emotions: Studying Social Movements as if People Really Matter." *Mobilization* 15:113–134.

te Brake, Wayne. 1998. *Shaping History: Ordinary People in European Politics, 1500–1700.* Berkeley and Los Angeles: University of California Press.

Tempi Moderni. 1960. "Modificazioni strutturali e politiche delPCI al suo IX Congresso." *Tempi Moderni* 2:1–22.

Thompson, E.P. 1971. "The Moral Economy of the English Crowd in the Eighteenth Century." *Past and Present* 50:76–136.

Tilly, Charles. 1978. *From Mobilization to Revolution.* Reading, MA: Addison-Wesley.

1984. *Big Structures, Large Processes, Huge Comparisons.* New York: Russell Sage Foundation.

1984a. "Social Movements and National Politics." Pp. 297–317 in *Statemaking and Social Movements*, edited by Charles Bright and Susan Harding. Ann Arbor: University of Michigan Press.

1985. "War Making and State Making as Organized Crime." Ch. 5 in *Bringing the State Back In*, edited by Peter Evans, Rueschemeyer Deitrich, and Theda Skocpol. New York and Cambridge: Cambridge University Press.

1986. *The Contentious French.* Cambridge, MA: Harvard University Press.

1990. *Coercion, Capital, and European States, AD 990–1992.* Cambridge, MA: Blackwell.

1992. "War and the International System, 1900–1992." in *CSSC Working Paper No. 134.*

1993. *European Revolutions, 1492–1992.* Oxford: Blackwell.

1995. *Popular Contention in Great Britain, 1758–1834.* Cambridge, MA: Harvard University Press.

2000. "Mechanisms in Political Processes." *Annual Review of Political Science* 4:21–41.

2002. "Event Catalogs as Theories." *Sociological Theory* 20:248–254.

2004. *Social Movements, 1768–2004.* Boulder, CO: Paradigm Publishers.

2006. *Regimes and Repertoires.* Cambridge: Cambridge University Press.

2008a. *Contentious Performances.* New York and Cambridge: Cambridge University Press.

2008b. *Explaining Social Processes.* Boulder, CO: Paradigm Publishers.

Tilly, Charles, and Sidney Tarrow. 2007. *Contentious Politics.* Boulder, CO: Paradigm Publishers.

Tilly, Charles, Louise A. Tilly, and Richard Tilly. 1975. *The Rebellious Century, 1830–1930.* Cambridge, MA: Harvard University Press.

Tilly, Charles, and Lesley Wood. 2009. *Social Movements, 1768–2008.* Boulder, CO: Paradigm Press.

Tocqueville, Alexis de. 1942. *Souvenirs d'Alexis de Tocqueville.* Paris: Gallimard.

    1954. *Democracy in America.* (trans. Henry Reve, ed. Phillips Brady). New York: Vintage.

    1955. *The Old Regime and the French Revolution.* Garden City: Doubleday.

    1960. *Journey to America.* (trans. George Lawrence; ed. J. P. Mayer). New Haven, CT: Yale University Press.

    1988. *L'Ancien régime et la révolution.* Paris: Flammarion.

    1992. *Recollections: The French Revolution of 1848.* New Brunswick, NJ: Transaction Books.

    2007. *Democracy in America.* New York and London: W.W. Norton and Company.

Togliatti, Palmiro. 1954. "L'azione democratica e socialista nel Mezzogiorno." *Cronache meridionali* 1:401–422.

    1964. *Il partito.* Rome: Editori Riuniti.

    1964. *La via italiana al socialismo.* Roma: Editori Riuniti.

    1964. Sul movimento operaio internazionale. Roma: Editori Riuniti.

Touraine, Alain. 1969. *La société post-industrielle.* Paris: Denoel.

    1971. *The May Movement: Revolt and Reform.* New York: Random House.

    1973. *Production de la société.* Paris: Seuil.

Touraine, Alain, François Dubet, Zsuzsa Hegedus, and Michel Wieviorka. 1978. *Lutte edudiante.* Paris: Seuil.

Touraine, Alain, Zsuzsa Hegedus, François Dubet, and Michel Wieviorka. 1980. *La prophetie anti-nucleaire.* Paris: Seuil.

Touraine, Alain, François Dubet, Zsuzsa Hegedus, and Michel Wieviorka. 1981. *Le Pays contre l'Etat.* Paris: Seuil.

Touraine, Alain. 1981. *The Voice and the Eye: An Analysis of Social Movements.* Paris: Seuil.

    1984. *Le mouvement ouvrier.* Paris: Fayard.

    1991. "Commentary on Dieter Rucht's Critique." Pp. 385–391 in *Research on Social Movements: The State of the Art in Western Europe and the United States.* Boulder, CO: Westview Press.

Tournier, Maurice. 1992. "La loi dans la langue, loi de langue à travers une chronique de la grève des origins à 1848." *Langage et société* 60:17–48.

Traugott, Mark. 1995. "Barricades as Repertoire: Continuities and Discontinuities in the History of French Contention." Pp. 309–323 in *Repertoires and Cycles of Collective Action*, edited by Mark Traugott. Durham, NC: Duke University Press.

2010. *The Insurgent Barricade*. Berkeley and Los Angeles: University of California Press.

Tsebelis, George, and John Sprague. 1989. "Coercion and Revolution: Variations on a Predator-Prey Model." *Mathematical Computer Modeling* 12:547–559.

Tsutsui, Kiyoteru, and Hwa-Ji Shin. 2008. "Global Norms, Local Activism, and Social Movement Outcomes: Global Human Rights and Resident Koreans in Japan." *Social Problems* 55:391–418.

Tuma, Nancy, and Michael Hannan. 1979. "Dynamic Analysis of Event Histories." *American Journal of Sociology* 84:820–854.

Turner, Ralph, and Lewis Killian. 1987. *Collective Action*. Englewood Cliffs, NJ: Prentice Hall.

Uba, Katrin. 2009. "The Contextual Dependence of Movement Outcomes: A Simplified Meta-Analysis." *Mobilization* 14:433–448.

Uba, Katrin, and Fredrik Uggla. 2011. "Protest Actions against the European Union, 1992–2007." *West European Politics* 34:384–393.

Usher, Douglas. 2000. "Strategy, Rules and Participation: Issue Activists in Republican National Convention Delegations, 1976–1996." *Political Research Quarterly* 53:887–903.

Valenza, Pietro. 1958. "Aspetti del Fanfanismo in Lucania." *Cronache meridionali* 5:858–867.

1960. "Alcuni problemi del rinnovamento del PCI nel Mezzogiorno." *Cronache meridionali* 7:7–14.

Vallely, Richard M. 1993. "Party, Coercion and Inclusion: The Two Reconstructions of the South's Electoral Politics." *Politics and Society* 21:37–68.

2004. *The Two Reconstructions: The Struggle for Black Enfranchisement*. Chicago: University of Chicago Press.

Van Stekelenburg, Jacquelien, Conny Roggeband, and Bert Klandermans, eds. 2012. *The Changing Dynamics of Contention*. Minneapolis and St. Paul: University of Minnesota Press.

Vasi, Ion Bogdan. 2009. "Social Movements and Industry Development: The Environmental Movement's Impact on the Wind Energy Industry." *Mobilization* 14:315–336.

Vernus, Michel. 1988. "La F.C.P.E. en Mai 1968." in *Colloque sur Acteurs et terrains du mouvement social de 1968*. Paris: CRSMSS.

Vertovec, Steven, and Robin Cohen (Eds.). 2002. *Conceiving Cosmopolitanism: Theory, Context, and Practice*. Oxford: Oxford University Press.

Villari, Rosario (Ed.). 1961. *Il sud nella storia d'Italia*. Bari: Laterza.

Von Bülow, Marisa. 2010. *Building Transnational Networks: Civil Society and the Politics of Trade in the Americas*. New York and Cambridge: Cambridge University Press.

Wahl, A. 1988. "Le mai des footballeurs." Pp. 142–156 in *Colloque sur Acteurs et terrains du mouvement social de 1968*. Paris: CRSMSS.

Waldinger, Roger, and David Fitzgerald. 2004. "Transnationalism in Question." *American Journal of Sociology* 109:1171–1195.

Waldron, Jeremy. 1992. "Minority Cultures and the Cosmopolitan Alternative." *University of Michigan Law Review* 25:5–14.

2000. "What is Cosmopolitan?" *The Journal of Political Philosophy* 7:227–243.

Walgrave, Stefaan, and Dieter Rucht. 2010. *The World Says No to War: Demonstrations Against the War on Iraq*. Minneapolis and St. Paul: University of Minnesota Press.

Wallerstein, Immanuel. 1974. *The Modern World System: Capitalist Agriculture and the Origins of the European World-Economy in the Sixteenth Century*. New York: Academic Press.

Walt, Steven. 1996. *Revolution and War*. Ithaca, NY: Cornell University Press.

Walters, Ronald G. 1976. *The Antislavery Appeal: American Abolitionism after 1830*. Baltimore, MD and London: Johns Hopkins University Press.

Wapner, Paul. 1996. *Environmental Activism and World Civil Politics*. Albany, NY: State University of New York Press.

Waterman, Peter. 2001. "Internationalists in the Americas: Agitators, Agents and Communicators." Unpublished Paper Presented to the Tercer Congreso Internacional de Latinoamericanistas en Europa, Amsterdam, the Netherlands.

Weber, Max (Ed.). 1991. *From Max Weber: Essays in Sociology*. New York: Routledge.

Weingast, Barry. 1998. "Political Stability and Civil War: Institutions, Commitment, and American Democracy." Pp. 148–193 in *Analytic Narratives*, edited by Robert Bates et al. Princeton, NJ: Princeton University Press.

Weyland, Kurt. 2009. "The Diffusion of Revolution." *International Organization* 63:391–423.

Wickham-Crowley, Timothy. 1992. *Guerillas and Revolution in Latin America: A Comparative Study of Insurgents and Regimes since 1956*. Princeton, NJ: Princeton University Press.

Wildavsky, Aaron. 1974. *The Politics of the Budgetary Process*. Boston: Little Brown.

Wilentz, Sean. 1984. *Chants Democratic: New York City and the Rise of the American Working Class, 1788–1850*. New York: Oxford University Press.

Williams, Heather. 2003. "Of Labor Tragedy and Legal Farce: The Han Young Factory Struggle in Tijuana, Mexico." *Social Science History* 27:525–550.

Woloch, Isser. 1994. *The New Regime. Transformations of the French Civic Order, 1789–1820s*. New York: W.W. Norton and Co.

Wood, Gordon S. 1991. *The Radicalism of the American Revolution*. New York: Vintage

——— 2009. *Empire of Liberty: The Early Republic, 1789–1815*. New York and Oxford: Oxford University Press.

Wood, Lesley J. 2003. "Breaking the Bank and Taking to the Streets—How Protesters Target Neoliberalism." *Journal of World-Systems Research* 10:69–89.

Wood, Leslie J. 2007. "Breaking the Wave: Repression, Identity, and Seattle Tactics." *Mobilization* 12:377–388.

Zagoria, Donald S. 1971. "The Ecology of Peasant Communism in India." *American Political Science Review* 65:144–160.

Zald, Mayer N. 2000. "Ideologically Structured Action: An Enlarged Agenda for Social Movement Research." *Mobilization* 5:1–16.

Zald, Mayer N., and Roberta Ash. 1966. "Social Movement Organizations: Growth, Decay and Change." *Social Forces* 44:327–341.

Zald, Mayer N., and Michael Berger. 1987. "Social Movements in Organizations: Coup d'Etat, Bureaucratic Insurgency and Mass Movement." Ch. 8 in *Social Movements in an Organizational Society*, edited by Mayer Zald and John McCarthy. New Brunswick, NJ and Oxford: Transaction Books.

Zippel, Kathrin. 2006. *The Politics of Sexual Harassment: A Comparative Study of United States, the European Union, and Germany*. Cambridge and New York: Cambridge University Press.

Zolberg, Aristide. 1972. "Moments of Madness." *Politics and Society* 2:183–207.

Index